AGAINST THE CURRENT

AGAINST THE CURRENT

Selected Writings 1939–1996

Pierre Elliott Trudeau

Edited by Gérard Pelletier
New Translations by George Tombs

"The Asbestos Strike" (pp. 42-66): From *The Asbestos Strike* edited by Pierre Elliott Trudeau, translated by James Boake. Translation © James Lewis & Samuel (James Lorimer & Company Ltd.) 1974. Reprinted by permission.

"Approaches to Politics" (pp. 67-78): From *Approaches to Politics* by Pierre Elliot Trudeau, translated by I.M. Owen. Translation © Oxford University Press Canada 1970. Reprinted by permission of Oxford University Press Canada.

"Two Innocents in Red China" (pp. 116-31): From *Two Innocents in Red China* by Jacques Hébert and Pierre Elliot Trudeau, translated by I.M. Owen. Translation © Oxford University Press Canada 1968. Reprinted by permission of Oxford University Press Canada.

"The United States" (pp. 295-96): Copyright © 1968 by the New York Times Co. Reprinted by permission.

Canadian Cataloguing in Publication Data

Trudeau, Pierre Elliott, 1919–
    Against the Current: selected writings 1939–1996

Includes bibliographical references and index.
ISBN 0-7710-6979-0

1. Canada – Politics and government – 1939–   .*
I. Pelletier, Gérard, 1919–   II. Title.

FC600.T78 1996   971.064   C96-931271-7   F1034.2.T78 1996

The publishers acknowledge the support of the Canada Council and the Ontario Arts Council for their publishing program.

Typesetting by M&S, Toronto
Printed and bound in Canada

McClelland & Stewart Inc.
The Canadian Publishers
481 University Avenue
Toronto, Ontario
M5G 2E9

1 2 3 4 5 6   01 00 99 98 97 96

Contents

Part VI – Einstein and Ralston Prize Lectures

Foreword by Pierre Elliott Trudeau

I cannot say exactly when I became a contrarian, nor why. I do remember, however, that in my early years, far from going "against the current," I was more inclined to do and say the conventional thing and to devour gratefully every morsel of knowledge that came my way, whether from my parents, my friends, my teachers, or my Church. My childhood having been a happy one, I felt no need for "le doute méthodique."

It was during my teens that I began to change. I still had a thirst for knowledge, but I was looking for consistency too: things had to make sense. The word of an authority was not proof enough: I became argumentative. Fortunately for me, the "authorities" understood, as did my father: if I could justify my disagreement or my disobedience, I would be let off easily.

The sea-change came when I returned to Canada, in my late twenties, after several years of studying and travelling abroad. My province had become a citadel of orthodoxy with a state-of-siege mentality. To remain a free man in Quebec, one had to go against the current of ideas and institutions. I began writing in *Cité libre* and in *VRAI*. I edited and contributed to *The Asbestos Strike*. In doing research for this latter book, I came to the realization that the élites in Quebec in the 1920s and '30s had mainly been preaching outdated and unreal doctrines; that they were trying to lock the Quebec people into an authoritarian society.

In 1960, at long last, the dissenters and the people prevailed: the Quiet Revolution brought us into the modern world – for a while.

Alas! Thirty-six years later, nationalist politicians increasingly feel oppressed by "Ottawa" and misunderstood by "les Anglais": they have gone back to the state-of-siege mentality with their own politically correct orthodoxies. Opposing voices are becoming scarcer. And that is why I thought it might be useful to publish some of my writings before they are buried under the prevailing monolithic doctrines.

In the pursuance of my task, I am enormously indebted to my friend Gérard Pelletier, whose wise judgement was responsible for the choice of texts, and whose great patience was often tested in digging them out of various archives.

Introduction

Throughout his life (except during his long political career), Pierre Elliott Trudeau has never stopped writing. The texts brought together in this volume bear eloquent witness to that fact. From articles published in the monthly newspaper of his college to his most recent statements in the press on current events, all of these texts reveal the passion of a man who has always sought to express his thought with both force and clarity.

Hubert Beuve-Méry, founder of the Paris daily newspaper *Le Monde*, said of writing that it was "the best place for reflection to take place." I can personally testify that such has been the case for the author you are about to read. Whether he wrote about his love for canoeing or about the first stirrings of his political thought, he gave shape to his ideas by committing them to paper – no matter what effort that required of him. He did not write easily. He invested a lot of himself in searching for the most appropriate word, the most evocative turn of phrase. He was never happy with a first draft; he worked and reworked his texts right up to the deadline. Sometimes it even happened that, a day or two after submitting an article, he would visit the print-shop, desperate to change a few words that no longer suited him.

Every event of his life, every phase of his intellectual evolution, inspired texts of a very personal nature. The articles of his early youth are ripe with the emotions of that age, whether they describe climbing a mountain on skis (before ski-lifts were invented!) or reading a scientific work. Even the essays he wrote on serious economic and political subjects are rarely cool in tone, and certainly never detached. Instead, these are the words of a man of commitment, words bearing the imprint of the author's convictions, likes and dislikes.

Pierre Elliott Trudeau wrote nothing between November 1965, when he entered political life, and June 1984, when he left it. This can doubtless be explained by the fact that neither ministers nor heads of government have time to devote to writing. When they do take up the pen, it is to annotate, and more likely to correct, the drafts prepared for them by bureaucrats, or to scribble in the pages of a personal diary.

As prime minister, Trudeau definitely spent a lot of time correcting drafts; but I do not believe he devoted a single second to a diary. In the preface to his memoirs, he writes: "Even in those years [his earliest term as prime minister], friends who were aware of my background as a writer and an editor would express the hope that I was keeping a journal or at least making notes, so that when it was all over I would, in their words, 'write a book about all this.' My response to that was always a definite No. I was not in politics to acquire material to write a book."

As a result, there is a twenty-year gap in this collection. That is why, despite the subtitle chosen for this book, we have had to include passages from speeches and interviews from print and electronic media. It seemed important to us to bring up subjects which Pierre Elliott Trudeau would certainly have dealt with in writing, if he had had the leisure to do so.

We have tried to take these very diverse texts published over a half century and place them as accurately as possible in their setting. And so we have quoted from prefaces and critical reactions to the author's writings that appeared at the time of first publication, or a few years later when they were republished, to enable the reader to place everything in its proper perspective.

Here, then, is a choice of texts which we consider representative not only of the thought of their author, but also of the periods in which they were written. From the several thousand pages Pierre Elliott Trudeau has published by now, we have gathered a selection that shows his diverse styles – discursive, critical, polemical, and humorous.

Have a good read.

GÉRARD PELLETIER

PART I

Studies and Travel

The writings of one's youth are always marked by candour and somewhat precious turns of phrase. But definite progress can be detected in Trudeau's writing, from articles in the Collège Jean-de-Brébeuf monthly or Le Quartier latin, the student weekly at the Université de Montréal, to his first travel accounts, published in Le Devoir – progress towards greater precision and simplicity, culminating around 1950 in a fully mature style.

Relative Utopia

＞＜

We stopped a moment before beginning the final climb. The oblique light seemed to raise the snow-bedecked and gleaming mountain till it loomed above us.

At the summit, a forest of fir trees crowded together; one might have imagined an impregnable castle, and the sentinel, clad in white and bearing a spiked helmet, keeping the watch step by step.

Climbing up the mountain on skis is always a long moment of reality. At first, you enjoy calculating the angle of elevation and the strength of your own breathing; a little higher up, you gauge the weight of your haversack and the distance covered so far; then, as the slope continues upwards, you feel encouraged by the calmness of your shadow moving along the snow.

Once the climb is over, the idea of coming down again radiates in the mind, and reality seems less brutal than before. Scanning the forest that blocked the passage to the promised land, I found a breach. We entered.

It was all silence and shadow.

Our first steps were tentative; then I was startled by the boldness of my skis as they hit the virgin snow.

Our pathway widened, however, and soon we stopped in an immense, luminous crypt – under azure vaults and all carpeted with ermine. Close to the sum-mit, a squirrel moved about; a pine branch shook, loosening silvery dust which sparkled in the sunshine. A bird chirped. I was both surprised and relieved to learn that such absolute stillness and silence could be broken without violence.

Out of curiosity, I explored an opening between two dazzling white coniferous trees. I saw that it led to a clearing where fairies come to dance; I saw their footprints on the ground and so I immediately withdrew.

Once we reached the edge of the wood, we believed we were in some blue-tinged imaginary country. The sky was losing its azure veil, which slipped delicately to the ground. Along an endless horizon, mountains without number massed together, like gigantic dunes in the desert.

Huge, tapered pines broke through the firmament here and there, some poking through holes for the stars; a heavy and obscure fluid was already flowing along the bottom of the valley. It was time to hurry.

Chest swelling, bent forward, arms relaxed, we headed back earthward, with ever-increasing speed.

A sailor only braves the elements, and a scholar can do no more than ob-serve their force; an artist scarcely knows what Beauty is; a genius is only a man in the end. But the Skier is a god who makes toys of mountains, who takes gravity into his own hands to do with it what he will, who laughs off the abyss and takes ferocious pleasure in taunting it. The Skier knows the joy of the explorer and scientist and superman. Pressed ahead by his haversack, his shoulders rounded, his knees tightly held together, his hands close to his thighs, his cheeks whipped by the dry air, and his tuque worn low over his eyes, he clears a path through imprecise nature, leaving behind a long whirlwind of pulverized clarity.

It seems incredible but it is nonetheless true that the Skier should fear ecstasy. His gaze fails, he abandons his body to all unknown forces and drifts infallibly in the pathways of space and time. What a magnificent sport, what an incomparable thing to do: one mogul was enough to send me hurtling into the sky, and from the sky neither mountain nor valley could be seen, only the lights of the village that glowed like a handful of pearls at the bottom of a lake or the Big Dipper hanging like a sign in the sky and the numberless stars like snowflakes.

...Alas! It is the fate of mortals that they can cast off reality for only a brief moment. Blessed is he who completes his heavenly flight with a drop into the coolly real but soft snow.

It falls on others to fall otherwise: a leg rapturously envelops a maple tree, followed by forty days in a cast. Skis of ash, crutches of oak. Utopia is no more.

Brébeuf monthly (1939)
Translated by George Tombs

Where Are Indians From?

>‹

Naturally I am the one to have been asked to review Paul Rivet's *Les Origines de l'homme américain*.

Since who among you – unless I exclude a small number of law students – would be able to read intelligently that "beyond beregma, the line continues to rise and only begins to bend at the level roughly of the latter third [this "roughly" is admirable!] of the sagittal angle; from this point right on to the iliac, the line flattens out somewhat but does not fall off precipitously [how reassuring!] so that the change of direction is harmonious." And I somehow can't imagine your enthusiasm at the news that Sapir managed to establish a relationship between the No-Dene group of languages and Sino-Tibetan, thus confirming an older work by Hill-Tout on the relationship between the Dene and Chinese languages which had not seemed conclusive.

I planned initially to warn you away from the work of this eminent scientist, who is director of the Musée de l'homme. However, considering that the settlement of pre-Columbian America should not remain some virginal enigma for the students of our continent, I undertook to make a précis, from which the following passages are drawn.

In the first two chapters, a brief and scholarly criticism of geological and palaeontological theories puts the problem of the origins of our Indians in focus, after which the author concludes: "The American Indian is not native; he arrived from the Old Continent, and only began to appear in the New World at the end of the quaternary period, after the retreat of the great glaciers; he was only able to reach it by using routes which exist in our day, since America got its current shape in that remote period" (p. 54).

The third chapter provides even more nuance. First, Rivet the archaeologist manages "to eliminate once and for all any hypotheses suggesting that America was peopled by civilized races: Jews, Syrians, Tartars, Egyptians. . . ." After which Rivet the anthropologist, the ethnographer, the linguist, examines the theory of migration via the American Northwest. He accepts the hypothesis of Asian immigration, but then he profoundly modifies it, believing that "other ethnic elements . . . must have intervened after that, in a later period . . . and the extraordinary polymorphism of populations can be explained in large part by the cross-breeding that resulted" (p. 69).

Chapters IV and V are concerned with the northernmost and southernmost of the primitive peoples, respectively: "the migration of Australians to South America, on the edge of Antarctica, finds a curious parallel in the migration of Arctic peoples along the edge of the frozen Ocean, leading to the establishment of Eskimos in northern America" (p. 87).

A third ethnic contribution is then revealed in the sixth chapter: "the Malayo-Polynesian, whose migration did not follow the land route but followed the bold and moving maritime route instead." And in addition to migration, there was trade between Polynesia and America. "Why be surprised that the Polynesians, who were the most prodigious navigators in the world, should have pushed their voyages straight over to the American coast? They had a perfect knowledge of currents and winds, knew how to navigate by the stars, travelled by night and frequently made non-stop voyages over distances of 2000 miles. . . . To locate the tiny Polynesian islands in the immensity of the Ocean, they made a landmark of the little cloud which forms above the islands, at

3600 metres altitude, and which a trained eye can make out from 120 nautical miles offshore" (p. 120).

Finally, a seventh chapter recounts the heroic settling of Greenland by the Norsemen, who were repulsed by the climate and glacial attitude of the Eskimos. The ending of this intrepid adventure is quite cynical: "this resulted in no significant change in indigenous civilization. All that survived of so much human effort and suffering, it seems, was more diverse vegetation . . ." (p. 112).

Mr. Paul Rivet reaches his short and lucid conclusion with the hope that "old Europe and young America alike will learn to appreciate what they owe to Indian civilization." These last lines surely express the most noble appeal to sentiments of brotherhood among men: "More than at any time in the past, the sentiment of great human solidarity needs to be exalted and strengthened. Every man must understand and know that under every latitude and under every longitude, other beings, his own brothers, have contributed to making his life sweeter and easier, whatever the colour of their skin or the shape of their hair."

. . .

This book is short, logical, clear, and straightforward. It is worth reading for the simple reason that nothing in it is useless. Of course, as I mentioned at the beginning, the uninitiated will find technical terms and esoteric proofs – but the main body of the exposition is easily understandable.

. . . Ah! Authentic Science is so wonderful!

Le Quartier latin, 12/11/43, p. 4
Translated by George Tombs

The Ascetic in a Canoe

><

I would not know how to instil a taste for adventure in those who have not acquired it. (Anyway, who can ever prove the necessity for the gypsy life?) And yet there are people who suddenly tear themselves away from their comfortable existence and, using the energy of their bodies as an example to their brains, apply themselves to the discovery of unsuspected pleasures and places.

I would like to point out to these people a type of labour from which they are certain to profit: an expedition by canoe.

I do not just mean "canoeing." Not that I wish to disparage that pastime, which is worth more than many another. But, looked at closely, there is perhaps only a difference of money between the canoeists of Lafontaine Park and those who dare to cross a lake, make a portage, spend a night in a tent and return exhausted, always in the care of a fatherly guide – a brief interlude momentarily interrupting the normal course of digestion.

A canoeing expedition, which demands much more than that, is also much more rewarding.

It involves a starting rather than a parting. Although it assumes the breaking of ties, its purpose is not to destroy the past, but to lay a foundation for the future. From now on, every living act will be built on this step, which will serve as a base long after the return of the expedition . . . and until the next one.

What is essential at the beginning is the resolve to reach the saturation point. Ideally, the trip should end only when the members are making no further progress within themselves. They should not be fooled, though, by a period of boredom, weariness or disgust; that is not the end, but the last obstacle before it. Let saturation be serene!

So you must paddle for days, or weeks, or perhaps months on end. My friends and I were obliged, on pain of death, to do more than a thousand miles by canoe, from Montreal to Hudson Bay. But let no one be deterred by a shortage of time. A more intense pace can compensate for a shorter trip.

What sets a canoeing expedition apart is that it purifies you more rapidly and inescapably than any other. Travel a thousand miles by train and you are a brute; pedal five hundred on a bicycle and you remain basically a bourgeois; paddle a hundred in a canoe and you are already a child of nature.

For it is a condition of such a trip that you entrust yourself, stripped of your worldly goods, to nature. Canoe and paddle, blanket and knife, salt pork and flour, fishing rod and rifle; that is about the extent of your wealth. To remove all the useless material baggage from a man's heritage is, at the same time, to free his mind from petty preoccupations, calculations and memories.

On the other hand, what fabulous and undeveloped mines are to be found in nature, friendship and oneself! The paddler has no choice but to draw everything from them. Later, forgetting that this habit was adopted under duress, he will be astonished to find so many resources within himself.

Nevertheless, he will have returned a more ardent believer from a time when religion, like everything else, became simple. The impossibility of scandal creates a new morality, and prayer becomes a friendly chiding of the divinity, who has again become part of our everyday affairs. (My friend Guy Viau could say about our adventure, "We got along very well with God, who is a damn good sport. Only once did we threaten to break off diplomatic relations if he continued to rain on us.

But we were joking. We would never have done so, and well he knew it. So he continued to rain on us.")

The canoe is also a school of friendship. You learn that your best friend is not a rifle, but someone who shares a night's sleep with you after ten hours of paddling at the other end of a canoe. Let's say that you have to be lined up a rapid and it's your turn to stay in the canoe and guide it. You watch your friend stumbling over logs, sliding on rocks, sticking in gumbo, tearing the skin on his legs and drinking water for which he does not thirst, yet never letting go of the rope; meanwhile, safely in the middle of the cataract, you spray your hauler with a stream of derision. When this same man has also fed you exactly half his catch, and has made a double portage because of your injury, you can boast of having a friend for life, and one who knows you well.

How does the trip affect your personality? Allow me to make a fine distinction, and I would say that you return not so much a man who reasons more, but a more reasonable man. For, throughout this time, your mind has learned to exercise itself in the working conditions which nature intended. Its primordial role has been to sustain the body in the struggle against a powerful universe. A good camper knows that it is more important to be ingenious than to be a genius. And conversely, the body, by demonstrating the true meaning of sensual pleasure, has been of service to the mind. You feel the beauty of animal pleasure when you draw a deep breath of rich morning air right through your body, which has been carried by the cold night, curled up like an unborn child. How can you describe the feeling which wells up in the heart and stomach as the canoe finally rides up on the shore of the campsite after a long day of plunging your paddle into rain-swept waters? Purely physical is the joy which the fire spreads through the palms of your hands and the soles of your feet while your chattering mouth belches the poisonous cold. The pleasurable torpor of such a moment is perhaps not too different from what the mystics of the East are seeking. At least it has allowed me to taste what one respected gentleman used to call the joys of hard living.

Make no mistake, these joys are exclusively physical. They have nothing to do with the satisfaction of the mind when it imposes unwelcome work on the body, a satisfaction, moreover, which is often mixed with pride, and which the body never fails to avenge. During a very long and exhausting portage, I have sometimes felt my reason defeated, and shamefully fleeing, while my legs and shoulders carried bravely on. The mumbled verses which marked the rhythm of my steps at the beginning had become brutal grunts of "uh! uh! uh!" There was nothing aesthetic in that animal search for the bright clearing which always marks the end of a portage.

I do not want you to think that the mind is subjected to a healthy discipline merely by worrying about simplistic problems. I only wish to remind you of that principle of logic which states that valid conclusions do not generally follow from false premises. Now, in a canoe, where these premises are based on nature in its original state (rather than on books, ideas and habits of uncertain value), the mind conforms to that higher wisdom which we call natural philosophy; later, that healthy methodology and acquired humility will be useful in confronting mystical and spiritual questions.

I know a man whose school could never teach him patriotism, but who acquired that virtue when he felt in his bones the vastness of his land, and the greatness of those who founded it.

Originally published in French in *Journal JEC*, June 1944. English translation published in Borden Spears, ed., *Wilderness in Canada* (Toronto: Clarke, Irwin & Company, 1970), pp. 3–5.

Letter from Mesopotamia

><

Bouclée, bouclée l'Antiquité
JEAN COCTEAU

Ur is not a village but a dot in the desert where the single track from Basrah to Baghdad becomes two tracks for a while and allows trains to pass each other. I was the only passenger to get off: I quickly met the "station" master and left my rucksack in his care: in two hours, the sun would be unbearable and make carrying any baggage intolerable. From beyond the clouds hugging the eastern horizon hovered now the first glimmering of day; and in the opposite direction I could make out the flattened mound and knoll of Ur of the Chaldees, a city already two thousand years old by the time the prophet Abraham was born there, some two thousand years before Christ.

The Desert
Distances are deceptive in the desert, just as they are at sea: the mound was higher and farther away than I had at first imagined, since I had to walk more than an hour on crusty sand; and although I had enveloped my head in a *sheffea wa egal*, that marvellous Bedouin headgear which would shield me from sunstroke, I was shivering in my shorts and shirt. Among the pits and digs, I sought a passage to the foot of the ziggurat, a pyramid-shaped construction at the top of which the Sumerians had

13

the habit of erecting their temples. After walking up the hundred steps leading to the top, I ate my meal of the day, two eggs and some dates, and then started identifying the different districts of Ur. Often only the outline of the walls could be made out, and I thought that at last I had found a city where the destruction was more complete than in the Warsaw of our day.

Three Arab drifters interrupted me, given the prospect of extracting some money from this stranger in their midst. I greeted them with the usual "Samalah alecum," touching forehead and heart with my fingers, then pretended to be completely indifferent to them. My attitude disconcerted them somewhat and they looked for something to do. But they quickly began acting up, since they had definitely not walked three miles in the desert, nor climbed so high above the plain, armed with sticks, simply to catch butterflies.

Bakshish!

They surrounded me and by signs asked to see my papers (which they wouldn't have been able to read in any case!), looked me up and down, inquired into the purpose of my visit, indicated where I could find water, proposed to accompany me there, etc. But I saw what was on their mind and, just when they were about to demand "bakshish" (a tip which is paid more often to have some peace and quiet than to reward any services actually rendered), I motioned to them to sit down and, showing my torn shirt, stretched out my hand and pleaded: "Bakshish!"

This reversal of roles completely startled them. And once they had regained their composure, they began to get on my nerves, scrutinizing my clothes, making ready to rummage through my pockets. Suddenly I seized the curved double-edged dagger one of them wore in his belt and pretended to examine it. This counterattack annoyed them and they started loudly demanding that I follow them to the railway station, where, they said, the police were looking for me. I did in fact follow them to the top of the narrow stairway leading down the ziggurat, where, once they had gone ahead, I remained towering above them.

They were outraged at this deception and started yelling more than ever. But I replied with phrases borrowed from every known language, and a few others besides, sometimes raising my voice, alternating between sweet talk and melancholy; I recited poetry, performed drama, started a speech. Each time I took a breath, they tried to put in a word edgewise, but I started up again, with still more sparkle in my eyes and more forceful gestures.

This put-on of mine worked. The three louts feared madness more than any handgun, and beat an anxious retreat down the steps without letting me out of sight. I was ruthless. I was determined to witness the complete obliteration of their self-respect and I had all the force of a firebrand. They didn't dare look at the crazed and wildly gesticulating silhouette looming above them. They fled into the desert to escape my wrath, focusing their eyes straight ahead and, if I may say so, keeping their tail between their legs.

Exploration

I was quite alone and Ur was all mine. First I explored the walls of the temple. While I swayed on the wall of the charming convent which Nabonidus had built for his daughter, a brick, held fast for twenty-five centuries, broke loose and flung me into the bedroom of the lovely priestess of Nanna. I wanted to avoid any fuss and so hastened off to the residential district, where I savoured the streets and alleys, walking from a house to a store, from a room to a courtyard. My boots pounded the shards of urns littering the ground. I examined bricks fashioned from straw and sun-baked terra-cotta, still bearing words in cuneiform script. I picked up tiny shells which reminded me that once, long ago, the Persian Gulf had reached this far. In an oratory where once the Prophet had prayed to Jehovah, I replied to a litany of flies.

My mind wandered as I came down "the street called straight" (the streets had all been named by Woolley, an archaeologist both imaginative and celebrated); then a big fox decided to play hide-and-seek with me, and just as a forceful leap of the imagination transported me to the age of our father Ibrahim, this darn fox knocked over some bricks and I jumped four feet in the air, not to mention four thousand years!

The Mausoleum

A visit to the mausoleum is the key to the expedition. Imagine a huge building with thirty rooms, and beneath each of them an enormous vault where the royal remains were buried, along with priceless treasures, and sometimes even courtesans. Steep stairs led down into some of the cellars but not into others, and I had to let myself drop down perpendicular shafts. At first I was reluctant to enter, because the vaults were so crumbled and worn. And then: so what! If they had held up for forty centuries, I would be safe visiting them for another five minutes. In fact, there was nothing worth seeing there, but I derived some satisfaction from getting down to the antediluvian level (the depth to which the foundations had been driven). An acrid smell wafted in the air, a lizard fled at my approach, wings flapped somewhere. I looked at the swaying bricks. Let's get back up to the flood, I told myself as I came out again suddenly. And I remembered Isaiah: "But wild beasts will lie down there, and its houses will be full of howling creatures . . . and there satyrs will dance."

I could not bid farewell to Ur without once more climbing the ziggurat. I wanted to get another bird's-eye view of the ordered rubble which had long ago been one of the most civilized cities of Antiquity! I wanted to gaze at the other mound of Eridu along the horizon, which the Ancients deemed to be the oldest in the world. I also wanted to reflect on the previous day I had spent among the ruins of legendary Babylon, precious jewel of Nebuchadnezzar, of Cyrus and Alexander; moulded brick bas-reliefs, Daniel's den; the great hall of Belteshazzar's feast, the hanging gardens, seventh wonder of the world. And of the Tower of Babel itself, all that was left was a slight depression in the ground, in the shape of a huge rectangle. Irony of the gods! Bricks destined to reach up to the sky have finally ended up part of the low-lying huts of Arabs today. "The mills of the gods grind slowly, but they grind exceedingly small."

Archaeology

Of course, some treasures did indeed survive the invaders and bandits of Antiquity. They lie sleeping in the museums of Europe, where other thieves and conquerors will one day seize them. *Sic transeat* . . . But archaeologists will always be obsessed with digging, and the compulsive rite of digging will continue to feed their frustrations in particular. Every bump may conceal treasure – every single bump. Nothing is ever finished: dig just another six inches . . . And in removing earth, they build up other mounds, and may leave behind a shovel, which will have archaeologists from the year 10,000 thinking that humanity in the twentieth century had not made much progress since palae-olithic times.

In the middle of the stairs, I threw a stone at the fox lurking below: I kept an eye on him until he ran clear out of the city walls of Ur.

Once I got to the top of the ziggurat, I saw a huge black bird lunge into the air after leaving droppings on a column where once offerings to the moon goddess had been placed.

At midday the vertical sun offered no shade. I was completely alone in the wide burning desert, from which the Euphrates had a few centuries ago withdrawn. *Vanitas vanitatum, omnia vanitas . . .*

Le Devoir, 12/2/49, p. 9
Translation by George Tombs

Just Back from Moscow

>‹

Pierre Trudeau participated as an economist in a conference held in Moscow. After his return, he published a seven-part account in* Le Devoir, *of which the second part follows. He introduced the series with the following words:*

"For many people, the Soviet Union is Hell and it takes some pact with the Devil just to set foot there. This prejudice has prevented many economists and businessmen from going to the international economic meeting in Moscow.

"But as both a lawyer and an economist, I deplore the idea of rejecting pacts without looking at them carefully. Why hide the fact? If I were offered the safe conducts that Dante apparently had, I would gladly go to Hell in search of a few statistics on damnation."

Self is hateful.
PASCAL

---

* Rencontre économique internationale de Moscou, 1952.

18

If the flexibility of an administrative system can be gauged by its ability to deal with a special case, then I have to give some credit to the Soviets, because I am the very embodiment of a living special case. Instead of taking the plane from Paris to Prague, and then on to Moscow, the way people do when they set out from France, I decided to take the train to Austria.

For reasons which reason alone cannot comprehend, I ended up in Linz, at the edge of the American zone. I then had one hundred miles of Soviet territory to cover before reaching the Czech border, and I asked the [occupation] authorities for all necessary authorization.

The French told me it was impossible. The British proposed an alternative solution which was completely unworkable. The Americans advised me to try my luck, predicting all the while that I would wake up in the mines of Siberia. So it made sense to ask the Soviets directly.

I Get Through!

I crossed the Danube; as soon as I was caught up in the military cogs, I quickly covered the distance separating me from the Kommandantur. Once there, all I had to do was discuss the matter with a Russian officer whose German was just as rusty as mine. I was in for a surprise! He let me through without the slightest formality. And I reflected that the Danube, at Linz, was about as wide across as the distance from Washington to Moscow, and that people on one bank knew nothing about what was happening on the opposite bank.

When I reached Prague at three in the morning and was the only traveller arriving from Austria, I was sure I would catch somebody unprepared. Not at all. I was met at the station, ushered to magnificent lodgings, fed, issued a Soviet visa, and sent to Moscow with exemplary speed and courtesy.

In Moscow, the machine did an admirable job of dealing with my case. (But just wait for the end of the story . . .)

I arrived four days early at the conference and was received with open arms and installed at the new Sovietskaya Hotel, a true master-piece in the *parvenu* style.

I had an interpreter, a chauffeur, and a Ziss (a startling imitation of a deluxe Chrysler) at my disposal. And when I was invited to take on the city, I put my hosts off somewhat by asking for a map of Moscow (which totally defied my attempts at translation) and by indicating that I wanted to walk about alone. I have to say that I was not encouraged to go it alone, and everything was done to organize my time. However, nobody interfered with me; only once did I have the pleasure of making fun of a man following me, but he could just as well have been a gaping onlooker as a policeman. And since I managed pretty well with the subway and buses, I could go wherever I wanted to in Moscow.

At Mass!

On Passion Sunday, I announced that I intended to go to Mass. People were a little astonished that I still believed in old wives' tales like that, but after a few phone calls I was given information regarding the place and the time. In all, during a month's stay in the USSR, I went to Mass on four Sundays, in three different places. I also entered a synagogue and many Orthodox churches. Other conference delegates told me that they went to Protestant churches.

On feast days, these temples are full to the rafters – but full only of old people. Freedom of worship has not been snuffed out, but a lack of religious instruction means that Christianity here is cut off from its young people. Except in Georgia, however, where young people still seem to be pious.

I continued asking all sorts of special questions. I wanted to attend a trial, speak to priests, study the economic foundations of the Gosplan, meet university students, etc. I was never turned down, although the self continued to be hateful, and even insolent.

I Commit Sacrilege

I questioned a judge about his salary and lifestyle. I subjected professors to an examination of economic doctrines. I scoffed at trade-unionists for not being able to go on strike. On the Kolkhoz, I was more interested in the hovels of peasants than in modern stables. I constantly broke away from the group when we visited the Kremlin, opening doors and following corridors in the hopes of finding some lovely icon to look at.

Another time, I was impressed to see, in city and country, in public places and even private ones, effigies, busts, statues, photos, paintings, engravings, mosaics, embroidery, bas-reliefs, done in cardboard, ebony, ivory, marble, sculptured grains of rice, and I don't know what else, representing the Father of the People, the Idol of the Working Class, the Leader of Universal Socialism, the Liberator of the Oppressed, the Chief of History, the Guide of Democrats, the Wise, Eminent, Sweet, Strong, Infallible, the Great Comrade Stalin; I was so impressed, in fact, that I affectionately threw a snowball at a statue representing him in a particularly good-natured pose.

What a scandal! My hosts reacted with pain rather than with anger. Which left me free to continue speaking of Tito and Tomsky, asking for the works of Trotsky in libraries, and generally making tactless remarks.

Le Devoir, 16/6/52
Translation by George Tombs

PART II

Early Political Writings

"Functional Politics," the first article published in Cité libre *(July 1950), ushers in a long series of political writings. Other articles for the same journal would follow, as well as numerous essays, a few reports drafted at the request of union federations and other private organizations, and many commentaries on current events. The following texts are spread out over more than a decade, the first in 1965, the balance from 1950 to 1962.*

Interest in Public Affairs

><

Plato said: "The cost of not showing an interest in public affairs, is to be governed by people worse than oneself."

Actually, there are two kinds of active involvement in public affairs: outside involvement, which consists of critically examining the ideas, institutions, and people who, together, compose the political reality; and inside involvement, the result of becoming a politician oneself.

The people who choose the first option and play the role of political critics have to develop their thoughts to the limit. They would quickly lose their independence, and especially their usefulness, if they stopped to consider the enemies they might make by speaking out, or the doors that their words would close to them. That is why we have spoken and written harshly of all Canadian political parties, without exception – as a way of pushing politicians along the road of progress.

Once the political critic decides to take action, he will inevitably join a political party he has already opposed; it's fair enough that his opponents should remind him of this apparent contradiction. There is no tragedy in the fact that the author was recently criticizing the Liberals – unless it is claimed that a political critic should never enter active politics, thereby preventing political parties from seeking out independent minds and passionate observers of politics.

Cité libre 17/80 (October 1965)
Translation by George Tombs

Functional Politics

✦

For a long time, the sole principle guiding our action was adversity. Our politics consisted in saying "No" and we quite rightly regarded as leaders those who organized effective resistance. Our people were then surrounded by real dangers – above all, ethnic and religious assimilation – and for us the nation's welfare could be defined in terms of contradictions.

But it is not enough to avoid evil; we also have to do good. A Church would be an impostor if it stayed forever in the catacombs. Similarly, in politics you cannot stay below ground too long. An excess of unhappiness will snuff out the spirit, and heroic resistance will degenerate into beast-like stubbornness. That unfortunately is what happens to some peoples who have struggled too much, and take virtue itself to be a negation.

I sometimes wonder if French Canada is not headed for this kind of dead end. Some of our leaders maintain political power by protecting the people from exaggerated and often imaginary dangers. Others gather the flock together and brandish threats of eternal damnation. In other words, it seems less important to make friends than to denounce enemies: communists, the English, Jews, imperialists, centralizers, demons, free-thinkers, and I don't know what else. "That over there is forbidden," we hear; "this over here is not allowed." But who will speak of sins of omission? Who will own up and say, "Father, I am guilty of not doing good?"

"After all," some people will say, "we have held onto the language and faith of our fathers: isn't that something positive?"

What a damnable lie! – illustrating, moreover, the way we mix up quality and quantity. An impartial study of history will show that we started to lose everything the day our enemies became subtle enough to deprive our negations of any justification. Our language has now become so impoverished that we no longer notice how badly we speak it; I sometimes wish some of our people would blush because they can't make themselves understood in France. Our shaky faith is no longer apostolic; eminent prelates have so little confidence in grace that they discourage university students from pursuing their studies abroad – in foreign countries of iniquity. It should come as no surprise that people can lose faith itself without so much as leaving the country.

There are not many ways out of this dead end. If for a moment we stop being afraid of the thought of danger, if we stop upholding our traditions while slandering everything that is opposed to those traditions, we will have to consider what positive actions can support our beliefs.

We want to bear witness to the Christian and French fact in America. Fine; so be it. But let's get rid of all the rest. We should subject to methodical doubt all the political categories relegated to us by the previous generation: the strategy of resistance is no longer conducive to the fulfilment of our society. The time has come to borrow the "functional" discipline from architecture, to throw to the winds those many prejudices with which the past has encumbered the present, and to build for the new man. Let's batter down the totems, let's break the taboos. Better yet, let's consider them null and void. Let us be coolly intelligent.

Cité libre 1/1 (June 1950)
Translation by George Tombs

Reflections on Politics in French Canada

✦

This passage is from a special issue of Cité libre *devoted to the Quebec general election of July 16, 1952. The Union Nationale handily won the election, with 35 per cent of the popular vote, sixty-eight seats out of the Assembly's ninety-two, and corrupt electoral politics in full swing. This corruption reached a peak four years later.*

Our deep-seated immoralism has to be explained.

After all, we claim to be a Christian people. We subscribe to ethics which rigorously define our duties towards society and our neighbour. We do not fail to respect civil authority, and we generally live in a climate of obedience to law. We punish treason and assault in the name of the common weal and of natural law; we explain communism in terms of the faltering of faith; we consider war to be the ransom of sin.

In short, our ideas on the order of society are shaped by Catholic theology, and our personal values generally bear witness to the sincerity of these views – with one exception. In our relations with the State, we are really quite immoral; we corrupt bureaucrats, we blackmail members of the Assembly, we put pressure on the courts, we cheat the tax-collector, we turn a blind eye when it seems profitable to do so. And when it comes to electoral matters, our immoralism is absolutely appalling. The peasant who would be ashamed to enter a brothel sells his conscience for a bottle of whisky. The lawyer who calls for the maximum penalty when the parish poor-box is emptied out is proud to have added two thousand phony names to the electoral list. And stories of electoral dishonesty have so filled the childhood of our collective memory that they hardly shock anyone anymore.

It is not enough to say that "democracy does not catch on among Latin peoples" or that "Nordic peoples have a greater sense of civic-mindedness than we do": we have to find out why that is the case. Where French Canadians are concerned, I believe the answer is to be found in our political history.

Our parliamentary democracy is essentially of British origin. After the Conquest, the conquerors and conquered were more or less agreed that English political institutions should be progressively imported, but for reasons which in my view are diametrically opposed. Canadians of British origin saw self-government as the most noble way to govern the relations between men: their dignity as free citizens would settle for nothing less. However, the institution of self-government did not have any particular attraction for French Canadians: prior to 1763, the country had known only authoritarian government; and even at the municipal level, the peasant had, so to speak, never participated actively in public affairs.

French Canadians did not develop a penchant for politics in the nineteenth century because of some sudden enthusiasm for responsible government. We had one sole passion: survival. And when viewed from this perspective, universal suffrage could very well prove to be a useful instrument. Moreover, by importing the English parliamentary system one piece at a time, our secret goal was not only to use it, but also to abuse it. Let others seek the ideal government: we were ready to use any and every means available. (Frank Scott recently expressed this idea in the review *Esprit*, without being the least bit insulting, when he wrote that French Canadians "have used democracy instead of adhering to it as a doctrine.")

But English parliamentary rule rests on quite clear premises: two parties seek the same common end, but by different means; they establish ground rules according to which the majority party will organize the pursuit of that end, on condition that it will step aside whenever the other party's means become more acceptable to a majority of the electorate.

The rules presuppose an agreement on the end worth seeking as well as the periodic opportunity for the minority to become the majority. However, there has never been any agreement in Canada on the common end, because the French Canadians have always insisted on absolute equality of political rights with English Canadians. And that is something which the governors before the Act of Union, as well as English-Canadian members of Parliament afterwards, had never wanted to consider. Moreover, the alternation between majorities and minorities could never work, because ultimately the majority/minority cleavage reflected a stable ethnic breakdown of the population far more than changes in voting patterns.

Our people faced just two alternatives. Either sabotage the parliamentary machine by means of systematic obstruction, the way the Irish did at Westminster; and who knows? perhaps this pure method might have got us Laurentian home rule and we would have honest politics by now – within an insignificant State. Or appear to play the parliamentary game, but without considering ourselves morally bound by its fundamental postulates; this was the choice of our ancestors, who refused to confine their Canadianism to Lower Canada alone.

They understood that, for a long time to come, the government of the people and by the people would not be *for* the people, except, above all, for the English-speaking part of the people. From then on, they adhered to the social contract with mental reservations: they did not believe there could be any "general will" without an ethnic pact; and since there was no hope for them of sharing as equal partners in a Canadian common weal, they secretly decided to pursue their own French-Canadian weal. Which meant breaking the rules of the Canadian weal in order to safeguard the French-Canadian weal. In other words, they formed a community within the community. From the Union government onwards, the people seemed to lose interest in any ideology other than nationalism. For the people, the terms "Tory" and "Clear-Grit," "Conservative" and "Liberal," related less to techniques of administration than to a see-saw which made upping the ante and extracting concessions all the easier; instead of dealing in ideological terms, people came to speak simply of "bleu" and "rouge." That is why the Church's condemnation of liberalism and of the advantages of reciprocity for our people did not prevent Laurier from winning in 1896 and from losing in 1911: our people did not vote for or against a philosophical or economic ideology but only for the champion of our ethnic rights; first Laurier, then Bourassa.

Unfortunately, cheating is habit-forming. A subtle form of casuistry allowed us to break the rules of the political game, until ultimately the game itself slipped out of the whole realm of morality. We had done so well at subordinating the Canadian public weal to the French-Canadian weal that we lost any sense of moral obligation to the former. Apart from times of strife (Riel, the separate-schools question in the West, conscription), during which we instinctively massed together to fight for survival within the whole community, everyone pursued his own interest, to the detriment of the community. In other words, our sense of civic responsibility was perverted.

This genesis of our lack of civic-mindedness has important religious dimensions. We have to admit that Catholics, collectively, have rarely been pillars of democracy – I say that to our shame, and without seeking to prejudge the future. Catholics manage to confuse spiritual and temporal questions, and thus have a hard time settling on any single truth when the time comes to count votes. In countries with a large Catholic majority (Poland, Austria, Spain, Portugal, Italy, South American republics), Catholics often only avoid anarchy by means of authoritarian rule, whereas in those countries where they are not as strong (France, Germany, The Netherlands, Belgium, the United States, Canada) they accept the separation of Church and State as a stopgap measure; they devote their civic energies to the pursuit of the

Catholic weal; and, as a group, they are notable neither for their morality nor for their political insight.

Cité libre 2/3 (December 1952)
Translation by George Tombs

On Economic Domination in

International Relations

>-<

The following paragraphs are taken from a statement made at the annual meeting of the Institut canadien des affaires publiques, at the beginning of the 1950s.

. . . In the great majority of cases, foreign domination means: American. If we stick to the manufacturing industry, we see that this influence tends to be concentrated in an ever-smaller number of large corporations: of sixty Canadian companies with equity of $25 million and over, American capital represents 42 per cent of the number and 60 per cent of the value.

The meaning of these figures is obvious: in key sectors of the Canadian economy, non-residents are in a position to take decisions quite foreign to the welfare of Canadians. The foreigner will determine whether our oil wells will be exploited or capped, whether our ore will be refined here or elsewhere, whether our factories will be automated or not, whether our products will reach world markets or not, whether our workers are free to exercise their right of association or not. The foreigner will decide . . . and will collect the profits. In the postwar years, for example, 55 per cent of dividends paid by all Canadian companies were distributed to non-residents; at the same time, these people automatically laid their hands on two-fifths of the accumulated and retained profits, thus strengthening their hold on our economy.

. . .

In conclusion, we can see that a country under the control of a dominant economy can turn things to its advantage only by planning. That is why Canadian nationalism should turn to economic interventionism and why politicians should think more of general welfare than they think of campaign funds.

But that may be too much to expect. Canadians want an economic system offering all the advantages of a policy of state intervention without actually having a planned economy . . .

Address, Institut canadien des
affaires publiques (1953)
Translation by George Tombs

On Constitutional Problems . . . in 1953

>—<

In 1953, the Fédération des unions industrielles du Québec asked Pierre Elliott Trudeau to draft a report for submission to the commission of inquiry set up by the Government of Quebec to study constitutional problems. In his preface to the second edition of the report, the author wrote: "It is only fair to add that a report like this had to be the fruit of a collective effort. As in any democratic movement, the ideas that form the substance of the report were studied and developed during discussions with the federation, and especially with its executive. . . . As far as originality in the thinking and perseverance in the execution are concerned, the real author (of whom I would like to have been a better student) was the Quebec labour movement."

Here are a few passages from the report.

The federation is first and foremost an association of industrial workers. However, if the federation appears in this report, as much as in its daily actions, to specifically promote guarantees of material living conditions, that shouldn't lead anyone to conclude that the workers do not attach much importance to spiritual matters. On the contrary, the workers want to safeguard the respect of all human values; and they

36

uphold the inviolability of the person as the basis of civil and political society. That is why they want to use the Canadian Constitution in order to protect the individual's inviolability from arbitrary rule. In particular, they are deeply committed to the democratic system and to the liberties on which that system is based, such as the freedom of belief, of thought, of the press, of assembly, and of association. They uphold the equality of all before the law. And they maintain that Canada's real character – the union of two large ethnic groups – calls for an intelligent and open kind of federalism. . . .

The Fédération des unions industrielles du Québec does not have a narrow objective. Our association seeks nothing less than the fulfilment of each worker's potential; however, the federation is realistic and knows that such an ideal cannot be attained simply by means of declarations of principle and exhortations to virtue.

The federation is made up of men and women who, throughout their life, must devote the greater part of their energies to their own material security and that of their family. And it knows that the imperative of survival has a greater impact than constitutional guarantees on the religious, cultural, and political evolution of a people; living, after all, comes ahead of philosophizing. . . .

Labour Legislation

One of the specific objectives of labour unions is to obtain for workers the highest salaries compatible with progress and justice. It is a well-known principle that justice has a greater chance of being respected in an agreement between co-signatories who are on an equal footing. Consequently, the best labour contract results from the parties (employers and workers) discussing and negotiating as equals. And that is why workers organize themselves in labour unions.

As a result, labour legislation favouring trade-unionism benefits the entire community; not only do workers learn within their labour unions how to govern themselves, which is indispensable in a democracy, but they also obtain greater security and higher salaries, which makes them less dependent on relief from the State.

This is where the constitutional question comes in. The provinces are, as it were, rivals when it comes to attracting capital: each province tries to attract industry and to exploit its natural resources as best it can. But since investments automatically flow to wherever the return at the margin is the most attractive – where profits are the highest – there is a danger that provinces might get into a bidding war, forcing salaries downward. And since labour legislation falls under provincial jurisdiction (except in certain industries, such as railways), a short-sighted government might be tempted to base its economic-expansion policy on union-busting legislation: the other provinces would be forced to lower their standard of living, or risk being cut off from capital markets altogether.

The federation is opposed to any "injustice premium" and wants to see a minimum of equity in wage scales across the country. In particular, we should move towards legislation guaranteeing Canadians an equal right of association and related rights such as union accreditation and union security; there should also be minimum age and wage standards, and maximum limits on working hours. . . .

If all workers fully enjoyed these conditions, then the cause of many industrial conflicts would simply disappear, and competition between the provinces would neither provoke nor intensify class struggle.

There are two ways of developing the kind of national labour code we have outlined. The first consists in transferring jurisdiction in this area to the federal government. The second consists in the provinces agreeing to adopt certain common standards.

The federation's preference is for reform based on an agreement between the provinces, since no constitutional amendment would be required. Industrial legislation is closely linked to the law of contracts and, in the federal system, comes under provincial rather than federal jurisdiction. Each province is free to resolve problems raised by industrialization in its own way and according to its own lights; and the provinces can then share among themselves the most appropriate solutions they have come up with. . . .

This whole process naturally calls for frequent interprovincial meetings, exchanges, and agreements. But whereas the International

Labour Organization exists to coordinate legislation in different countries, no equivalent organization exists in Canada to institutionalize cooperation between the provinces. . . .

Fiscal Cooperation

There can be no stable prosperity or true autonomy in a federation without some kind of fiscal cooperation between governments. . . . This federal–provincial cooperation should be based on the following principles:

1. *The principle of fiscal proportionality*
Each government, whether federal or provincial, should have a fiscal right of taxation proportionate to the responsibilities under its jurisdiction in the taxable area under its territorial authority.

2. *The principle of financial equalization*
The federal and provincial governments on the whole should make sure that they all have adequate financial resources to carry out their tasks properly.

3. *The principle of economic stabilization*
No government should be in a position to prevent the implementation of a countercyclical fiscal policy that Canadians generally want.

Conclusion: An Open and Courageous Federalism

It will be noted that the federation is not so much trying to propose constitutional amendments as to show how the current constitution could help citizens and governments pursue the common weal together.

Clearly, the federation could have promoted many other reforms. For example, municipal and school regulations are extremely important for workers and their children who generally live in urban centres. . . . But the federation preferred to leave discussion of these problems to public bodies more directly concerned with them. . . . Which obviously doesn't preclude citizens from working on all fronts at the same time. Quite the contrary. Arguments supporting decentralization and inter-governmental cooperation would be more convincing, however, if practical benefits were first demonstrated within a province, at the level of municipal, school, and university regulations, etc.

The first objective of the autonomy movement is to open up and improve contacts between the governors and the governed. One of the first responsibilities of autonomists is both to increase the number of civic experiences at all levels and to help develop that critical sense which is required by sovereignty of the people. A movement for true autonomy will thus seek to give real powers to local governments, leaving a real degree of responsibility in the hands of the people and encouraging self-government in such semipublic bodies as labour unions, factories, cooperatives, etc. . . .

It is abundantly clear, then, that cooperation between the federal government and the provinces is indispensable, for the obvious reason that neither the Constitution nor administrative practice provides for an adequate and exclusive division between executive, legislative, and judicial functions of the federal government and the provinces. Since cooperation is inevitable, it seems reasonable to make that cooperation as effective as possible. It is time to stop seeing cooperation as a secret opportunity to reach for new powers, since that can only make for more acrimony all round. . . .

Therefore, the federation recommends that a first federal–provincial conference be held in order to discuss

1. setting up a federal–provincial secretariat;
2. fiscal cooperation;
3. labour legislation.

The government of the province should make a clear and detailed statement to this effect so that the other governments know what to expect. In particular, Quebec should make concrete proposals on how to solve the fiscal problem; it should also show that it is ready to make compromises on certain questions of constitutional jurisdiction.

The province could then say it was ready to accept that a declaration of human rights be entrenched in the Constitution, on condition that the rights of disallowance and reservation were done away with. The province could put forward a specific plan to patriate the Canadian Constitution, providing at the same time for an amending formula, on condition that the Senate became a more federalist and less unitary body, and on condition that the makeup of the Supreme Court depended directly on the Canadian Constitution rather than on federal laws alone.

Report of the Fédération des unions industrielles du Québec to the Royal Commission of Inquiry on Constitutional Problems set up by the Quebec government (1953).
Translation by George Tombs

The Asbestos Strike

><

In spring 1956 a study came out in Montreal on the asbestos strike, co-authored by nine people: professors, trade-unionists, and journalists, under the direction of Pierre Elliott Trudeau, who had written one-fourth of the study. André Laurendeau, then editor-in-chief of Le Devoir, *wrote a series of long editorials entitled "P.E. Trudeau's Hundred Pages" in which he was by turns critical, harsh, and full of praise. The series ended with the following words: "What comes out most strongly, quite apart from Trudeau's technical competence, is his love of liberty; he fully accepts liberty's risks as well as its advantages. A remarkable personality has appeared."*

The Ideas

Generally speaking, the leading ideas in a society tend to become embodied in its institutions and so identified with them that one cannot describe the thinking of its leaders without also revealing the propensities of the institutions which provide a context for their actions.

In Quebec, however, during the first half of the twentieth century, our social thinking was so idealistic, so a priori, so divorced from reality, in sum so futile, that it was hardly ever able to find expression in living and dynamic institutions. By isolating some aspects of this thought, we may show the reader just how little – at the time of the asbestos strike – people were prepared to accept, interpret, and influence realities in this highly industrialized province, as I have sketched it above.

In my analysis, I attach little importance to the few circles where liberal and realistic thought existed on the fringes of our monolithic ideology, as I call it. I am, of course, fully aware that such circles did exist. The profound repercussions of the asbestos strike on very different parts of our society later revealed the foresight and courage of those who had refused to accept our official thinking as an affirmation of eternal truths. This chapter, though, is not primarily devoted to handing out medals, but to describing a society which had arrived at a critical point in its development. Why does the upheaval we are study-ing have such a scope and importance? In my opinion, it is not because a few precursors were able to understand and influence reality, but because circumstances forced an entire people to choose one lifestyle (as I have shown above), while all its intellectual and moral training urged it to cling to another (as I will explain below).

The Main Focus

Up to the very end of the period studied in this book, nationalism was the main focus of almost all French Canadian social thought. This indisputable fact needs no explanation here. A people which had been defeated, occupied, decapitated, pushed out of commerce, driven from the cities, reduced little by little to a minority, and diminished in influence in a country which it had nonetheless discovered, explored, and colonized, could adopt few attitudes that would enable it to preserve its identity. This people devised a system of security, which became overdeveloped; as a result, they sometimes overvalued all those things that set them apart from others, and showed hostility to all change (even progress) coming from without.

That is why our nationalism, to oppose a surrounding world that was English-speaking, Protestant, democratic, materialistic, commercial, and later industrial, created a system of defence which put a premium on all the contrary forces: the French language, Catholicism, authoritarianism, idealism, rural life, and later the return to the land.

From this set of values, focussed by nationalism, the social theorists created an astrology which claimed to regulate the destinies of French Canada with all the precision of the celestial system. In this way, they reasoned, our providential mission would be accomplished.

These thinkers were building, in the twentieth century, a superstructure which combined, in a logical and homogeneous manner, all the social ideas that had proved useful to the French Canadians at a period in their past history. Meanwhile, the French Canadian people themselves were busy meeting the challenges to their existence offered by everyday reality. Individuals, after all, must first worry about making a decent living for themselves and their families, even if they have to upset a few mental constructs in the process. The result of this in practice was that nationalistic ideas were continually threatened with extinction, and nationalism survived as best it could. In the last century, for example, the exodus to American industrial centres dissolved a little pastoral dream. Authoritarianism was considerably shaken when Laurier was brought to power by a people to whom Monsignor Laflèche had preached, during the election campaign of 1896, that "no Catholic could, without committing a serious sin, vote for a party leader" like Laurier.

In the following pages, I do not intend to analyze what is sometimes (wrongly) called our "de facto nationalism." This is only the concrete result of the virtue of patriotic piety exercised, after a fashion, by an ethnic group, and one which men of action sometimes pretend to have served after the event. I shall, instead, be concerned with our "theoretical nationalism," as formulated and dispensed by those among us who were professional writers and teachers, and who were generally accepted as our leaders and intellectual masters.

In the present context, I can only mention a few people; they are, however, recognized as typical. Since I do not have the space to do justice to their thought as a whole, I feel I should say that these men are, almost without exception, worthy of respect. They have lacked neither honesty in their intentions nor courage in their undertakings; neither firmness of purpose, nor always imagination in their solution of problems. Surrounded by a materialistic civilization and confronted by politicians who were often shameless, the nationalist school was just about alone in constructing a *system of thought*. As I shall be chiefly concerned with social and economic questions, I shall rarely have a chance to mention the valid aspects of this thinking, but it would be wrong to conclude that I minimize the value of the services it was able to render. Was it, perhaps, necessary first to "save the race," so that others might later find what was worth saving in the man? The gestation of a culture is a matter of generations, and today's generation would perhaps have thought like those of yesteryear, if born twenty years earlier. Perhaps . . . but I do not want to judge anyone, and remote historical facts do not interest me very much. For the same reason, I will not shrink from emphasizing those aspects of nationalist thought which are a burden on the present, and harmful to free and honest action. In all fairness, however, I cannot undertake a criticism of this thought without offering its adherents this statement in their favour: there have been many varieties of "nationalists," but most of them were known by their spirit of loyalty, their faith in the intellect (if not always in man!), and a certain respect for culture. Had such men not concerned themselves with public affairs, our people would have had that much less experience of disinterested government.

Alas, the nationalists have been harmed by their very idealism. They loved not wisely but too well, and in their desire to obtain only the best for the French Canadians, they formulated a system of social thought which could not be realized and which, for all practical purposes, left the people without any effective intellectual guidelines. It is this social thought which I now wish to examine.

Nationalism as an Intellectual Discipline

In a sermon of 1902, which has become "the breviary of the French Canadian patriot," Mgr. Paquet declared: "It is our privilege to be entrusted with this social ministry, reserved for elite peoples. . . . Our mission is not so much to manipulate capital, as to handle ideas; not so much to light the fires of factories, as to maintain the luminous hearth of religion and of thought, making it to radiate afar. While our rivals are laying claim to the hegemony of industry and finance, we shall strive above all for the honour of doctrine and the palms of apostleship."

The policies and principles of this school of idealism could not be more succinctly and forcefully stated. Our intellectuals had to subscribe to them, and one after the other they all aspired to "the honour of doctrine." It reduced them to complete intellectual sterility in the end, for the only doctrine they were permitted to expound had to be derived from the most unproductive traditionalism.

One hundred years apart, two mentors of "the doctrine" established a rigorous framework for all research. In the conclusion to his *Histoire du Canada*, F.X. Garneau wrote: "May the French Canadians remain faithful to themselves; may they be wise and persevering; and may they not let themselves be seduced in any way by the glitter of social and political innovations! They are not strong enough to give themselves free rein in this field. It is up to the great peoples of the world to put new theories to the test." In 1945, this counsel of excessive caution had become, in the writings of Mr. Esdras Minville, an imperious *Gleichschaltung*: "It is not enough for us to desire equally the welfare of the nation; we must wish *unanimously* for the means to achieve it. . . ." As we shall see, a *unanimous* system of thought, as our nationalists understood it, could only be timid and reactionary.

Anyone whose thinking went beyond the limits of official nationalism or who tried to reshape it by changing a basic trait was thus automatically suspect: on all sides, he and his ideas were scrutinized. If he renounced nationalism, he was discredited and ignored; if he embraced it, his ideas were emasculated, then assimilated.

This happened to Edouard Montpetit and a few other young professors. Before World War I, they came back from Europe with the idea, rare at the time, that our people should enter the fields of industry and finance. This idea had been advocated in the nineteenth century by Etienne Parent, Edmond de Nevers, and Errol Bouchette, but had not yet found favour, although the yearly exodus of 20,000 people to the United States was due to the lack of industry in Quebec.

Greeted with hostility and suspicion, the young professors were accused of atheism, on the excellent grounds that they taught economic liberalism.

Finally, they succumbed to attrition. By consenting to "think nationally" in their scientific work, they arrested its development and gave official social thought the chance to overtake and engulf their own. Within a few decades, they were blithely teaching an obsolete science in our schools. In addition, a growing number of our thinkers had already begun to grapple with economic issues, in nationalistic terms of course.

In 1921 Joseph Versailles, a Montreal financier, addressed a convention of the Association catholique de la jeunesse canadienne-française (Catholic Association of French Canadian Youth [A.C.J.C.]) as follows: "Let us stop serving our enemies. With the help of material power and moral force, our race will win a place of honour. . . . To succeed, we must get our most promising youngsters to take up careers in business and finance." In the same year *L'action française*, then edited by Abbé Groulx, began a lengthy investigation of economic issues. In 1927, it carried a study of the French Canadians' economic status by Olivar Asselin. He concluded that, though French Canadians made up two sevenths of the Canadian population, they possessed only one seventh of the national wealth. "Given our numbers," he wrote, "we aren't half as rich as we should be."

During the Depression, economic nationalism was discussed more than ever. In 1934, according to *Le Devoir* of October 30, Abbé Groulx asked: "There are 2,500,000 French Canadians in Quebec. Is it inevitable, then, that all big business, all high finance, all the public utility companies, all our hydro power, all our forests, all our mines should belong to a minority of 300,000 individuals?" (Groulx, of course, is speaking of an *ethnic* minority. We should not regard this passage as a restatement of the principle: "Property is theft.") In the same year Athanase David, Secretary of the Province of Quebec, writing in *En marge de la politique* (Speaking of Politics), dared to say: "Has the day not come when the graduates of our classical colleges must no longer look upon commerce, industry, and finance as occupations unworthy of their culture and their education? . . . I believe that we must have money. With money, we can do the great things which we are meant to achieve on this continent." In 1936, Victor Barbeau assessed our situation in *Mesure de notre taille* (Sizing Us Up). He showed (p. 24) that "apart from the land, in all her desolate and ravaged immensity, apart from a few islets where we hold on by the force of inertia, we have nothing, you see, nothing. We do not even enjoy the use of the innumerable riches bestowed on us by God."

In a province which was 63% urbanized and already heavily industrialized, in a city which, in 1933, had a 30% unemployment rate and 280,000 people "on direct welfare," people saw the inadequacies of aspiring to "the honour of doctrine and the palms of apostleship" while despising industrialization. They began to think that the engineer, the merchant, and the businessman played as vital a social role as the priest, the doctor, and the lawyer. Because nationalism coloured our approach to these problems, however, we religiously avoided any solution that might challenge our basic assumptions.

Our assumptions about agriculture will illustrate our overall approach. Having suggested an *Achat chez nous* (Buy Quebec Products) program to solve our economic difficulties, Edouard Montpetit went on to say: "This will solve our problems in secondary industry, which will be largely supported by agriculture, the basic industry which furnishes the raw materials." Two months later, Olivar Asselin published some striking work, in which he attacked the sellout of our natural resources and the exodus to the United States, but arrived at this strange conclusion: "To keep the natural increase of the population in the country, it will not therefore be necessary to have new industries, if there is some way of keeping the farmers' sons attached to the soil." He preached colonization in Abitibi and wanted to postpone the employment of "our race" in big industry. Then, in 1928, in *L'action française*, Asselin, drawing on the conclusions of his inquiry of 1927, which we discussed above, was principally concerned with rural affairs. He did recommend a revolutionary policy, the eventual return to the State of natural resources exploited by private interests, but the greater part of his reforms dealt with agricultural methods and products, handicrafts, the country schools, and fisheries. Victor Barbeau declared that agriculture would have saved us from the humiliations of the Depression, and jeered at us for having "rushed to the fires that industry was lighting all over our hills." Athanase David was careful not "to ignore the fact that Quebec is above all a field, that it is and will remain an agricultural province." Henri Laureys, though Dean of the Ecole des hautes études commerciales (School for Higher Commercial Studies), hardly went any further: "To achieve its fullest development, Quebec agriculture must, by a certain industrial extension, strive for the expansion which is denied it by the facts of geography." In 1945 Father Arès, S.J., took stock of our overall situation in *Notre question nationale* (Our National Question). He wrote that the industrial revolution "was bound to be disastrous for our people . . . [because] we did not have money, we did not have any industrial and commercial tradition, we did not have any great technical schools. Above all, we did not have a clearly defined social and national doctrine." Arès, a theorist of nationalism, was ready to supply a social doctrine along the following lines: "This belittling of rural life is a great misfortune, because of the prime importance of the countryside in the lives of nations in general, and of our nation in particular. What Minville says is true: 'The countryside has always been a reservoir for the physical and moral forces of a nation. In our bustling, unsettled times, this is truer than ever. . . .' . . . From the social and moral standpoint the big city, especially in times of high unemployment, devours bodies and souls, disrupts family life, and arouses hatred and resentment. Social unrest and revolutionary ideas flourish in this environment."

The theorists told city workers that they were naturally inferior, and proclaimed that Quebec must pursue its vocation for agriculture, in spite of the fact that less than 5% of its surface area was said to be arable. Nevertheless, they had to suggest some cure for the "ills" introduced by industrialization.

Unfortunately, few were qualified for the task. Clergymen, journalists, lawyers, and accountants vainly tried to become sociologists and economists, but they could not free themselves from a social environment that was traditionalist, anti-modern, and imbued with authoritarianism and fuzzy thinking.

When, accordingly, they had diagnosed our intellectual, social, and economic plight with some vigour; had censured our people's lack of spirit and exhorted them to show initiative and perseverance; had preached the familial, rural, and national virtues; had spoken at length of reforming the educational system; had gone over time and again the ideas they clung to; then their social thinking stopped strangely short: they had not yet said anything about our absorption into the real world of the industrial revolution.

Now the same preoccupation with security that had made them incapable of resolving the problems of the new era by themselves also prevented them from studying the solutions other people were proposing.

Our official thinkers, with amazing constancy, ignored all the social science of their own day. To judge by their writings, we may say without exaggeration that until very recently they knew nothing of universal legal thought, from Duguit to Pound; nothing of sociology, from Durkheim to Gurvitch; nothing of economics, from Walras to Keynes; nothing of political science, from Bosanquet to Laski; nothing of psychology, from Freud to Piaget; nothing of pedagogy, from Dewey to Ferrière.

They filled in these gaps in their social thought with a set of ideas which they called the social doctrine of the Church.

"Our" Social Doctrine of the Church

We must distinguish clearly between Catholic social ethics as expounded by certain popes who have been particularly attentive to the upheavals of modern society and the social doctrine of the Church as it has been understood and applied in French Canada.

The first group of ideas does not concern me here; the second is exactly my subject. It is nothing more, in fact, than a continuation of our traditionalist assumptions, with a veneer of papal authority. Our official thinkers were scarcely willing to recognize the advent of industrialization and the conversion of the masses into a proletariat. They were totally unprepared to understand these phenomena and had great difficulty in seeing the profound significance of the social encyclicals, which were written to put an end to what Pius XI called the scandal of the Church. Consequently, in drawing on the social thought of the popes, our theorists adopted only formulas which might dignify our collective prejudices with a borrowed prestige.

This exploitation of papal authority for the sake of nationalism was favoured by a misunderstanding stemming from the popes' condemnation of capitalism. The popes reproached this system because it kept a certain proletariat in abject poverty and prevented most people from developing their truly human qualities; our clerical and nationalist doctrine seemed opposed to this system principally because it kept the French Canadians in a state of economic colonialism and prevented them from developing their truly nationalist qualities. Abbé Groulx, quoted by Father Arès with approval, said: "Here, not only classes are oppressed, but a nation. . . ." Still, Abbé Groulx was more realistic than many others, for he also said: "I am certainly not claiming that if our captains of industry or finance were drawn from our own people, we would be socially better off. . . . Social evil would remain social evil, but the passions which dangerously aggravate it would be entirely absent."

An indigenous capitalism would probably have spared us every misfortune likely to be accompanied by "passions"! Our captains of industry would have protected us from the worldwide economic depression and, had they failed in that task, they would not have aroused any resentment among the unemployed, so long as they were of the same blood! We see, then, that for our social thinkers, industrialization did not present any serious problem that was not already known at the time of that *Maria Chapdelaine* they so loved to quote; their complaint remained the same: "Strangers have surrounded us whom it is our pleasure to call foreigners; they have taken into their hands most of the rule, they have gathered to themselves much of the wealth. . . ." They could not, then, imagine that to become part of a world transformed by the industrial revolution, they would have to make a few modifications in their traditional ideas and methods. "For this is it that we must abide in that Province where our fathers dwelt, living as they have lived . . . nought shall suffer change. . . ."

In other countries, the social doctrine of the Church did much to prepare the way for the democratization of peoples, the emancipation of workers, and the progress of society. In French Canada, it was invoked in support of authoritarianism and xenophobia. What is more serious still, our doctrine made it impossible for us to solve our problems. On the negative side, it rejected any solution which might succeed among our "enemies": the English, Protestants, materialists, etc. On the positive side, it was content to set up conceptual systems bearing no objective relation to reality; the application of these systems was frequently impossible.

Negative Effects of the Doctrine

In the field of economics, we rejected those corrective measures for capitalism devised by the liberal economists of Sweden and England and recommended for our use by the federal civil servants in Ottawa. For example, one of the most tragic episodes of the Thirties was our complete confusion in the face of unemployment, combined with our unshakable opposition to any constitutional amendment that would make it possible for Ottawa to attack the problem seriously. Our economists even managed to see that the unemployed in Quebec obtained less relief from federal sources than those out of work in the other provinces. As Esdras Minville remarked, the province of Quebec "received less because it asked for less. . . . Quebec had a kind of instinctive fear of excessive expenses. . . . The other provinces, which do not have the same *traditional attitude towards expenditures*, seem on the contrary to have wanted to profit as much as possible from federal handouts: public works, etc."

Our efforts in the social field were extremely feeble as well. Like the popes, for example, we had long demanded family allowances, but our influence on the capitalist organization of our society was slight. In addition, we were obstinately devoted to the idea that the State was a bogeyman eager to devour the family. We were thus unable to introduce this reform either through private enterprise or social legislation, and family allowances – desired by the Church and constitutionally within the jurisdiction of the provinces – were ultimately offered to French Canadian families by the federal, "Protestant" government. Significantly, François Albert Angers, the most competent and estimable of our nationalistic economists, tried to preach the rejection of these allowances by personal example, on the grounds that they were a threat to paternal authority.

We should also mention the case of old age pensions. The federal act dates from 1927; the provinces decided, one by one, to permit their elderly inhabitants to profit by the scheme. The last province to act was Quebec: it waited until 1936. This should come as no surprise; as late as 1939, the most famous sociologist in French Canada taught the traditional doctrine in these terms: "Social welfare in the Province of Quebec is organized by *private initiatives*. The Catholics are generally agreed that this must continue to be so. Let the State intervene to supplement or to round out the program, not to oust it or dominate it. . . . The urgency with which different measures are required varies from people to people and from age to age."

Finally, in the area of politics, we condemned ourselves to an equally discouraging impotence, because our political ideas were imbued with authoritarianism and we continued to regard the State as an entity independent of its citizens. This native obstinacy in believing that even the provincial government (though elected by a French Canadian majority) could not be placed at our service and under our control is found even in a theorist who, to his credit, made a patient effort to rehabilitate democracy among listeners who scarcely believed in it. Maximilien Caron analyzes the grandeur and servitude of the State in these terms: "The masses are thus able to extort one concession after another [from the political parties]. These concessions ultimately weaken authority, gravely compromise the finances of the State, and bring about the ruin of the government. . . . The State, *almost always impotent*, is a witness to these fratricidal struggles [between rich and poor]." In a discussion of corporatism, the same author speaks of the legislative function of the State: "The regulation of society by corporations is a thousand times better than the cartel and state control of the economy. Corporative control is adopted in broad daylight, with the consent of the majority of those concerned, under the surveillance of government and of consumer protection groups." How, then, does this jurist believe that a democratic government ought to pass laws?

This attitude, combined with the pope's condemnation of atheistic socialism, gave us an excuse to reject the new Canadian social-democratic party, the Cooperative Commonwealth Federation (C.C.F.), though it was concerned neither with atheism nor philosophy, but offered us concrete political means for putting an end to the economic colonialism which our nationalism found so offensive.

In expounding the social doctrine of the Church, Cardinal Villeneuve rather neatly summed up our political thought. His judgments include the following: "The C.C.F. doctrine was condemned in a pastoral letter by Mgr. Gauthier, Archbishop of Montreal. The C.C.F. differs from communism mainly in that it does not seek to obtain its ends by violent means. . . . [As for Social Credit], the Church is neutral with regard to the Social Credit Party. . . . As for fascism, [Mussolini] has made a great contribution to saving the peace of Europe by his presence at Munich. The Italian mode of government involves certain dangers, it is true, but one should not forget that the democratic form of government involves certain dangers as well."

Obviously, expressions of doctrine of this kind – in a society where a bishop's opinion was equivalent to an order – were not likely to foster, in the people, that spirit of inquiry and liberty of judgment which are basic to democratic practice. Our thinkers seemed, at heart, to be deeply suspicious of the people, who had, in a way, betrayed their providential mission by abandoning the land – where they were starving – to go and work in the cities. Furthermore, in our interpretation of the social doctrine of the Church, political society was viewed much more in terms of elites and leaders than in terms of the political education of the masses.

This was, in fact, the era when the Editions de l'A.C.J.C. (Publications of the Catholic Association of French Canadian Youth) published their book *On demande des chefs* (We Want Leaders).

Elsewhere Abbé Groulx wrote in connection with the subject of "language and survival": "We have, however, a magnificent army of masters at our disposal. They are waiting only for a doctrine, a method, an impulsion. Who will be the mover, the supreme distributor of impetus, of will-power? Who will be the national leader, the de Valera, the Mussolini, whose policies are debatable but who, in ten years, have in psychological terms created a new Ireland and a new Italy, as a Dollfuss and a Salazar are in the process of making a new Austria and a new Portugal? Alas, we had better admit frankly: we do not have this national leader. Will we ever have him? . . . With anguished heart we shall demand this man of Providence, the man that every people needs. Meanwhile . . . etc."

The editors of *L'action nationale* put it as follows: "French Canada demands a leader. . . . Our survival urgently requires a leader, a real leader, with our traditions in his bones, strong in our faith, clear-headed, determined, high-spirited. May Providence bring him forth."

Albert Lévesque, an editor of nationalist publications, also wrote: "For some years, in fact, young people have been demanding leaders; they are even sorry that they have lacked some. They complain that there are no directives, and they beg their elders to provide them." In 1945, Esdras Minville wrote two volumes, *The French Canadian Citizen* (*Le citoyen canadien-français*), in which he called upon the elite to play a role of great importance. He had already distinguished, as one of the "peculiar qualities" of our popular mentality, "an acceptance, spontaneous so to speak, of authority and hierarchy in the family, in society, and in the State. *The French Canadians like to be governed.* . . .*"

Before we turn to an analysis of the positive content of our social doctrine, we ought to point out one final characteristic of it: an idealism bordering on schizophrenia. An escape by the high road offered the only exit from the blind alley where our social thought had ended up. Our ethnic group really had no influence on the private sector of the economy; we could always seek consolation in aspiring to the "palms of apostleship," but this course of action did not offer us an effective means of demanding improvements in a social order which assigned us the role of servants. Furthermore, we abhorred state intervention on principle, and we also rejected any political action likely to result in economic reforms, for the irrefutable reason that liberal economic reforms were proposed by the "English," socialist reforms by "materialists."

Still, we proudly aspired to ideal solutions, despite the great poverty of our social sciences. Our attitude was: "A Catholic is too rich to borrow from communists or socialists." Our social policies had hardly been successful, and yet we said: "Let's keep it [political power] for ourselves, entirely for ourselves. Let's tear it away from the domination of financial powers, from the tentacles of Ottawa." Our trade union movement may have been pretty feeble, but still we said: "Let's not abandon our workers to agitators from outside our borders."

Esdras Minville, in commenting on an investigation into "25 years of national life," summed up our economic position as follows: "The evident inability of the capitalist system to solve the painful problems from its own functioning, and the inhuman character of the so-called reforms advocated by the adherents of communism and totalitarianism of all kinds, have convinced [the French Canadians] of an elementary truth, that they can expect to obtain a solution to their problems from no one other than themselves. For the past few years, instead of looking to the outside world for directives, an orientation, a system of thought, or a doctrine, they have set out to find these things within themselves, in their own social philosophy and in the examination of their actual situation."

The young people were no less filled with national pride than their elders. André Laurendeau, in his *Alerte aux Canadiens français* (Warning to French Canadians), blamed Mr. Godbout for his acceptance of an amendment to the constitution enabling the federal government to deal (finally) with the problem of unemployment. He thus explained why it was necessary to prevent Ottawa from invading the field of social legislation. "In this event, a Protestant majority will screen the reforms which have been or are to be undertaken to make our social life conform more closely to Catholic morality. The dreams of corporatism will be shattered. Our hopes of readapting social legislation to the needs of the family will disappear for a long time (because Anglo-Saxon thought is more firmly individualistic than ours), and so will our hopes of altering that legislation to meet the needs of the human and geographical context (since Ottawa will legislate for the country as a whole and not for this or that part of it). . . . We cannot compromise on social legislation for any reason: *we need to control all of it*" (Laurendeau's italics).

This attitude is rather surprising, considering the retrograde attitudes which had always been typical of Quebec social policies. The search for self-government is truly an admirable step, provided that one fully intends to govern oneself. We must now look at what positive recommendations we made, as substitutes for those harmful reforms offered us by the outside world.

The Positive Message

I do not, of course, intend to consider each of the panaceas put forward by the social theorists of French Canada in the last fifty years. Some, like handicrafts, were too obviously futile to detain us. Others, like our opinions on immigration, amounted to a rejection and became associated with the negative effects of the doctrine. Still others, like certain statements on state control or nationalization, were too sporadic, timid, and especially too contradictory to amount to a really "positive message." Essentially, then, our nationalist "social doctrine of the Church" proposed the renewal of economic and social life by five means: the return to the land, small business, the cooperative movement, the Catholic trade union movement, and corporatism.

a) The return to the land

Any proposed remedy for the upheavals caused by industrialization almost always featured colonization and the return to the land. As I have already shown above, agriculturalism was an integral part of our nationalism, and anyone who wished to deal with our economic problems first had to sacrifice to the rural gods. Here, then, I will simply offer some other typical examples.

In a series of articles on the Depression, written in September 1931, Henri Bourassa recommended a return to the land as the principal remedy for the situation. In May 1933, *L'action nationale* informed us that the Ecole sociale populaire (People's School of Social Studies) had just worked out a program of social renewal; this led Father Alexandre Dugré, S.J, to remark: "We must be loggers or die; we must be farmers or be unemployed. . . . We must remain a race of farmers, or we will stop increasing, we will disappear."

We have already quoted the 1939 study, *La législation ouvrière et le régime social dans la province de Québec* (Labour Legislation and Social Services in the Province of Quebec). Its author, Esdras Minville, was farsighted enough to recognize the tendencies to industrialization in Quebec at quite an early date, but he still spoke of reform in the following terms: "From the sociological point of view, unemployment insurance and certain other measures of social legislation seem to us *more or less advisable* in the Province of Quebec. In an appendix to our brief on trade unionism, we have explained the seriousness of the *rural problem* in the Province of Quebec at some length. Most of the economists and sociologists who have studied the situation share our opinion: the present economic instability is rooted in the desertion of the countryside and the extreme congestion of the cities, particularly Montreal. Any measure tending to *improve the lot of the industrial worker even more*, or to give the illusion, at least, that the life of the urban worker is becoming more and more secure and easy, would almost fatally accelerate the *movement away from the countryside*, unless equal advantages were guaranteed to the rural population. . . ."

b) Small business

Edouard Montpetit declared: "My study of our needs has long convinced me that, in the field of production, we must stick to medium and small industry for now." Maximilien Caron touched on almost all our reforms in a paragraph: "Let us develop small and medium industry, applying the principles of the cooperative movement to assure success. By our efforts, our fellow citizens will become thoroughly convinced that a healthy prosperity must be based on sound corporatism. . . ." An American sociologist quotes the following extract from the sermon of a small town priest on St. John the Baptist Day: "The patriotic way for the true French Canadian to live is to save and become a small proprietor. English methods are not ours. The French became great by small savings and small business. Don't borrow the commercial ways of others." Henri Laureys, at the end of the talk cited earlier, expressed the hope that "the French Canadians will make a determined effort to enter the field of medium and small industry."

Minville also reports that many people say: "Let's take over small industry." He goes on to demolish this aspect of our doctrinal mythology: "The economists have never been able to give a satisfactory definition of small industry. We might also ask how small firms could meet the competition of big industry, and above all whether a community could ever attain enough independence, by small industry alone, in an economy planned and managed to suit big business, and dominated by it." Needless to say, these timely questions remained unanswered. Strangest of all, even their author seems to have forgotten them. In 1945, he suggested that a reform of the industrial system be an integration of part-time manufacturing into the rural economy: agriculture, logging, fishing . . .

c) The cooperative movement

Our theorists certainly deserve credit for realizing that cooperatives might have become – had we approached them differently – a means of emancipation for a people without capital, whose only leverage on the economic world was the force of numbers. In this field, Alphonse Desjardins and his pupils were admirable pioneers.

Although the cooperative movement was somewhat successful in the countryside and among the fishermen, it failed miserably in the cities, for a good reason. This institution presupposes a firm belief in democratic responsibility and in collective property. Our fear of socialism led us to stifle these ideas systematically, especially in the cities. In addition, people used the worst possible methods, it seems, in their attempts to win acceptance for the cooperative idea. Some apostles of the movement appear to have directed most of their efforts towards the St. John the Baptist societies and towards other organizations of small property owners and merchants. The idea of committing economic suicide for the sake of a hypothetical nationalism did not particularly appeal to this group. Others did spread their ideas among the workers, but their efforts came too late, in our industrial development. The cooperative movement was no longer capable, in itself (i.e., without the aid of political action), of winning a place in a world where capitalist institutions had complete control of the economy. The last straw was the Jesuits' strong campaign to make the cooperatives denominational. Such a policy did nothing to further the adoption of cooperatives in urban areas, with their variety of language and religion. The provincial leader of the Dominicans at the time came to the defence of Father Lévesque, who had been attacked by the Jesuits for recommending that the cooperatives be non-denominational: "I fear, though I have no positive proof, that some people want to turn the issue of religious affiliation into a narrow question of nationalism."

d) The Catholic trade union movement

One cannot exaggerate the role played by Catholic French Canadian trade unionism in the development of a working-class consciousness in Quebec. Largely through this movement, the Quebec worker has managed to formulate – in his own language and with his own concepts – problems and solutions in his particular industrial world. One would, however, almost be tempted to say that this result was a chance by-product ...

Catholic trade unionism, in fact, was not in the main an offspring of liberal thinking, an attempt to alleviate the real hardships afflicting our Catholic proletariat in Quebec. Like much of our social doctrine, our ideas on trade unionism emerged from a nationalist reaction against reforms which arrived from the outside world, after we, in our indifference, had neglected to apply them in time. Our denominational trade unionism was conceived by artificial insemination; its birth is not the most glorious episode in its history. The xenophobic, authoritarian, and unrealistic character of the movement is reflected in the words of the tireless zealot of the Ecole sociale populaire, who rationalized our long blindness as follows: "Necessity [of uniting after the Conquest] made the French Canadians one big family without distinctions of caste or class rivalry. Little by little, with the increase of the race, social differences were established among its members, but barely perceptible ones. There were no great gaps between the rich and the wage earners, such as one finds elsewhere; above all, no animosity divided them. . . . Because of these circumstances, the Church in Quebec was slow to establish trade unions. . . . Faced with new economic facts, such as the increasing cost of living and the development of foreign-owned joint stock industries, the Church *believed that the time had come* to organize the workers. The difficulties that it then encountered almost all originated [*sic*] with American organization. The employers had already suffered at the hands of the international trade unions, and their lack of social consciousness made them generally hostile to the movement. There were many workers who belonged to unions or who, though not members, had been won over to the ideas of neutrality spread among the masses by the unionists: they were not well disposed towards this undertaking. . . . But the difficult times are over. Thanks to the very clear directives of the bishops, based on the teachings of Rome, the energetic efforts of the chaplains, and the pious attitude of several managers and *a good number of workers*, Catholic organization of the workers is now doing well. . . ." Father Archambault concludes that "the elite acts upon the masses," and that to serve "the race and the Church," the doctrine should be preached everywhere in society: in the Church, in Parliament, in the press, among industrialists and financiers, *and even* (!) "in the factories where one finds a restless proletariat, which is too often embittered and menacing."

During the same Semaine sociale (Symposium on Social Issues), Mgr. Lapointe, one of the founders of our Catholic trade union movement, blandly remarked: "At the right time, when it was possible, the clergy did for the workers what they had done for all the citizens of other classes. Here again we must, I feel, admit that they have broken new ground with wisdom and foresight."

What, then, inspired Cardinal Taschereau to condemn the Knights of Labour (Chevaliers du travail), an act which, according to Alfred Charpentier (before he "converted" and became the first president of the Catholic trade unions), was due to "lack of reflection, haste, and incompetence"? Wonderful, indeed, is the "farsightedness" which – in Chicoutimi and Jonquière in 1913, for example – led "the Catholic authorities" to make "a most aggressive appeal" against the international unions, calling upon "the workers to cast them out with all their works, if they wished to keep their Catholic faith."

With the passage of years, the aggressive character lessened, of course, but the gist of the appeal was unaltered. In 1937, for example, during a strike in the Montreal garment industry, the religious authorities strongly supported the Catholic unions against the I.L.G.W.U. (International Ladies' Garment Workers' Union) by approving a collective agreement which violated the minimum wage law.

In 1938, Father Arès wrote in the *Petit catéchisme d'éducation syndicale* (The Little Catechism of Trade Union Education): "In the Province of Quebec, is the Catholic worker permitted to prefer the non-denominational union to the Catholic union? No, unless in leaving the non-denominational union for the Catholic union, he would suffer severely; for example, if he were to lose *the only job available* to him" (p. 28, my italics). In 1939, the sociologist Esdras Minville had this to say about international (American) trade unionism: "The unreligious character of the group makes it almost inevitable that the members will have to choose between two loyalties: to their religion or to their trade association." A bit farther on he added: "International trade unionism, given its doctrinal inspiration, is no more a guarantee of order than the revolutionary individualism from which it springs, or the communism towards which, by a natural tendency as it were, its ideas carry it." Mr. Minville candidly adds that his comments "are, in short, just a summing up of the great campaign waged last November [1937], in the French Canadian Catholic press and on the radio, in favour of national, Catholic trade unions." Turning, at last, to matters of fact, he admits that the "trade unionism" which he so nonchalantly libels "has not really gone so far or so fast as its principles allow it. Still, it is left-wing. Its demands have followed a pattern which shows its tendencies clearly enough, particularly where hours of work are concerned. Before 1872, it fought for the nine-hour day ... [and today] it is calling for the six-hour day and the thirty-hour week." There can be no doubt: this is the pattern of the purest bolshevism! The whole piece ends with a speech in favour of "the employer who has the same right to live as the worker."

Is there a fairer indictment of this phalanx of social thinkers than the words of a "neutral" trade unionist, reported by Mgr. Lapointe? "Abbé . . . for many years we have suffered, toiled, laboured for starvation wages. . . . When we complained of our poverty, and were greeted with rifle shots as rebels and revolutionaries, what were you doing? You counselled patience, pointing to heaven, and you read us some fine little sermons on respect for the social order. . . . Abbé, you offered us no solution. Then, organized labour from the States opened its arms to us, and we rushed into them. Today you say that's no good. Why didn't you say so before?"

Our sociologists ignored the destitution of the working class until they were led, by nationalism, to denounce the international unions. They now favoured a paternalistic labour movement, controlled by clergymen and employers. They advocated religious affiliation for the unions, because "without this system, *no authority will be able to enforce the principles of Christianity* in these organizations, where men of every opinion will come together. . . ." Forgetful of the deep scars they had left on the labour movement, and of the serious disturbances they had created in Christian consciences, our social thinkers again withdrew into the cosy myth of our providential mission. Bourassa concluded a series of editorials on the trade union movement with an appeal to working-class nationalism, isolationism, and social conservatism. It is not surprising that the next year found him denouncing "the plague of industrialization and its inevitable consequence, the depopulation of the countryside." Alfred Charpentier sent *Le Devoir* "a public profession of faith in the nationalism of the working class." He later wrote: "God, it seems, intended that our race should flourish in this part of the country, in spite of past persecutions, to become the purifying salt of the entire Canadian nation. . . . Providence calls upon our Catholic workers to do their part as well, namely, to lead a defence of this country's working class against the dangers which threaten it."

e) Corporatism
Corporatism is without a doubt the most important reform to delight our social thinkers. The greatest variety of men, in the most different circumstances, and for the most opposed ends, proclaimed the gospel

of corporatism. Their voices were as one, and they preached their futile homilies with unflagging enthusiasm. Nothing more starkly revealed the monolithic nature of our ideology.

From year to year, in connection with everything and nothing, lecturers at the Semaines sociales (Symposiums on Social Issues) found ways to apologize for corporatism. They included Mgr. Paquet and the future Mgr. Desranleau (1921), Jean Bruchési (1936), and Maximilien Caron (three times from 1938 to 1942). Caron relied upon such disparate authorities as Cardinal Villeneuve ("Corporatism all the way!") and the prime minister of the province ("Anything that brings us closer to corporatism is a step forward."). At the Semaine sociale of 1942, Gérard Picard was still speaking of trade unionism as a means of achieving a corporative organization of society.

The contributors to *L'action nationale* also went through a phase of hard-line corporatism. In November 1937, Roger Duhamel expressed the opinion that nationalism would emerge victorious from a national and Catholic trade union movement, which could reach full maturity within a corporative framework. The next year, a long inquiry into corporatism began. In the course of it, the greatest variety of learned doctors found themselves in agreement with one another: Abbé J.B. Desrosiers (in a Semaine sociale held at Collège Jean-de-Brébeuf, November 1937, he also recommended that family allowances be obtained through corporatism); François Hertel (who advocated a corporatist version of personalism; he still adhered to this doctrine in 1945, in his *Nous ferons l'avenir* [We Will Make the Future]); F.A. Angers (who held that the unions must develop towards corporatism). We should also add the names of other zealots who participated in this inquiry: Hermas Bastien, Gérard Filion, Esdras Minville. Father Lévesque was also part of the group; he recommended joint action by the adherents of the cooperative movement and the supporters of corporatism.

Father Arès devised a corporatist catechism, and in his trade union catechism, he emphasized (Question 45) that the trade union movement is a first step towards corporatism. Victor Barbeau made a remarkable inquiry into our economic hardships; he concluded it with a statement in favour of an economic and political order based on corporations. In the same year, the Jeunesses patriotes (Young Patriots) published a book on separatism, *Le séparatisme*, by Dostaler O'Leary. O'Leary called for "the establishment of a corporative regime in the Free French Canadian State." The Bloc universitaire (University Coalition), at its Duchesnay convention of 1939, passed a resolution that "each of our Schools of Social Sciences should make a special effort to interest all students in ... corporatism."

We could add to the list indefinitely, but the nature of our philosophic idealism is clear enough. Several decades of social thought are summed up almost in a word: corporatism. Since the word had crossed the lips of the Pope, and since the English were hardly enthusiastic about corporatism, we were glad to regard it as a universal panacea. Everybody was happy to recommend this miraculous remedy, which had the advantage of *not requiring any critical reflection*. Nobody felt that he had to search for an approach to social issues in tune with the course of history. Anyone who endorsed the fashionable prejudice was granted the title of Catholic and national sociologist.

I do not intend to deal here with the question of whether or not corporatism has some contribution to make to a political theory based on the idea of progress. Objective political economy and sociology have certainly not yet shown how a legal superstructure, which makes no essential changes in capitalist institutions, could reconcile the opposed interests of capital and labour, except in limited areas and for limited periods of time. Social and economic tendencies to monopoly, inherent in these reconciliations, would very likely create conflicts of interest (cartel against cartel, cartel against the consumers, etc.). These conflicts could be resolved only by oligarchy, eliminated only by dictatorship. It would therefore be most dangerous to attempt corporate organization, except among people whose democratic development was so far advanced that one could be utterly certain that special interests (the concern of the corporations) would be subordinate to the general interest (the concern of the State).

Now, most of our thinkers saw corporatism in a completely different light: they regarded it as a means to tame the *democratic* thrust of the trade union movement. They tolerated unions only because they believed that they would soon be contained by corporations. Our brand of corporatism was actually devised for an "elite," who saw it as a means to discipline popular movements and to maintain its authority over the masses organized in this fashion. The people were not at all taken in by this. When we finally made an objective inquiry into the results of nearly half a century of theoretical corporatism, we realized that defeat was total: "There is not one organization whose administrative structure corresponds exactly to the ideal type described by the militants."

The Book of Ecclesiastes still offers the finest comment on our social ideas in general in the half century before the asbestos strike: *mataiotès mataiotètôn, ta panta mataiotès.*

The Asbestos Strike (Toronto:
James, Lewis & Samuel, 1974)
Translation by James Boake

Approaches to Politics

⟩⟨

"Approaches to Politics" is the general title given to a series of twenty articles appearing in the newspaper VRAI from 1958 onwards. The English translation was not published until 1970, however. In his preface to this translation-reissue, Professor Ramsay Cook noted: "What is most impressive about the journalistic pieces is the ease with which obvious erudition is transformed into clear, simple statements of fundamental political philosophy."

When Madmen Think They Are Ministers and MPs

We can only think of Plato and Aristotle in grand academic robes. They were decent fellows, like others, laughing with their friends; and when they diverted themselves with writing their Laws and their Politics they did it for their own amusement. This was the least philosophical, the least serious, part of their lives; the most philosophical part was to live simply and quietly. If they wrote of politics, it was as if to make rules for a lunatic asylum. And if they made a show of speaking of great affairs it was because they knew that the madmen they were talking to thought they were kings

67

and emperors. They entered into their principles in order to miti-
gate as far as possible the damage done by their madness.
PASCAL

We are going to be governed whether we like it or not; it is up to us to see to it that we are governed no worse than is absolutely necessary. We must therefore concern ourselves with politics, as Pascal said, to mitigate as far as possible the damage done by the madness of our rulers.

The first – almost the only – question to ask is: how does it happen that one man has authority over his fellows?

Sermons and worthy books are always talking of respect for the human personality and of the inviolability of conscience. In the context of our Christian civilization, those phrases have no meaning unless all men are regarded as fundamentally free and equal, each man being of infinite value in himself, bound only by his own conscience; from which it must follow that neither authority nor obedience ought to be taken for granted. If my father, my priest, or my king wants to exert authority over me, if he wants to give me orders, he has to be able to explain, in a way that satisfies my reason, on what grounds he must command and I must obey.

This is not the place to go into the natural and supernatural sources of authority within the family and the Church. But whence comes authority in civil and political society? It is extraordinarily important to know this. For even the priest, collecting his tithes or building his church, can do so only under the sway of the civil power. You cannot marry or bring children into the world or educate them without conforming to the laws of the state. Neither the owner of a factory nor the president of a club nor the headquarters of a union can exercise the least authority except within the legal framework determined by the government. You can neither buy a newspaper, nor take a tram, nor live in your house, nor beat your wife (or your husband), nor baptize your children unless the law ratifies your action and weighs its import.

What, then, is the source of the astonishingly universal law that gives so much power to our political leaders? The question engrossed the first philosophers thousands of years ago, and it remains to be answered.

Some take the easy way out by reiterating that authority comes from God. They omit to explain why God conferred it on a Stalin or a Hitler; or why, in our democracies, God would choose to express himself through the intermediary of electoral thugs and big campaign contributors.

According to others, authority is founded on force. To quote Pascal again, "unable to make justice strong, we make strength just." This explanation is inadequate too. For no man or group of men can impose authority on a population against its will. When injustice reaches a certain point, even soldiers and policemen refuse to obey – as witness the French, Russian, Chinese, Indo-Chinese, and other revolutions.

Still others invoke natural law, affirming that authority rests on the nature of things. Like the divine explanation, this is an abstraction; while it is not false, it fails to explain the contradictory variety of forms of authority and law. In certain societies it is the grandfather who rules, in others it is the mother, in still others the queen's eldest son. Slavery is illegal here; elsewhere it is allowed. One country sanctions divorce, another forbids it altogether. Two years ago the Padlock Law[*] governed us in Quebec, today we are free of it. "The nature of things," then, is no great help in explaining how it is that Maurice can give orders to Pierre, and why something permitted here is forbidden elsewhere.

We must keep on looking, then. . . .

To Prevent Sedition . . .

It is dangerous to tell the people that the laws are unjust;
for they obey them only because they think them just. That is why
they must be told at the same time that they must obey them

---

[*] In 1956 Frank Scott had successfully challenged the Padlock Law before the Supreme Court. This law had been passed by the government of Quebec in 1937. On the pretext of preventing the incursion of communism into Quebec, Duplessis had given himself the discretionary power to padlock premises used by organizations alleged to be "communist."

because they are laws; just as they must obey superiors,
not because they are just, but because they are superiors. In this
way all sedition is prevented.

PASCAL

I have already shown that it is not enough to appeal to God or nature, fear or force, to explain the authority possessed by certain leaders and certain laws over the mass of people.

Some philosophers have tried to explain this authority by a kind of contract among the members of society, delegating authority to some of them. This notion has its attraction, bringing into our inquiry, as it does, the idea of consent: A has authority over B because B agrees to it. The obvious difficulty is that such a contract is an abstract idea, never having in fact been signed. In reality, man is born into society without having been consulted, and he has very little choice but to go on living in it.

Let us see, then, where our discussion has led us. On the one hand we say that all men are brothers, that is to say, equals. But on the other hand wherever we look, in whatever country we may be, we see that the great majority are subject to a small number of superiors who make the law for them. As Rousseau said, "Man is born free, yet everywhere he is in chains. . . . How did this change come about?"

To reconcile these contradictions and unravel our difficulties, we must begin by observing that society is a given fact for man. We cannot know if there has ever existed, or will ever exist, a species of man who does not live in society but courses the woods like a lone wolf. What we do see is that wherever men live they in fact live in society and depend on a social order. Not even the criminal can escape this order, for his ignorance of the criminal code and his dislike of prison do not prevent his subjection to those institutions. The nomad, the hermit, and the gypsy also depend on the social order on whose fringes they think they live; for there is no territory in the world that does not fall under the dominion of some sovereign power. The hermit's cave, whether he likes it or not, is regulated by the laws of possession and property. The gypsy cannot tell your fortune without liability under the law of contract.

And I have watched the nomads of the Asiatic steppe being required to pay duty to the Afghan treasury when their migrations took them into the Khyber Pass.

The human being, then, lives in the framework of society; and life in society cannot be pictured without subjection to an established order – that is, a government. It is in this sense that one can say that authority, philosophically speaking, comes from God or from the nature of things, since God has created man with a nature that compels him to live in society: subject, that is, to politics. Political authority comes from God in the same sense as the queen's authority in a beehive comes from God.

But we are not bees, nor are we ants, and that is why this answer by itself is not enough. Men stay free because *no one* is fully vested by God or nature with authority to rule his fellows. James I of England wrote big books to prove that he was king by divine right; he believed that his son Charles I could be too, but that did not prevent the English from cutting off his head. Louis XVI of France and Tsar Nicholas II of Russia ended their careers in much the same manner. And in democracies political parties and prime ministers that thought themselves eternal have been sent packing by the people, and will be again.

Human societies, then, differ from the beehives in that men are always free to decide what form of authority they will adopt, and who will exercise it. And it really is men who have the responsibility of taking these decisions – not God, Providence, or Nature. In the last analysis any given political authority exists only because men consent to obey it. In this sense what exists is not so much the authority as the obedience.

Tyrannicide, the Jesuits, and Father de Léry

It is one thing to show a man that he is in an error, and another to put him in possession of truth.

JOHN LOCKE

Certain men of learning have done me the honour of commenting on these essays. The comments are hostile, but what does that matter? Political discussion on the theoretical level is so rare in French Canada that any step in that direction is a step forward.

Father de Léry's article in *Relations* (April 1958) is especially welcome. He knows his subject, and he shows us that according to Catholic doctrine any patriot at all may assassinate an unjust and illegitimate tyrant. The case of a tyrant who oppresses his subjects, but did obtain power legitimately, is more complicated: only the "representatives of the people" can decree his death and arrange for his assassination.

The question of deciding who the "representatives of the people" are is a bit tricky, clearly. Father de Léry refrains from tackling it, unfortunately; and I must leave it to the theologians to sort out their little problem. For my part I am concerned only with the doctrine as a whole. At the beginning of the article under arraignment, I wrote that I disliked violence. Since it seems necessary to dot my i's, let me add that it repels me. That is precisely why, throughout this series, I am trying to raise politics to the level of conscience, and am preaching a political philosophy directed towards democracy and the obsolescence of the theologies of political assassination.

That is clear enough, isn't it? What is less clear is what is bothering Father de Léry. He complains that "three lines [by Trudeau] sufficed to incriminate eminent theologians, among them certain Jesuits. . . . We will need nearly a page to re-establish the facts."

Now, I incriminated nobody. There were no facts to re-establish, as is proved by the fact that Father de Léry recites in detail the theology of tyrannicide to which I made only a passing allusion, quoting Canon Boillat – who expounds exactly the same doctrine as Father de Léry. My purpose became quite clear in the rest of the article: to establish that "it is the duty of citizens . . . to examine their consciences on the quality of the social order they share and the political authority they acknowledge."

I am sorry that such a brief foray into theology was enough to trouble the consciences of the Jesuits of *Relations*. True, I was thinking of Mariana[*] when I wrote the essay, but I was also thinking of Suarez[†] and of the great Cardinal Bellarmine, who did so much to establish a distinction between the spiritual and the temporal with regard to the authority of the clergy. And I was thinking just as much of their remote predecessors, of the theologians, like William of Occam, who laid the foundation of the theories that made it possible to set bounds to the despotism of princes. In short, some theologians (not excluding certain Jesuits) have played a leading role in the evolution of political thought, and it is partly thanks to them that the liberty of the citizen has managed to prevail over the absolutism of kings. Merely because, at certain periods, they have had to consider the theory of assassination is no reason for them to have a guilty conscience today.

But Father de Léry seems perfectly well aware of these matters, and if left to himself would certainly have felt no call to blush for the Jesuit Mariana, whose book "was many times republished *by the Protestants.*" (The italics are *Relations*'s.) It follows that Father de Léry's article was written under orders, as sometimes happens among the Jesuits. Somebody must have told him that Trudeau was a malcontent and that his articles were considered to have a Protestant tendency. Hence the tone of refutation that the good father felt obliged to adopt in writing, in effect, the same thing I did!

The pity of all this is that neither you nor I found out what Father de Léry thought about democracy, or about the theory of legal sovereignty that I outlined in my articles. *Relations* has before now been able to take up the cudgels most effectively against the political immorality of our society; but might not my remarks of two weeks back have some application to that magazine? "It is utterly useless to preach electoral morality to a people while minimizing or ridiculing the idea of popular sovereignty."

---

[*] Juan de Mariana (1536–1624), Spanish Jesuit whose thesis that it was lawful to overthrow a tyrant contributed greatly to the suspicion with which Jesuits were regarded, especially after the assassination of Henry IV in 1610.

[†] Francisco Suarez (1548–1617), Spanish Jesuit who denied the divine right of kings; James I of England had one of his books burned by the common hangman.

Commentaries on the history of theology have their place, certainly, in a magazine like *Relations*. But if that magazine is ever again tempted to do me the honour of commenting on my *VRAI* articles, I venture to hope that it might be to touch on some of their more important aspects. As for the criticism of a prudent friend, which Father de Léry recommends to me at the end of his article, I should like it to be offered by someone who would not hesitate to depart a little from the vocabulary of an instructor in "Philosophy II" speaking of democracy and concluding that monarchy is the only perfect form of government.

Contempt of the Legislature

> *If the people are silent, you call them content; if they protest*
> *you say that they are given to disorder; and in the one case as in*
> *the other they can look to you for nothing.*
> GLADSTONE

Democracy is superior to other political systems, as I have explained, because it solicits the express agreement of the people and thus avoids the necessity of violent changes. At each election, in fact, the people assert their liberty by deciding what government they will consent to obey.

Hence we must shun the concept of the state as a machine to command obedience and impose order. The truly democratic state should rather *court* obedience and serve the citizens' loyalty by maintaining an order that they will think just. Under these conditions the exercise of force (army, police, prison) cannot become a *habit* of government. My idea of a state "made to measure" applies thoroughly here: the state must use force only to the extent that individuals or organizations try to use it themselves against the common good. If it is true that in the last analysis the state must retain the monopoly of force, the purpose is less to use it than to prevent someone else from usurping the thunderbolts.

The detractors of democracy are wrong, then, in equating this form of government with anarchy, disorder, and impotence. The democratic state is a strong state; but its strength, being based on agreement, can be exerted only in the direction desired by the consensus of citizens.

Now, what is it that the citizens desire? That is the question that every democratic government must ask itself constantly. And it is in this respect that the democratic state, better than any other, turns to account the creative liberty of people living in society. For if it is to establish an order that citizens will agree to support, the state must go further than merely investigating their needs; it must also encourage them to demand what they consider just. In this way democracy becomes a system in which all citizens *participate* in government: the laws, in a sense, reflect the wishes of the citizens and thus turn to account the special wisdom of each one; the social order to some extent embodies all the wealth of human experience that the citizens possess.

In such a state the liberty of citizens is an end in itself. The authorities don't think of it as an annoying phrase; on the contrary, they want it, and encourage it as the surest guide to the common good.

And that defines just how remote from the democratic spirit are the political *mores* of Quebec. With very few exceptions, and at any level of authority you care to pick, you find only distrust of freedom and hostility towards its exercise. Thus the people are trapped in the dilemma Gladstone was talking about: if they suffer in silence, the authorities think, "Here's a nice little society, content with its low wages, its slums, and its ignorance"; and if they dare to complain they are blamed for succumbing to the agitation of dangerous "leftists."

The government that goes by the name of Union Nationale is the manifest master of this technique; it stands supreme in its contempt for freedom. It is not merely that it spits on the right of association (the anti-union laws), harasses free speech (the padlock law), despises human dignity (beatings by the provincial police), but, more than all this, it insults the spirit of democracy in its most solemn sanctuary, the parliament. I hold no brief for the Liberal opposition – on the contrary its mediocrity is partly to blame for the ills we suffer. But I

choke with indignation at the humiliations inflicted on that opposition. The point is that in a parliamentary democracy the opposition
is the last and most important bulwark against arbitrary tyranny;
through it the people reserve the right to criticize from moment to
moment the way they are governed – through it they nip legislative
and administrative abuses in the bud. And the Duplessis government,
by buffoonery, contempt, accusation, insult, intimidation, illegality,
and fraud, has prevented the parliamentary opposition from performing its functions and has therefore gagged the people in the
persons of their best-accredited representatives. If it is alleged that
these words constitute contempt of the legislature, I can always be
summoned to appear at the bar of the assembly. And they will learn
that a free citizen does not suffer without protest the degradation of
his liberties.

For a Living Democracy

> *I know no safe depository of the ultimate powers of the society*
> *but the people themselves; and if we think them not enlightened*
> *enough to exercise their control with a wholesome discretion, the*
> *remedy is not to take it from them, but to inform their discretion.*
> THOMAS JEFFERSON

At the end of this first series of articles, which is based on the
Declaration of Principles of the Rassemblement, democracy appears as
the logical outcome of a policy aimed at preventing tyranny, avoiding
violence, doing justice to all, encouraging the full flowering of personality, and turning to account the creative liberty of every citizen.

That is not to say that democracy is a perfect form of government:
you just have to look around you . . . What holds us to democracy is
not that it is faultless but that it is less faulty than any other system. If
the people use their sovereignty badly, the remedy is not to take it away
from them (for to whom could we hand it over who would offer a better
guarantee for *all* citizens?), but rather to educate them to do better. To

be precise, democracy is the only form of government that fully respects the dignity of man, because it alone is based on the belief that all men can be made fit to participate, directly or indirectly, in the guidance of the society of which they are members.

However, we must refrain from making undue claims for democracy; that would be the best way to discredit it. For instance, democracy does not claim that majority rule is an infallible guide to *truth*. Nor does it claim that the average citizen is capable of resolving the extraordinarily complicated problems that face modern governments.

As for majority rule, the fact must be faced that it is a convention, possessing simply a practical value. It is convenient to choose governments and pass laws by majority vote, so that those who exercise authority can feel assured of having more supporters than opponents – which is in itself some guarantee that the social order will be upheld. It is true that from one point of view the majority convention is only a roundabout way of applying the law of the stronger, in the form of the law of the more numerous. Let us admit it, but note at the same time that human groupings took a great step towards civilization when they agreed to justify their actions by counting heads instead of breaking them.

And this must be added. Democracy genuinely demonstrates its faith in man by letting itself be guided by the rule of fifty-one per cent. For if all men are equal, each one the possessor of a special dignity, it follows inevitably that the happiness of fifty-one people is more important than that of forty-nine; it is normal, then, that – *ceteris paribus* and taking account of the inviolable rights of the minority – the decisions preferred by the fifty-one should prevail. But the majority convention has only a practical value, I repeat. Democracy recognizes that one person may be right and ninety-nine wrong. That is why freedom of speech is sacred: the one person must always have the right to proclaim *his* truth in the hope of persuading the ninety-nine to change their point of view.

On the second claim falsely attributed to democracy, the point is that parliamentary democracy does not require a decision from its subjects on each of the technical problems presented by the complicated art of government in the modern world. It would be a delusion to look to a vote of the citizens to settle the details of, for example, a fiscal policy, a war budget, or a diplomatic mission. The citizens as a group can judge such measures only by their effects – real or apparent – on the happiness of the group.

That is why modern democracies hardly ever resort to the plebiscite – which requires each citizen to decide on what is often too technical a question. In contrast, the electoral system asks of the citizen only that he should decide on a set of ideas and tendencies, and on men who can hold them and give effect to them. These sets of ideas and men constitute political parties, which are indispensable for the functioning of parliamentary democracy.

But the study of parties, and of their responsibilities in the democratic education of citizens and in the guidance of the nation, opens up a new direction for our approaches ...

Ramsay Cook, ed., *Approaches to Politics* (Toronto: Oxford University Press, 1970)
Translation by I.M. Owen

Some Obstacles to Democracy in Quebec

>‹‹

The first paragraph of the following passage, perhaps the most frequently quoted paragraph in P.E.T.'s political writings, sums up his analysis of tensions which have marked the relations between English-speaking and French-speaking Canadians. The article was first published in 1958, in the Canadian Journal of Economics and Political Science; *was subsequently included in Mason Wade, ed.,* Canadian Dualism *(Toronto: University of Toronto Press, 1960); and was republished eight years later in John Saywell, ed.,* Federalism and the French Canadians *(Toronto: Macmillan, 1968).*

Historically, French Canadians have not really believed in democracy for themselves; and English Canadians have not really wanted it for others. Such are the foundations upon which our two ethnic groups have absurdly pretended to be building democratic forms of government. No wonder the ensuing structure has turned out to be rather flimsy.

The purpose of the present essay is to re-examine some of the unstated premises from which much of our political thinking and behaviour is derived, and to suggest that there exists an urgent need for a critical appraisal of democracy in Canada. No amount of inter-group back-slapping or political *bonne-ententisme* will change the fact that democracy will continue to be thwarted in Canada so long as one-third of the people hardly believe in it – and that because to no small extent the remaining two-thirds provide them with ample grounds for distrusting it.

I

French Canadians are perhaps the only people in the world who "enjoy" democracy without having had to fight for it. Before 1763 they had known only an authoritarian rule, implicitly founded on a belief in the divine right of kingship. The people were subjects of an autocratic monarch and were governed by administrators responsible only to him. Their church was also authoritarian, their seigneurial system was quasi-feudal, and even on a strictly local plane the farmers and towns-folk had never been active participants in public affairs. As Gustave Lanctot demonstrated: "The *habitants* of New France had no experience of common action in political matters. With no organization whatsoever that could group and direct them they had become accustomed to submitting without question to the ordinances of the intendants, to the orders of the governors and to the edicts of Versailles."[*]

That whole political structure was challenged in 1760 *by an outside force*. And its gradual replacement by forms of sovereignty which were to give an ever widening place to the principles of self-government was first brought about not by the Canadiens but by the English colonists. It was the latter who protested against the Act of 1774 and demanded an elective assembly; it was the former who circulated petition after petition in opposition to such an assembly. In 1788, Lord Dorchester advised the Colonial Office that only one-fifth of the total

---

[*] *L'Administration de la Nouvelle-France* (Paris, 1929), p. 140. See also F. Ouellet, "M. Michel Brunet et le problème de la conquête," *Bulletin des recherches historiques* (June 1956), p. 99: "La société canadienne à l'époque de la Nouvelle-France avait vécu sous l'absolutisme le plus complet."

population wanted a "change of laws and form of government"; and fully three-quarters of the French Canadians were actively opposed to such a change.

Consequently, when the Constitutional Act of 1791 ushered in – after a fashion – representative government, the Canadiens were neither psychologically nor politically prepared for it. As Durham later remarked, they were being initiated to responsible government at the wrong end; a people who had not been entrusted with the governing of a parish were suddenly enabled through their votes to influence the destinies of the state. And as was natural with a vanquished people, they valued their new form of government less for its intrinsic value than as a means to their racial and religious survival. Thus, though the elections of 1792 failed to evoke much enthusiasm in the Canadiens, they were quick to realize that, though their ethnic group composed 94 per cent of the population, it had elected only 68 per cent of the Assembly; and that furthermore they were in a minority in both the non-elective bodies – the Legislative and Executive Councils, where the seat of power truly rested.

Such a situation, soon to be aggravated by Governor Craig's despotic disposition, stifled what otherwise might have been a nascent belief in democracy. French Canadians felt that they had been deceived by the pre-1791 propaganda extolling the virtues and powers of representative assemblies; and they would forevermore look with distrust at majority rule, so called. True, they soon took to the electoral process like ducks to water; and 1837–8 even found many of them fighting and dying to uphold its logic. But such conduct cannot be ascribed to a sudden miraculous conversion to parliamentarianism. They had but one desire – to survive as a nation; and it had become apparent that parliamentary government might turn out to be a useful tool for that purpose. Consequently, in adopting piece by piece the British political system, their secret design was not merely to use it, but to abuse it if need be.

Such abuse was apparent in the extremism of the assemblies which opposed first Aylmer's and then Gosford's conciliatory attitudes, and brought the racial issue to a head. Though the *Quatre-vingt-douze*

Résolutions reflected the republicanism of the leaders of the revolt, there is little doubt that the effectiveness of the document among the people stemmed mainly from the anti-British violence which it contained. And whereas the Mackenzie rebellion in Upper Canada was a clear struggle for democratic self-government, most of Papineau's followers took up their pitchforks to fight for national self-determination. It was because of that issue that Durham observed: "I expected to find a contest between a government and a people: I found two nations warring in the bosom of a single state: I found a struggle not of principles but of races."*

The Canadiens fought at Saint-Denis and Saint-Eustache as they would eventually rally for electoral battles or parliamentary debates whenever their ethnic survival seemed to be imperilled, as men in an army whose sole purpose is to drive the *Anglais* back. And, as everyone knows, the army is a poor training corps for democracy, no matter how inspiring its cause.

That is not to deny the existence of radical currents in French-Canadian political thought. For instance, one cannot ignore the fact that during part of the nineteenth century a significant section of the *bourgeoisie* was notoriously *rouge*. But if historical events are any guide at all to the discovery of underlying ideologies, it seems fair to assert that the dominant ideologies in French Canada turned out to be more nationalistic than democratic. A lengthy study would be necessary to show how French-Canadian radicalism was crushed, mainly by agreement between the English-Canadian governing class and the French-Canadian higher clergy. Quite typical of such a pincers operation was the seizure of *Le Canadien* by Governor Craig, and the approval of that seizure by the Bishop of Quebec. The end result was that, for the mass of the people, the passage from French to British rule was remembered – not unnaturally – more as an enslaving defeat

---

* See F.R. Scott, "Canada et Canada français," *Esprit* (Paris) (August 1952); and also P.E. Trudeau, "Réflexions sur la politique au Canada français," *Cité libre* (December 1952). I have drawn heavily from this earlier article of mine in a few of the following paragraphs.

than as a liberation from Bourbon absolutism; regardless of how liberal were·the conqueror's political institutions, they had no intrinsic value in the minds of a people who had not desired them, never learned to use them, and finally only accepted them as a means of loosening the conqueror's grip.

How then were the French Canadians to use the arsenal of democratic "fire-arms" put at their disposal? There were two possibilities: sabotage of the parliamentary works from within by systematic obstruction which, like the Irish strategy at Westminster, might lead to Laurentian Home Rule; or outward acceptance of the parliamentary game, but without any inward allegiance to its underlying moral principles. The latter choice prevailed, no doubt because the years 1830 to 1840 demonstrated that sabotage would lead to suppression by force. Moreover, a show of co-operation would have the added advantage of permitting French Canada to participate in the governing councils of the country as a whole. Such a decision guided most French-Canadian politicians after the union of Upper and Lower Canada, and continued to do so after Confederation.

Fundamentally, all French-Canadian political thinking stems from these historical beginnings. In the opinion of the French in Canada, government of the people by the people could not be *for* the people, but mainly for the English-speaking part of that people; such were the spoils of conquest. Whether such a belief was well founded (an issue I shall discuss in the following section) is entirely irrelevant to the present argument. So the Canadiens believed; and so they could only make-believe in democracy. They adhered to the "social contract" with mental reservations; they refused to be inwardly bound by a "general will" which overlooked the racial problem. Feeling unable to share as equals in the Canadian common weal, they secretly resolved to pursue only the French-Canadian weal, and to safeguard the latter they cheated against the former.

In all important aspects of national politics, guile, compromise, and a subtle kind of blackmail decided their course and determined their alliances. They appeared to discount all political or social ideologies, save nationalism. For the mass of the people the words Tory and Grit,

Conservative and Liberal, referred neither to political ideals nor to administrative techniques. They were regarded only as meaningless labels, affixed to alternatives which permitted the auctioneering of one's support; they had no more meaning than *bleu* and *rouge*, which eventually replaced them in popular speech. French Canadians on the whole never voted for political or economic ideologies, but only for the man or group which stood for their *ethnic* rights: even condemnation of liberalism by the Church did not prevent Mercier and Laurier from being elected in 1886 and 1896; and the advantages to Quebec's economy of Laurier's reciprocity did not prevent Bourassa from being returned as an anti-imperialist in 1911.

In such a mental climate, sound democratic politics could hardly be expected to prevail, even in strictly provincial or local affairs where racial issues were not involved. For cheating becomes a habit. Through historical necessity, and as a means of survival, French Canadians had felt justified in finessing at the parliamentary game; and as a result the whole game of politics was swept outside the pale of morality. They had succeeded so well in subordinating the pursuit of the common weal to the pursuit of their particular ethnic needs that they never achieved any sense of obligation towards the general welfare, including the welfare of the French Canadians on non-racial issues. Consequently, apart from times of racial strife such as the Riel Rebellion, the schools question, conscription, the plebiscite, and the like – when the Canadiens banded together avowedly to fight for survival within the national whole – they came to regard politics as a game of every man for himself. In other words, their civic sense was corrupted and they became political immoralists.

The foregoing explanation of the lack of civic-mindedness must not be taken to exclude religious factors. French Canadians are Catholics; and Catholic nations have not always been ardent supporters of democracy. They are authoritarian in spiritual matters; and since the dividing line between the spiritual and the temporal may be very fine or even confused, they are often disinclined to seek solutions in temporal affairs through the mere counting of heads. If this be true in general, it is particularly so in the case of the clergy and laity of Quebec, influenced as they were by the Catholicism of nineteenth-century France, which largely rejected democracy as the daughter of the Revolution.

But there was a quite separate reason why the Church in Quebec was suspicious of popular sovereignty. When Canada passed into British hands, the Church naturally concerned herself with safeguarding the faith by protecting her authority. And, as it turned out, she discovered that her position had in a sense improved. For after the débâcle of 1760 she remained alone as a social beacon to give strength and guidance to a vanquished people, and to the victor she had the potentialities of a formidable opponent. So, after difficult beginnings, both powers found it advantageous to work out a *modus vivendi*. Loyalty was bartered for religious freedom, and the Church was as good as her word. During the wars of 1775, 1812, 1914, and 1939, the Catholic hierarchy preached submission to His Majesty's government; they even launched an appeal against the Fenian raiders in 1870. And at the time of the 1837 rebellion, they used their powers to check the *patriotes*.

When the faith lay safe, no distant call to democratic liberty held much appeal to the churchmen. The reason may have been partly that the torch of freedom so often appeared to be borne by enemies of the faith, as in the case of nineteenth-century revolutionaries whose staple stock-in-trade was anti-clericalism. But more profane rivalries are not to be discounted. Until the rise of democratic politics, a French Canadian's only access to positions of command lay through holy orders; but with the coming of the politicians, a career was opened to the Canadiens whereby they might compete with ecclesiastical authority. It is no coincidence that leaders such as Papineau, Mercier, Laurier, and even Bourassa, to say nothing of a host of lesser men, all incurred varying degrees of ecclesiastical censure.

A conquered people therefore not only faced a state which they feared as the creature of a foreign nation, but also belonged to a church which distrusted that state as a rival power and as a child of the Revolution, liable to be dominated by anti-clericals, Protestants, or even socialists. The resulting popular attitude was a combination of political superstition and social conservatism, wherein the state – any state – was regarded as an ominous being whose uncontrollable caprices were just as likely to lead it to crush families and devour crucifixes as to help the needy and maintain order.* Electoral processes for the mass of the people remained mysterious rituals of foreign origin, of little value beyond that for which the individual can barter his vote: a receipted grocery bill, a bottle of whisky, a workman's compensation, a contract to build a bridge, a school grant, a community hospital. For it is noteworthy that in Quebec, a school or a hospital is not expected by the citizens as of right, being their due from an obedient government and for which they pay, but as a reward for having returned a member to the Government benches.** And many a respectable citizen or prelate who would deem it dishonourable to sell his vote for a keg of beer thinks nothing of advising his *gens* to barter theirs for a load of bricks.

I see little use in illustrating these latter points, not only because that task was excellently done after the last Quebec general election† but also because such illustrations would not, *per se*, prove my point that French Canadians as a people do not believe in democracy, for other people who do profess to believe in democracy have none the less succumbed to corrupt electoral practices, the system of spoils, and so on. I prefer to quote some recent†† and typical instances which exemplify not

---

* That and that alone can explain why nationalist Quebec has never dared to translate into public ownership and a demand for the welfare state its unending clamour for economic emancipation; and why a people – so moral in other areas – has no sense of moral obligation in its relation to the state.

** This doctrine was given its classic expression and official sanction in Mr. Duplessis's speeches to the electors of Verchères during the 1952 elections, and to those of Shawinigan during the 1956 elections.

† See André Laurendeau's series "La Politique provinciale," *Le Devoir*, July and August 1956, during the course of which appeared the devastating denunciation written by the abbés Dion and O'Neil. See also Pierre Laporte's lengthy investigation "Les Elections ne se font pas avec des prières," *Le Devoir*, October and November 1956. For material on the 1952 provincial elections see *Cité libre*, December 1952.

†† The present paper was first drafted in August 1956. As time went by I began to add references to current events, but soon discontinued this practice as it added more to the length than to the strength of my demonstration. Consequently my *recent* and *typical* instances are more typical than recent.

corruption, but the complete lack of a democratic frame of reference for French-Canadian political thinking.

On the morning of the last provincial general election (June 20, 1956), the following was read over radio station CBF during the program called "Prières du matin: Elévations matutinales":

> Sovereign authority, by whatever government it is exercised, is derived solely from God, the supreme and eternal principle of all power. . . . It is therefore an absolute error to believe that authority comes from the multitudes, from the masses, from the people, to pretend that authority does not properly belong to those who exercise it, but that they have only a simple mandate revocable at any time by the people. This error, which dates from the Reformation, rests on the false principle that man has no other master than his own reason. . . . All this explanation about the origin, the basis, and the composition of this alleged [!] sovereignty of the people is purely arbitrary. Moreover, if it is admitted, it will have as a consequence the weakening of authority, making it a myth, giving it an unstable and changeable basis, stimulating popular passions and encouraging sedition.*

My original draft was written when the national Liberal Party was at the height of its glory. The accusations I shall level at it later on in this paper remain historically valid; but I must recognize that I felt less cruel in writing them a few years ago than I do in publishing them now. If it be a sop to anybody, I sadly add that the campaign waged by the Conservative henchmen in Quebec for the election of March 1958 has hardly given me reason to hope that by the sole grace of the new régime there will be a rebirth of democracy in "la belle province."

* This program apparently is under the guidance of the Comité interdiocésain d'Action radiophonique. To sociologists, it is no doubt an interesting example of the intermeshing of two institutions as different as the Church and the Canadian Broadcasting Corporation. I need hardly add that Catholicism is not *per se* incompatible with democracy; as a matter of fact, many a Catholic would claim that democracy follows naturally from the Christian belief that all men are brothers and fundamentally equal. But the historical fact remains that the clergy in Quebec made no such deductions. On the contrary, the foregoing quotation shows a remarkable continuity of thought with the anti-democratic theories which Mgr. Plessis imparted to Quebec

Think *that* over before you cast your vote!

French-Canadian lack of concern for the liberties and traditions of Parliament was admirably brought out during the pipeline debate of 1956. The *Toronto Star*, the *Telegram*, the *Globe and Mail*, the *Ottawa Journal*, the *Citizen*, the Montreal *Gazette*, and many other English-language papers were all pressing for Mr. Speaker's resignation, but *L'Action catholique*, *Le Droit*, and *Le Devoir* looked with disdain on such childishness. Mr. Lorenzo Paré, a parliamentary correspondent of some repute in French-Canadian circles, wrote: "There is no reason to stir up a great parliamentary crisis over such a trifling matter. . . . The most surprising thing is that it has been prolonged for so long and that during all these weeks the Commons has displayed a spectacle of surprising childishness." *Le Devoir*'s two parliamentary *courriéristes* had the same reaction. Mr. P. Laporte wrote: "To aggravate matters the English press and the opposition have succeeded in making the real fundamentals of the problem disappear from sight. . . . Mr. St. Laurent has put things back into focus. He has practically said that it amounted to a tempest in a teapot." And Mr. P. Vigeant:

Catholics 150 years earlier. F. Ouellet has written with considerable insight on "Mgr. Plessis et la naissance d'une bourgeoisie canadienne" in a paper presented to the Congrès de la Société canadienne de l'Histoire de l'Eglise catholique at Chicoutimi in August 1956. The following opinions of Mgr. Plessis are quoted from that paper. In 1799 the Bishop warned the faithful that if they were not protected against the influences of revolutionary France, "the fatal tree of liberty will be planted in the middle of your town, the rights of man will be proclaimed; . . . you will be free, but it will be an oppressive freedom that will give you for masters the dregs of humanity and grind into the dust the respectable leaders who now possess your affection and your confidence." In 1810 he denounced "the system of the sovereignty of the people" as "the most false and most absurd" of sophisms, and told his flock that "J.C., in giving you a religion designed to lead you to heaven, has not asked you to control and supervise the sovereigns under whom you live." In 1815 and 1823 he was still writing against the constitution of 1791, "a constitution ill-suited to the genius of Canadians and which has had no other real effect than to render the governed insolent toward the governors. The spirit of democracy and of independence has won the people, has passed from them to the clergy, and you see the fruits of it."

It is a situation that has been explained quite badly to French Canadians. One must have been brought up from childhood in the cult of parliamentary institutions in order to react vigorously to incidents that seem, at least to us, to be quite secondary. Respect for the Speaker of the House . . . is something surprising to us. . . . These incidents illustrate quite well the difficulties that face our representatives at Ottawa in adapting to English parliamentary institutions whose functioning . . . has so little in common with our French genius.

Indeed, had the crisis over the Speaker's office aroused any considerable excitement at all in Quebec, it most surely would have been interpreted as a racial attack on Mr. Louis-René Beaudoin!

An unusual approach to civil liberties might also be considered as typical of French Canada. At the time of the decision on the Jehovah's Witness case, enforcing freedom of religion, public opinion in Quebec was quick to point out that the judges of the Supreme Court had been somewhat divided along racial and religious lines. The judgment of the Supreme Court on the Padlock Law drew the same kind of reaction. For instance, *Montréal-Matin* emphasized Judge Taschereau's dissent, and spoke of a Communist victory, good news for all revolutionaries in Quebec; Mr. P. Sauriol of *Le Devoir* (March 19, 1957) questioned whether "the Supreme Court would be as careful in an opposite case when it would be a question of protecting provincial jurisdiction from a federal intrusion" and underlined "one of the most profound differences that exist between us and English Canadians. . . . It is a question of knowing whether the defence of freedom must go as far as defending and respecting an alleged right to propagate error."

Writing about the debate on the subservience of the C.B.C. to the party in power, and the whole issue of freedom of opinion, Mr. Gérard Filion of *Le Devoir* (April 10, 1957) remarked that if opposition parties were looking for an electoral issue,

they have probably taken the wrong road as far as French Canada is concerned. Public opinion among us is not usually aroused by this kind of dispute. This is probably wrong, but that is how it is. On the other hand, the general feeling in French Canada is that Mr. St. Laurent was right to [protest to Mr. Dunton in order to] put in his place this young greenhorn who, though only recently come to our country, wants to give us a lesson on our duties toward the Empire.

If I have quoted heavily from *Le Devoir*, the reason is that it is generally recognized even in English Canada as a truly independent daily of exceptionally high intellectual standards. But it should go without saying that in the lesser French-Canadian press, democracy, if it is known at all, is known as an evil. Mr. Duplessis's paper, *Le Temps* (Quebec, September 24, 1956), in condemning the Rassemblement, accused it of the greatest of all sins: leading the people "vers la laïcisation et la démocratisation." Another weekly refers to citizens as "subjects" and preaches realism:

> The true masters of a province or of a country are and will remain the money powers. . . . It is no longer necessary to be deeply scandalized about the favouritism that grows with political partisanship. Whether in a democracy or in a monarchy . . . there normally develops between him [the head of the government] and his subordinates a camaraderie, sometimes even a sincere friendship, that leads to compromise and favouritism at the expense of others, and in the end at the expense of the people. This is not an ideal situation, but it is a very human one, and it would be unrealistic to dream of a government that could maintain itself in power for any length of time without some sort of favouritism.

Mr. Léopold Richer, long-time parliamentary reporter, and now director of *Notre Temps*, a self-styled "hebdomadaire social et culturel" with (until recently) a wide support among the clergy, is prone to mock "the new religion of democracy," and uphold authority everywhere. The following case is interesting because Mr. Richer was indignant at the "libertarianism" of what many a democrat might feel to be a rather authoritarian conception of civil government. Mr. G. Filion had written in *Le Devoir*: "Freedom is not a gift but something that must be won. The only freedom is that which has been torn from authority." At which Mr. Richer fumes: "Have you read this? Did you understand it? . . . It is defiance of established authority, whether religious or civil. It is sedition. It is revolt. Gérard Filion has been reduced to preaching revolution openly. Either he does not understand the true meaning of his words . . . or else one must regard him as an extremely dangerous journalist." And so on.

If I were to quote all the material proving that French Canadians fundamentally do not believe in democracy, and that on the whole neither the pulpit, nor the Legislative Assembly, nor the radio, nor the press is doing much to instil such a belief, I would "exhaust time and encroach upon eternity." In 1958, French Canadians must begin to learn democracy from scratch. For such is the legacy of a history during which – as a minority – they hammered the process of parliamentary government into a defensive weapon of racial warfare, and – as Catholics – they believed that authority might well be left to descend from God in God's good time and in God's good way.

II

Parliamentary democracy I take to be a method of governing free men which operates roughly as follows: organized parties that wish to pursue – by different means – a common end, agree to be bound by certain rules according to which the party with the most support governs on condition that leadership will revert to some other party whenever the latter's means become acceptable to the greater part of the electorate. The common end – the general welfare – which is the aim of all parties may be more or less inclusive, and may be defined in different ways by different men. Yet it must in some way include equality of opportunity for everyone in all important fields of endeavour; otherwise "agreement on fundamentals" would never obtain. For instance, democracy cannot be made to work in a country where a large part of the citizens are by status condemned to a perpetual state of domination, economic or otherwise.[*] Essentially, a true democracy must permit the periodic transformation of political minorities into majorities.

In Canada the above conditions have never obtained. As to ends, the French Canadians would never settle for anything less than absolute equality of political rights with the English Canadians, a demand which, as I shall show below, was never seriously considered by the Colonial Office before the advent of responsible government, nor by the English-speaking majority since then. In brief, one-third of the nation disagreed with the common good as defined by the other two-thirds. Consequently parliamentary government was unworkable, for, given this situation, there arose a fundamental cleavage between a majority and a minority which could therefore not alternate in power.

It may be that after 1760 the French were just as unrealistic in their demands as the English were uncompromising in their attitude. The point remains that the English-speaking Canadians, rightly considering that self-government is the noblest way of regulating social relations among free men, proceeded to claim its benefits for Canada, but only after serving standing notice on the French that such benefits were not for members of a subject race.

It is a matter of record that the purpose of the Royal Proclamation of 1763 was complete assimilation of the French Canadians; yet it was through that instrument that the French Canadians first became acquainted with representative government. "The proclamation tacitly assumed such an influx [of English settlers] by providing for the estab-lishment of English law and by promising an assembly." And when Governor Murray tried to protect the *habitant* against the voracious

---

[*] With others, Elton Mayo, *The Social Problems of an Industrial Civilization* (London, 1949), p. xiii, has observed that "representative government does not work satisfactorily for the general good in a society that exhibits extreme differences in the material standards of living of its various social groups. . . . [Nor can] representative government be effectively exercised by a society internally divided by group hostilities and hatreds."

English merchants, the latter "demanded the immediate calling of an assembly for whose candidates the French might be allowed to vote, but of which only Protestants were to be members." Of such an assembly, Maseres, the incumbent Attorney General, was to write in 1766: "An assembly so constituted [because of the laws against popery] might pretend to be a representative of the people there, but it would be a representative of only the 600 new English settlers, and an instrument in their hands of dominating over the 90,000 French." Instead of [providing] an assembly the Quebec Act of 1774 was brought down, welcomed by the Canadiens, but attacked by the English colonists for being undemocratic and establishing popery. Such attacks could only impart a peculiar understanding of democracy to a people who through the act had only received what they considered their birthright: freedom of faith and of language.

When at last French Canadians were initiated into the sanctuary of representative government, by the Constitutional Act of 1791, they discovered that it did not mean majority rule through an elected assembly, but rule by the representatives of the conquering minority, nominated to the Executive and Legislative Councils. Moreover, at its very first meeting, the elected Assembly itself split along ethnic lines over the language qualifications of the Speaker. The history of democracy in Lower Canada from 1793 to 1840 was that of one long process of warping. As Mason Wade puts it, the English colonists "were badly scared men." In 1793, Richardson, the able leader of the Opposition, was to explain: "Nothing can be so irksome as the situation of the English members – without numbers to do any good – doomed to the necessity of combating the absurdities of the majority, without a hope of success." In 1806, the English merchants raised the cry of "French domination" because of a tax they disliked, and during the fray the Montreal *Gazette* and the Quebec *Mercury* were summoned to the bar of the Assembly for contempt of that body. In 1810, Chief Justice Sewell proposed the establishment of high property restrictions upon the franchise, to prevent French dominance in the Assembly; the union of Upper and Lower Canada for more prompt and certain anglicization. Governor Craig also regretted the presence of a French majority in the

Assembly, proposed various schemes for reducing it, and advocated the playing of one ethnic group against the other.

As is well known, the situation deteriorated steadily until it led to the rebellion of 1837–8. When the smoke of battle had cleared, Lord Durham observed that

> the most just and sensible of the English . . . seem to have joined in the determination never again to submit to a French major- ity. . . . The English complained that they, a minority, suffered under the oppressive use to which power was turned by the French majority. . . . They assert that Lower Canada must be *English*, at the expense, if necessary, of not being *British*. . . . Nor have the English inhabitants forgotten in their triumph the terror with which they suddenly saw themselves surrounded by an insurgent majority. . . . Their only hope of safety is supposed to rest on systematically terrifying and disabling the French, and in preventing a majority of that race from ever again being predominant in any portion of the legislature of the Province.

That latter design was finally realized through the Act of Union in 1840.[*] A single legislative council was appointed and a single assembly was elected, with equal representation for Upper and Lower Canada, in spite of the fact that the latter province had 650,000 inhabitants against the former's 450,000. Moreover, English was to be the sole official language.

The final irrational upsurge of the frightened minority occurred in 1849, when the passing of the Rebellion Losses Bill unleashed the English-Canadian riots which led to the pelting of Governor Elgin, the burning of the Parliament buildings, and the Annexation Manifesto. But a year or so later, demographic change had at last made English-speaking Canadians the more numerous ethnic group; and forever after

---

[*] It had been advocated many times before: by Sewell and by Craig (1810), by the Duke of Richmond (1819), by Lord Dalhousie (1820). And it had almost succeeded in 1822, when a petition was signed by some fourteen hundred English-speaking Montrealers.

they were able to preach the grandeur of true democracy and to back up their preachings by their own virtuous submission to majority rule. Unfortunately, it was then too late for French Canadians to unlearn their first seventy-five years of schooling, during which time the notion of representative government had been identified with domination by an English-speaking minority. And they could hardly be expected to greet as the millennium the advent of representation by population in 1867, which could only mean continued domination, but this time by an English-speaking majority.

Future events confirmed French-Canadian scepticism with reasonable regularity: the wanton use of majorities to do away with a bilingual legislature in Manitoba, and with *droits acquis* over separate schools in various provinces; the formation of a Union Government in 1917 to ride roughshod over the whole of French Canada; the use of the plebiscite in 1942, by which English Canada pretended to absolve the Liberals from their twenty years of solemn (if unwise) pledges to the French Canadians; the long-standing practice of favouring immigration from the British Isles as opposed to that from France.[*] Such examples of the use of majorities as a bludgeon to "convince" minorities should remind us that if French Canadians made the mistake of using democracy as a tool of ethnic warfare, the English Canadians offered them the wherewithal to learn. In all cases where fundamental oppositions arose on racial lines, the French felt that a stronger force (first an army and later a majority of citizens) could always be mustered against them. Of course it would be wrong to conclude that cultural relations between the two groups in political matters were a complete failure. The converse is happily the case. But sadly enough, even in cases where complete

---

[*] As early as 1763 the implicit assumption of British policy was that the French group was to be swamped by immigration (see McInnis, *Canada*, p. 130). Durham recommended that policy in his famous report (p. 180). And the laws of Canada favoured it until after the Second World War, when P.C. 4849 was amended by P.C. 4186 (September 16, 1948) and by P.C. 5593 (December 10, 1948). In fairness, it must be added that the French on either side of the Atlantic were not militant advocates of migration to Canada; but the fact of inequality under the law is not changed for all that.

co-operation has seemed to exist between the French minority and the English-speaking majority, within the framework of the national parties for instance,[*] democracy appears to have been thwarted.

Towards the end of the nineteenth century a well-known combination of factors brought French Canadians *en masse* into the fold of the Liberal Party. The choice of Laurier as leader and the way the Conservatives handled the Riel Rebellion convinced the French-Canadian voters that their ethnic survival could be better guaranteed by the Liberals than by the Conservatives. And so, in every federal election from 1891 to 1958 Quebec returned a majority of Liberals to Ottawa, nearly always an overwhelming majority.[†]

I shall not belittle the amazing astuteness, foresight, and (in the very early days) courage that made such a performance possible. No doubt the Liberals received great help at various times from their bungling Conservative and socialist opponents; but they still deserve credit for preventing the growth in Quebec of a federal nationalist party, even at the height of Mercier's and later of Bourassa's influence, and even when the Bloc Populaire was in full sway. For they learned to cater to French Canada's intuition that its destinies would be better protected at Ottawa by a more or less independent bloc within the party in power than by a nationalist party, bound, because of its ethnic basis, to remain forever seated on Opposition benches.

But power entails responsibilities; and there is no doubt that the Liberals tragically failed to shoulder theirs. A party cannot have the approval of a majority of the electorate for well over half a century without accepting much of the blame for that electorate's political immaturity. If French Canadians even today have learnt so little about democracy, if they twist its rules so shockingly, if they are constantly

---

[*] The following remarks apply mainly to the Liberal Party, since for nearly seventy years French-Canadian representation in the others was not numerically significant. At the present time, it is too soon to generalize about the Conservative Party.

[†] Provincially the Liberal grip on power was only broken in 1936, when an even more "nationalistic" party was born.

tempted by authoritarianism, it is to a large degree because the Liberal Party has been miserably remiss in its simple political duty. Instead of educating the French-speaking electorate to believe in democracy, the Liberals seemed content to cultivate the ignorance and prejudice of that electorate.[*]

I should not like to apportion blame between French- and English-speaking Liberals in this regard. The gravest faults no doubt fall squarely on the former. It is they who have failed to inject valid democratic concepts into the innumerable campaigns waged during the present century. On the contrary, forgetful of the common weal, they have always encouraged Quebeckers to continue using their voting bloc as an instrument of racial defence, or of personal gain. Their only slogans have been racial slogans. Until 1917 their cry was: Vote for a party led by a French Canadian. After 1917 it was: Vote against Borden's party. This cry was still used in recent years, though between 1947 and 1957 more sophisticated politicians were able to revert to the French-Canadian leadership slogan, as well as to attack the Conservatives for being "anti–French Canadian Protestants and imperialists" and the C.C.F. for being "anti–French Canadian atheists and centralizers." And it was largely on the strength of such slogans that they were elected.

But the fact remains that throughout most of its existence the federal Liberal Party was overwhelmingly an English-speaking party. And that majority in my view should bear the blame for serious faults of omission with respect to the backwardness of democracy in Quebec. They might, *à la rigueur*, be excused for not having liked to poke into the hornet's nest of their French-Canadian bloc. But the pity is that they seemed to encourage such a state of affairs. The shameful incompetence of the average Liberal M.P. from Quebec was a welcome asset to

---

[*] There were some rare exceptions. For instance, a short but meritorious effort was made during the Second World War by groups that founded the Institut démocratique, but it was soon to perish. Today, a minority within a splinter group is trying to build a democratic Fédération Libérale provinciale with the help of a weekly, *La Réforme*; both are still very far from the electorate. Whether the Liberal débâcle at Ottawa will strengthen the provincial reformers remains an open question.

a government that needed little more than a herd of *ânes savants* to file in when the division bell rang. The party strategists had but to find an acceptable stable master – Laurier, Lapointe, St. Laurent – and the trained donkeys sitting in the back benches could be trusted to behave. Even the choice of front-benchers very often smacked of shysterism. Excepting the French-Canadian leader, who was usually a man of quality, many ministers of that ethnic group were chosen not so much for their ability to serve democracy as for their ability to make democracy serve the party; their main qualification was familiarity with machine politicians and schemers, and until lately they were traditionally put at the head of patronage departments such as the Post Office and Public Works. To sum up, English-speaking Canadians have long behaved in national politics as though they believed that democracy was not for French Canadians.

That this is so is forcefully confirmed by English-Canadian behaviour in local politics in Quebec. In precisely that province where the people had been historically conditioned to believe that government is a function of wealth and power, rather than of the will of the majority, it so happened that the English-speaking Canadians had wealth and power but not numbers. In such circumstances, it was perhaps inevitable that the English-speaking element should choose to govern with what means they had, rather than be thankless apostles of democracy, preaching in the wilderness that they had partly created. None the less, the net result is that incredible amounts are spent in Quebec at every election, many times more per capita than in other provinces.[*] Now it is all very well to denounce the dishonesty of voters who accept refrigerators and television sets in exchange for their votes, but it must be recognized that the offering of bribes is just as detrimental to democracy as the taking of them. So the question remains: Who makes those bribes possible?

---

[*] This is common knowledge among professional politicians. Attempted estimates for the 1952 provincial elections can be found in G. Pelletier and P.E. Trudeau, *Cité libre* (December 1952), pp. 35 and 61. Guesses at amounts spent in the 1956 elections have ranged from $15 million to $25 million, though this seems hard to believe.

As the President of Quebec Beauharnois stated, after his company had contributed three-quarters of a million dollars to various campaign funds: "Gratefulness was always regarded as an important factor in dealing with democratic governments." Of course, to some extent party funds come from French-Canadian business men and seekers after petty favours. But the *real* money comes from huge corporations and wealthy enterprises that give willingly to parties which, apart from being an insurance against socialism, promise (and deliver) favourable labour laws, exemptions from property taxes, special franchises, valuable contracts without tender, mining or hydro rights of inestimable value in exchange for a row of pins – to say nothing of openly tolerating profitable infringements of the law (as in the case of timber-cutting regulations). Those powerful financial interests are not to any extent directed or owned by French Canadians. Thus it is somewhat paradoxical to observe that wealthy, upper-class, English-speaking Quebeckers may sometimes return an Opposition member in their riding, thereby rejecting as individuals the undemocratic practices of the Duplessis government; but as directors and managers of wealthy concerns what a part they must play in making his elections a success!

Perhaps the prize example of such political schizophrenia is found in the Montreal *Star* and the Montreal *Gazette*. Unparliamentary procedure at Ottawa or undemocratic practices by national politicians are denounced with the vigilance which befits truly democratic organs. But these papers never have editorials on, indeed often neglect to report, the innumerable cases of violation of parliamentary and democratic rights which are standard procedure for the Government they support in Quebec. It is safe to assume that a person whose reading of politics was limited to the *Star* and *Gazette* would never realize that the Premier constantly shouts orders to the Speaker of the Lower House, and has even participated in a loud voice in the conduct of the Upper House; that he vociferously commands the Speaker to expel members from the House on the flimsiest of pretexts; that several times during debate he has accused an honourable member of ingratitude for sitting on the Opposition benches after having, as a student, received assistance from the Government side; that he has introduced retroactive and vindictive legislation, sometimes bearing on individual adversaries (for example the Guindon bill, and the Picard bill[*] in 1954; and since then the concerted legislative warfare against elected municipal representatives belonging to the Civic Action League); that he frankly tells the electorate that they will not get roads or bridges in their riding if they return a member of the Opposition; or that during the last provincial campaign his party repeatedly branded the Liberals as Communists because 'their friends in Ottawa' had given money to the Colombo Plan instead of to the farmers of Nicolet.[†]

Indeed it is hard to escape the conclusion that if in the past English Canadians went far to instil a distrust of representative government in French-Canadian minds, in the present they are doing precious little to eradicate that distrust and to spread the gospel of honest parliamentarianism in Quebec.

III

In the two foregoing sections I will perhaps have managed to displease all Canadians. Both French and English may claim that I put too much blame on their particular ethnic group. But that would be silly, for under the democratic form of government all citizens are jointly and severally responsible for the procedures by which they choose their

---

[*] Both Gérard Picard and Léo Guindon were prominent labour leaders in Québec and declared non-parliamentarian opponents of the Union Nationale provincial government. Premier Duplessis directed the Legislative Assembly to vote two bills into law whose sole and obvious purpose was to punish each of these two gentlemen for their opposition to his government. – Ed.

[†] These are miscellaneous examples of fairly recent occurrences. Concerning the "discretion" of the English press in relation to more distant instances, see a pamphlet by F.R. Scott. *The Montreal* Star *and the C.C.F.* (Montreal, 1944). See also G. Pelletier "La Grève et la presse," in *La Grève de l'amiante*. As of late, this topic has drawn more and more attention. For instance, see the indignant editorials by P. Vigeant and G. Filion, *Le Devoir*, February 21, December 7, 1957; and André Laurendeau's editorials on "La Théorie du roi nègre." Also, probably for the first time in English, the subject was dealt with in a very remarkable editorial, "The Shame of English Canada," which appeared in the *McGill Daily*, February 26, 1958.

leaders; all men are to blame who fail in their duty of denouncing unde-mocratic practices and shady politicians.

Democracy is not easy, even under the best of circumstances. But it is no consolation to know that under other climes other pitfalls beset democratic ways. It is important for Canadians to realize what particu-lar pitfalls beset *them*. And there is no doubt that the unpleasant facts I have evoked play an important part in conditioning Canadian political behaviour on both sides of the ethnic barrier. I have tried to pry those facts away from the back of the collective minds of French and English Canada, and fit them into an explanatory hypothesis, for I believe that such exercises are necessary if Canadians are to know how to provide the whole of Canada with a common and enduring democratic faith.

If my hypothesis is right, the current vogue for preaching political morality in Quebec will by itself be of little avail. For so long as people do not believe in democracy there is no reason why they should accept its ethics. Political behaviour in Quebec can be described as immoral, objectively speaking; but subjectively the people are not conscious of wrongdoing, and consequently they see no reason to change that behaviour.

But this essay has run its course; further thoughts would lead me towards ground where men of action take over. And this book is no place to publish a tract for the times.

John T. Saywell, ed., *Federalism and the French Canadians* (Toronto: Macmillan, 1968)

Diefenbaker Aloft in a Balloon

><

It is too early to pass a definitive judgement on the policy of our federal government. After more than a generation in the Opposition, the Conservative party naturally needs time to understand the wheels of administration and to put its distinctive imprint on our legislation.

But it is not too soon to pass judgement on Mr. Diefenbaker's style: his reach has exceeded his grasp.

Mr. Diefenbaker came to power surrounded by a team without government experience; he had to take control of a State bureaucracy largely shaped by the Liberals. For precisely those two reasons, he could have chosen to govern without making any waves during the years he needed to learn how to become a statesman. And nobody would have blamed him. If he had acted this way, if he had chosen to mature through a slow and reasoned process, the Conservative leader might have ended up giving his party a true historical dimension.

Instead, the party is now on the way to becoming a hodgepodge of loud-mouths and flashy individuals, a pack of lawyers charging so much per mile and of businessmen charging so much per square foot, in other words, a traditional party of Canadian politicians.

In fact, Mr. Diefenbaker has decided to reach farther than his grasp. Elected with the strongest majority since Confederation, he had a hard time tolerating a single shred of the Liberal legend. He seemed determined to completely wipe out everything down to the very shadows of our recent political history.

The Shadows

First, there was Mr. Pearson, a Nobel Prize–winner, a man respected in all the chancelleries of the world, and Leader of the Opposition. Mr. Diefenbaker had to rush out and eclipse Pearson by becoming a giant on the international scene. So he announced his vision for the Commonwealth, a powerful confederation of sister-nations reaching around the planet, whose strength comes from the number and diversity of its members, brought together nevertheless by an adherence to common traditions. Some Tory newspapers in London did their best to take this vision seriously, and Mr. Diefenbaker set out on an inspired journey, ready if necessary to take over the moral leadership of the Commonwealth.

Unfortunately, his balloon started coming down over Asia, and especially over Pakistan, a country whose poverty, disorder, and anti-parliamentary governments showed him that a common policy was full of hazards. From then on, he was never heard to speak of the Commonwealth, except, for example, when he used it to justify the fact that we did not vote in the United Nations against South Africa's policy of apartheid.

Then, there was Mr. Howe, that veritable satyr of trade and finance, who had left an indelible imprint on the direction of our economy. Mr. Diefenbaker decided that any trace of this man had to disappear, and he hastily announced a radical new 15 per cent realignment of our international trade. This was a real farce in terms of political economy; but Great Britain pretended to go along by proposing a free-trade agreement between our two countries. The protectionist lobbies quickly put a stop to all this babbling talk, which was absurd and dangerous (for them); in fact, they did such a good job that they succeeded in wiping out ten years of Canadian efforts at the GATT to reduce tariff barriers in international trade.

Then, there was Mr. St. Laurent, one of the main architects of NATO, and the man who had patriated part of the Canadian Constitution by means of Amendment No. 2 in 1949. In an attempt to quickly outdo the former Liberal leader on the strategic front, Mr. Diefenbaker hastily got us into commitments in NORAD with such rash zeal that our country is now in a state of military dependence setting us back one hundred years. And now, on the constitutional front, Mr. Diefenbaker says he will patriate the British North America Act.

Patriating the Constitution

It doesn't take a genius to see that Mr. Diefenbaker's latest balloon will lose air as pitifully as the previous ones. He has already retroactively brushed off the statements of his parliamentary assistant, Mr. Martineau, as "unofficial" (his assistant's flight in panic was really very revealing). Which leaves no doubt as to the completely ephemeral character of the Conservative leader's new vision.

For my part, I feel no need to discuss the constitutional question since it will soon join the heap of Mr. Diefenbaker's failed visions for the Commonwealth, international trade, and our independence from the United States.

What a shame it all is. Personally, I was convinced that King and St. Laurent had stayed too long in office and turned the Liberals into a party both arrogant and not democratic enough. And since the Conservatives were all that was left to fight the Liberals, I hoped that Mr. Diefenbaker would be a man to renew political thought to some extent, in various different areas.

Things have turned out differently. Since he gained power, Mr. Diefenbaker has announced a host of very welcome initiatives. Apart from the ones already mentioned, these initiatives include a bill of rights, a tendency to commute the death penalty, the reception of refugees suffering from tuberculosis, the transformation of federal–provincial relations, and opposition to nuclear tests.

On Balloons

In all these cases, and many others besides, Mr. Diefenbaker's measures have seemed generous but unfortunately have remained largely at the level of good intentions. They have been aerostats full of hot air and pushed along by the wind, but which have inevitably crashed, along with their pilot, before getting very far.

For example, on the death penalty, the federal cabinet has a tendency to act on humanitarian grounds. But nothing indicates that this tendency is being followed up with a legislative policy. And if this latter policy is not developed, humanitarian practice will not be praised without reservation; it will be a form of discrimination which is dangerous for social order and hated by the people who do not benefit from it.

The same goes for federal–provincial relations. The Conservatives have shown themselves incapable of any original thought on the subject. They are struggling to resolve the problem of grants to universities by closely imitating the spirit and letter of the Liberals; that is, they are resorting to a kind of deductibility which has completely lost sight of the anticyclical mechanism which was the main reason for the original fiscal agreements.

Mr. Diefenbaker's good intentions have flopped so often that flops are without a doubt the leading characteristic of his style; and as Buffon says, the style makes the man. He believes that inspiration dispenses him of the need to think, he has neither the patience nor the humility to make more haste and less speed, he doesn't feel the need to surround himself with men able to ground Canadian politics in real reflection.

Laurendeau says that Canadians seem destined to speak "joual"; we could just as well say that, for a long time to come, Canada seems destined to be governed in a sloppy fashion.

Cité libre 11/26
(April 1960)
Translation by George Tombs

On the Idea of Political Opposition

⤞⤝

I was amazed that a good number of "opposition" figures should accept seats from the Union Nationale, whether on the Superior Council of Labour, the Task Force on the Administrative System of Montreal, or the Commission of Inquiry on Hospital Insurance.

Let me make myself understood: I am not in any way challenging the moral integrity of these people, since some of them are my friends; I do question their political wisdom. I have to insist on proceeding, however, even though I found only two or three people who share my amazement, and a lot of others who consider me a nit-picker.

A Definition

In a parliamentary democracy, the opposition figure makes a profession of believing that the party in power is wrong to be there; not necessarily because this party always acts badly, but because another party would often do better. Consequently, whether the opposition figure sits in Parliament or is active in politics in some other way, he has to systematically and relentlessly criticize the government's mistakes, and use all reasonable arguments and legal means so that eventually the people will elect another party to office. Thanks to parliamentary custom, the opposition figure is not given over to anarchy. On the contrary, by participating in parliamentary committees, by discussing draft bills, by proposing amendments, by voting, "Her Majesty's Loyal Opposition" participates, as it were, in the life of the State; people outside of Parliament who are busy strengthening Opposition parties also participate in a less direct way.

On rare occasions, it sometimes happens that the party in power will ask an opposition figure to join a commission of inquiry or a consultative body. The latter will accept, if he considers that he will be in a better position to serve the common weal by becoming a councillor of the party in power than by remaining in the Opposition parties. But in so doing, he will cease to be an opposition figure.

And this is the point where it is worth repeating my amazement at the fact that some people accepted to become councillors and commissioners of the Union Nationale government.

My amazement is not directed at "independent" people: professors, lawyers, or other "experts" who clearly remain outside of politics and who temporarily find themselves in a situation like that of State bureaucrats. But what can be said of those claiming to be opposition figures? Of people who have been telling us for the last five, ten, and fifteen years that the Union Nationale had to be destroyed at all costs? Who bandied about words like "fascism" and "dictatorship"?

And here in the very bosom of the Task Force on the Administrative System of Montreal, and the Commission on Hospital Insurance, some of them have become salaried employees of the Union Nationale government. Just before the election, they have given up all political activity; more than that, they will hold all manner of hearings and inquiries, diverting away from the political arena a lot of attention and collective energy that could have served to strengthen the Opposition.

And other people have accepted to work for the Superior Council of Labour, and participate in the development of the Union Nationale's labour policy. On this point, the law explicitly states that the council is a "consultative" organization; its members deal with "subjects about which the public administration wishes to be better informed": they completely depend on the minister of labour, who has absolute control of the range of subjects dealt with by the council. It is clearly understood that councillors do not have to approve in advance whatever the Union Nationale does. But they are completely responsible for the measures proposed by the council; and as long as the government acts on their proposals, they will be hard-pressed to criticize laws or other government measures based on the very democratic decisions they have taken.

From Corporatism to Illegality

I have no idea how the corporatists will take to all this . . . But for someone like me, who still believes in parliamentary democracy, one person is ultimately responsible for labour policy: and that person is the minister of labour, who stands by the whole cabinet. The job of an opposition figure is to kick the minister out, along with his cabinet. Those who have accepted positions as the minister's councillors are *pro tanto* in his service. The law leaves no grounds for doubt on this point; and if it did leave such grounds, everything would become clear enough in practice.

In fact, from the very first meeting of the Superior Council of Labour onwards, the honourable Barrette completely compromised his new buddies with his anti-parliamentary actions, by announcing that "any unanimous decision made by the Superior Council of Labour will become law" (*Le Devoir*, March 30, 1960). This statement, in the finest traditions of the Union Nationale, treated the Legislative Assembly and the representatives of the people as if they simply did not exist. But not one councillor objected.

Then, as if to guarantee that the council was an accomplice of the Union Nationale in the latter's habit of misappropriating public funds, the first official act of the council was an illegal one. Whereas the law formally prohibits the payment of a salary to members of the council, the councillors voted for the following remuneration: $50 a day for those who did not have to travel, and for the others $100 for the first day and $75 for days following. It is clear that by fixing their "expenses" at such arbitrary and high levels, the councillors are trying to pay themselves a hidden salary; in other words, they are guilty of misappropriating public funds. I know very well that some working-class and university councillors voted against this scale of "expenses" and they deserve credit for the fact; but since the scale was approved by a majority, it inevitably took effect.

With the end result that, from their first meeting onward, former opposition figures acquiesced in spite of themselves to anti-parliamentary actions, illegality, and the misappropriation of public funds, and they stood by what is probably the most reactionary and corrupt government the province has known since Confederation.

Weakening the Opposition

Of course, I would be prepared to admit that on rare occasions an opposition figure might accept to sit on a royal commission of inquiry; he could be named by a government whose integrity he more or less respected. But he should never do so if his temporary defection seriously weakened the Opposition; since whatever contribution he might make to the commission of inquiry would not amount to much compared with keeping the Opposition lively and vigorous.

But in the province of Quebec the Opposition is so weak that it seems pointless to come even briefly to the assistance of the Union Nationale. Especially since some of the people who have accepted positions as councillors of the Union Nationale are the same ones who just recently – and quite rightly – were accusing this party of systematically undermining the very foundations of parliamentary rule.

What bizarre logic! Barely a year ago, a half-dozen of the citizens who have just accepted nominations from the Union Nationale were then denouncing as reactionaries and cowards the people who promoted the union of democratic forces in the hopes of strengthening the Opposition. It was supposedly unthinkable that legitimate Opposition figures should hold talks with Opposition parties as dubious as the Liberal Party or Civic Action!

However, I can't imagine Paul Gérin-Lajoie or Léon Patenaude[*] accepting an offer from the Union Nationale government to sit on one of these "consultative organizations" (that is what the law calls them) where our "real Opposition figures" are now to be found.

Besides, I couldn't help noticing that when the P.S.D. [Parti Social Démocrate – Quebec branch of the CCF] Congress was held in Montreal at the beginning of April, and where the creation of a new Opposition party was discussed, the so-called real opposition figures were conspicuously absent, even though two of them were supposed to be on the programme as guest speakers.

A Remarkable Strategy

I am sorry to say that I can only conclude from all this that the Union Nationale is led by extraordinary strategists (unless the Opposition is made up of unbelievably naïve people). Because the nominations just mentioned are simply masterful for two reasons.

First, on the very eve of an election, the Union Nationale has succeeded in tying up the leaders of several opposition groups with other activities; in so doing, the party has at the very least succeeded in taking the edge off the vehemence and frequency of their attacks, and has possibly reduced them to complete silence. (Consider the examples of anti-parliamentary actions and illegality outlined above.)

Second, at a time when people are discussing whether to merge the P.S.D. and the C.T.C. [Congrès du travail canadien – Canadian Labour Congress] to create a new left-wing party, the Union Nationale has succeeded in steering several leaders of the left in Quebec away from this plan. On the long term, however, this could prove extremely serious: if the new party is launched on the national scene without the effective participation of Quebec, well, this new party will inevitably

---

[*]   Paul Gérin-Lajoie was Quebec's first minister of education and Léon Patenaude was president of the Publishers' Association – Ed.

be perceived by Quebeckers over the next twenty-five years as an "English and foreign" party, just the way the P.S.D. has been perceived for the last twenty-five years.

At that rate, roads and bridges shall pass away, but the Union Nationale shall not pass away.

Cité libre 11/27 (May 1960)
Translation by George Tombs

The Identity Card Is Back

><

At irregular intervals in Quebec, the question of the identity card gets into the headlines, and never fails to receive the support of well-meaning citizens and organizations.

This time round, like the time six years ago, the municipal administration has come out in favour of cards; and on all sides decent citizens are bustling about, saying it is a good idea. Which is why I have to take up the same old arguments, and remind them that it is actually a bad idea.

The plan is basically to use the identity card to prevent electoral fraud, and people naturally forget that a host of institutions would find it convenient to use the card to identify the people they are in contact with, for the simple reason that it is there. As a result, without anyone really noticing, and because it is convenient, the identity card will become just as much a requirement in Quebec as it is in military dictatorships and police states.

I know that my opponents will not agree. They would like to have this card for electoral purposes above all, and use it if need be only to identify victims of accidents, criminals, bank clients, etc.

"Oh, So You're a Jew!"

Which doesn't sound bad at all, obviously: a harmless little card I could pick up every three or four years (but which would contain information enabling an officer to identify me, if I am voting, and a priest to give me extreme unction in the event of an accident, if I am a practising Catholic; enabling a policeman to badger me, if I have a police record, and a banker to cash my cheques, if I am solvent; enabling the police force to keep tabs on me, if I read Karl Marx, and a hotel manager to keep me out of his establishment, if I am a Jew.)

This cavalier attitude is shocking. It is also shocking to consider that, in the absence of political education there is no deep-seated emotion to convince democrats they should oppose such a measure. It would be enough to study the experience of Europe, or even our own experience during the war, to see that a system of civil and criminal identification would have to be permanent and generalized to be effective, especially in a highly mobile society like our own.

It would involve tight controls on the citizens, who would clearly have to report to a registration office each time they moved, changed jobs, or changed their civil status. Then the office would have to be able to quickly and correctly locate and identify each citizen; in other words, for each citizen there would have to be a corresponding file with a complete description: photo, signature, fingerprints, physical characteristics, biographical data, and police record.

"Your Papers, Please."

And, above all, the police would have to take measures to detect fake identity cards, to update expired cards, and to surprise negligent cardholders and forgers. In other words, the card would have to be produced on request at any time, and any doubtful case would have to be subjected to search, and every infraction would have to be punished with a fine or imprisonment.

In short, every citizen would have to be constantly ready to justify his presence, his actions, and his conditions to an authority: the State, the Office, the Police, the Boss.

"Nothing to worry about, less than nothing!" we hear? Good folk object to this kind of argument, saying that "the identity card will only protect the decent citizen and harm the criminal." So if a person has a clear conscience, he shouldn't have any objection to explaining every move he makes to the police. Which is like saying that, if a person is not a communist, he has no grounds to criticize the Padlock Law or bills 19 and 20 . . .* Personally, I do not consider that Quebec political society has given sufficient guarantees of its democratic maturity for me to gladly recognize the right to make an inventory, a numbered catalogue, of every single citizen.

"He Doesn't Even Have Any Papers!"

I'll tell you a little story that is typical of our civic mentality. A few years ago I spent two hours in the jail of one of our cities, because I refused to identify myself to a policeman who gruffly accosted me, although I was out for a walk just five hundred feet from my house.

As long as this type of police mentality prevails in Quebec, I can only say that it is hypocritical and irresponsible and totally unconvincing when people claim to be improving our electoral system by cheerfully handing over to the police the ultimate instrument of indoctrination and control.

I deplore electoral dishonesty as much as the next person. And if the identity card was absolutely the only way to attack these evils, I might have to accept it. But Quebeckers have already suffered a lot from petty officiousness, and I do not understand why anyone should recommend adopting coercive methods without even trying to exhaust other methods. For a hundred years already our lethargy has given corrupt politicians free rein to dominate the electoral scene; should our first awakening of interest in political morality be to impose yet more restrictions on our own liberty rather than to act directly against corruption?

---

* The Padlock Law authorized the Québec government to padlock premises occupied by organizations suspected of being communist. Bills 19 and 20 were conceived to limit labour unions' freedom of action – Ed.

"Take Him Away . . ."

Let's start by getting the Penal Code applied with the same severity in cases of election fraud as for bank robbery. Let's make sure electoral lists are properly put together. Let's study various registry and enumeration systems for electoral purposes. Let's try, above all, to create some kind of political conscience in Quebec.

There are few countries left in the world where citizens can still live their lives with a minimum of restrictions; without doubt the logic of the thermonuclear age and the universe of the concentration camp will sooner or later put an end to our anachronistic freedoms. But please, let's give in only with regret, and at the latest possible date; and let's make sure the first concessions are not imposed on us by a handful of political amateurs struggling to prove their good intentions to us.

Cité libre 11/33 (January 1961)
Translation by George Tombs

Two Innocents in Red China

><

In fall 1960, Pierre Trudeau and Jacques Hébert wrote a short book, Two Innocents in Red China *(published in 1961), after travelling for several weeks in China. It would be the last travel account by Trudeau before his entry into politics. Many people in the West still considered China very mysterious; the two authors brought to their travel experience a combination of humour and attentive observation, deep understanding, and sharp critical judgement.*

By the time the book was translated and reissued in August 1968, Trudeau already lived at 24 Sussex Drive in Ottawa. He felt the need to explain in an introductory note that "this book was not written by the Prime Minister of Canada or by any official, but by two private citizens responsible only to themselves for inaccuracies or indiscretions." He also added a tongue-in-cheek disclaimer: "If there are any statements in the book which can be used to prove that the authors are agents of the international Communist conspiracy, or alternatively fascist exploiters of the working classes, I am sure that my co-author, Jacques Hébert, who remains a private citizen, will be willing to accept entire responsibility for them."

That China is still an object of fear is betrayed even in everyday conversation. Before our departure, people seriously told us: "You are courageous to go over there!" At first we thought this was mockery, directed against frivolous travellers by those who were courageously keeping their noses to the grindstone. But no; other expressions used taught us what daring we were apparently displaying: "Have you made your will? Accidents happen so quickly." "It is easier to go behind the iron curtain than to come out again." "Aren't you afraid of being held as hostages?"

In all humility we couldn't bring ourselves to take these stories seriously. Besides, we each had in our possession a document belonging to the Canadian government, in which the Secretary of State for External Affairs of Canada requested under his seal and "in the name of Her Majesty the Queen" that the authorities of "all countries" should "allow the bearer to pass freely without let or hindrance" and should "afford the bearer such assistance and protection as may be necessary." Armed with such a precious safe-conduct, we didn't see why we should be bothered at presenting ourselves at the border of any country at all. Besides, as the ensuing history is going to show, the Chinese took infinite precautions to ensure our return home safe and sound. They seemed to be afraid that, if one of us chanced to drown in the Grand Canal or idiotically fell off the Great Wall, a certain section of the Western press would draw dramatic conclusions about the danger of restoring diplomatic relations with a country where the life of a "French-Canadian Catholic" was held so cheap.

In reality the only fear that we might possibly have thought reasonable was that of being denounced and vilified by compatriots on our return *ex partibus infidelium*. And it is a fact that out of a hundred French Canadians invited to go on this trip the previous spring (true, this was before the fall of the Union Nationale government), fewer than twenty dared to answer, and more than half of them refused.

But it must be said that on this score the authors of the present volume were pretty well immune to reprisals by this time. Since both of them had been generously reproved, knocked off, and abolished in the integralist and reactionary press in consequence of earlier journeys behind the iron curtain, the prospect of being assassinated yet again on their return from China was hardly likely to impress them.

All in all, we two, who had never travelled together before but between us had been four times round the world, sailed nearly all the seas, explored five continents extensively, and visited every country of the earth except Portugal, Romania, and Paraguay, discovered that we entertained the same outlandish philosophy of travel: we believed that those who have toured a country observantly and in good faith are in some danger of knowing more about it than those who haven't been there.

And it seemed to us imperative that the citizens of our democracy should know more about China. If when we were children the grown-ups had told us anything besides rubbish on this subject, and if they themselves had ever been encouraged to reflect that the unthinkable sufferings of the Chinese people deserved something more from the West than postage stamps, opium, and gunboats, China today might be a friendly country. And an important part of Western policy wouldn't have to be improvised in the back rooms of Washington and Rome on the basis of information gathered in Hong Kong and Tokyo by agencies that clip and collate various items from Chinese newspapers. So we thought some supplementary information, and an effort at compre-hension, might be of some use.

It is true that, not speaking the innumerable Chinese dialects really fluently, we would be largely at the mercy (and it *was* a mercy!) of inter-preters; that we would see only what the authorities would let us see; and so on. But the same reservations apply to the testimony of Canadian tourists in Spain, Egypt, or the Holy Land; yet nobody dreams of telling them that they would talk more sense about these countries if, instead of going there, they had kept their slippers on and stayed in Notre-Dame de Ham-sud or Sainte-Emilienne de Boundary-line.

For what has been seen has unquestionably been seen; what was translated was translated by a Chinese official interpreter, so that it does at least tell us what he himself thinks. Besides, we didn't lack points of comparison: the combined total of our earlier sojourns in

Asia came to nearly two years, partly spent in pre-Communist China and partly in Taiwan.

We know that to some people the mere fact of going to China and staying there at the expense of the Communists is enough to vitiate any testimony. Such people clearly rate their own and others' honesty dirt cheap.

There remain some individuals with the peculiar notion that good faith towards China amounts to bad faith towards the non-Communist world. To this argument we have no answer, except that this is not the way we understand human nature. We don't ask such people to read us or to believe us; and if they still persist in denouncing us we ask them first to reflect on the consequences of a purely negative anti-Communism.

For years anti-Communists of this kind have applied themselves to discrediting any evidence that might suggest that the Russians were not stone-age barbarians. Then, suddenly, the Soviets put gigantic Sputniks in orbit around the earth, photographed the other side of the moon, and confounded world opinion with their scientific progress. It is evident, then, today that Western governments would have done well to have listened more carefully to travellers who told of the progress of the USSR, and to have put rather less trust in the witch-hunters; for since it was our policy to regard Communism as an enemy or at least a rival, it would have been on the whole less dangerous to overestimate than to underestimate this enemy's intelligence.

It is partly to prevent the repetition of these errors with regard to the Chinese People's Republic that the authors have written the present work. Those who take seriously the precept "Love thy neighbour as thyself" cannot object to our reporting such success as the Chinese government is having in leading its people out of several millennia of misery. For it is always our fellow-humans that progress of this sort benefits – whatever their political allegiance may be.

But there will still remain some readers to accuse us – according to whether they are fanatically pro- or anti-Communist – of having said too much that is bad or too much that is good about today's China. We accept this certificate of impartiality – and we nonsuit both parties. Let each of them console themselves with the thought that our testimony (if it is as biased as they will say) can only help to weaken their particular enemy by exaggerating his superiority!

And now, the journey begins.

At 10.30 Mr Hou is shepherding his little flock back to the hotel. "Tonight the crowd will be too dense and excited," he says; "you would be dangerously jostled." But the Leader of the Canadian group swears to himself that he will have none of that. What? The Chinese Fourteenth of July, and he is not to storm the Bastille?

As the party leaves the Tien An Men gate, Trudeau hides for a moment behind a pillar, then darts towards the crowd that is swirling round the square. In an instant he is caught up, sucked in, and swallowed by the maelstrom of people, and lost to Mr Hou.

What happened after that we shall never know exactly, nor are we convinced that Trudeau remembers it clearly himself. He took part in weird and frenzied dances, in impromptu skits, in delightful flirtations; he described exotic orchestras, costumes of the moon-people, strange friendships, and new scents; he told of jackets of (imitation) leather, dark tresses, inquisitive children, laughing adolescents, brotherly and joyful men. Then he spoke of a weariness that imperceptibly settled on the city along with the dust, no longer kicked up by millions of dancing feet; he spoke too of lights being extinguished, voices growing hoarse, dances that gradually lost their speed and groups that grew steadily smaller; of trucks filled with soldiers at the end of their leaves, of busloads of departing peasants, of small parties straggling along the streets, of light footsteps in deserted alleyways, of dark lanterns, of the end of the masquerade; and of a very long walk through a sleeping capital in the small hours of the morning.

Having stealthily entered the hotel, our Leader steps into a hot bath. Just as he is congratulating himself on his incognito escapade, there is a knock on the door.

Trudeau opens the door a crack and perceives the stern visage of

Mr Hou, and Mr Wen himself, vice-president of the Chinese People's Association for Cultural Relations with Foreign Countries. Out of deference for this important dignitary, the bather puts on his underpants and invites the gentlemen to come in.

A conversation in gestures ensues, but doesn't get very far. At last Trudeau understands that he is supposed to put his trousers on. But just as he becomes convinced that he is going to be sent to Mongolia, Mr Wen introduces a magnificent young woman, thoroughly intimidated. So that's it! – she is the only interpreter they could dig up at this late hour.

In impeccable French, the girl translates Mr Wen's anxious reproaches. "You could have got lost or had an accident, walking all by yourself at night."

Trudeau can no longer resist teasing: "Clearly I would have felt less lonely with a pretty girl like you at my side." But the interpreter is impervious to this kind of thing, and translates to Mr Wen the compliments intended for her. Misunderstanding spreads, confusion becomes universal, the Plan is destroyed, the General Line takes on peculiar aspects, and Trudeau speaks of a Great Leap Forward to his tub. Decidedly this is not the night for building socialism.

Canton

> *It is the teachers who have caused the disorder in the world.*
> CHUANG TZU

THURSDAY, 13 OCTOBER

A long day on the train, with nothing worth reporting except increasing warmth. After the rather gloomy autumn of the north-east, it is good to taste the delightful climate of south China.

We take advantage of the journey to reflect on the economic plan. The train is on its way; we have to listen to each other. The reader is better off: he can leave the train, and the paragraphs that follow, and pick us up again tomorrow. So we'll see you at Canton station at six o'clock in the morning.

We recall that at the end of each meeting there was one question we always asked, in one form or another: "In a planned economy, and when prices and production are not regulated by supply and demand, who makes the decision – and how? How does the carpet factory or automotive works know how much to produce and when to expand? How does the commune divide its yield between its own members and the State? Who decides the scale of wages and the rate of profit?" And always we got the same answer: the Plan. The Plan was the source of every attitude, the fountainhead of all decisions, the bosom in which every anxious manager could find security.

Well (*jiga, jiga*), in a country where entrepreneurial talent is exceedingly scarce, such a system has its points. When the local manager doesn't have to worry about his raw materials or his markets, when his payroll and his rate of investment are decided by others, he can devote his efforts to increasing production. That is to say, he will concentrate all his energies on fulfilling or exceeding the Plan. And that is why, on the one hand, competition within each factory will be encouraged by all kinds of banners, rolls of honour, and improvised fanfares; and on the other, the workers will be encouraged to invent all kinds of gimmicks to improve output. The result can only be increased production – in certain sectors of industry or certain areas of the national economy. But in practice this also means bottlenecks.

And in fact do you remember those fields strewn with engines, those endless streets cluttered with railway coaches and tubing, in Shenyang? Those were glaring examples of bottlenecks in the execution of the Plan. Yet the economists and engineers we questioned refused to see them as anything but glorious indications of continuously increasing productivity. Their attitude endorsed a combination of economic waste and technical efficiency that would make any Western economist or entrepreneur shudder.

But the Chinese gloried in it! And perhaps they weren't altogether wrong. After all, the Chinese industrial revolution was just born, and already it was growing at a staggering rate. Perhaps that couldn't have been done without imbuing managers and workers with a single obsession – to surpass the Plan.

The workers work, the managers manage, and the problems that result from bottlenecks and dislocations land in the laps of regional and national planners. On them devolves the task of readjusting the Plan from year to year and from month to month. Certainly it's not easy, under a system where rather blunt administrative tools have to take the place of precise economic indicators. But they must console themselves by quoting Chairman Mao: "In our country an economic plan is drawn up every year to establish a suitable ratio between accumulation and consumption, and to attain equilibrium between production and the needs of society. . . . This equilibrium and this unity are partly broken every month, every quarter, requiring a partial readjustment. Sometimes, when the arrangements made fail to correspond to reality, contradictions occur and the equilibrium is disrupted. That is called committing an error. Contradictions appear unceasingly, and are unceasingly resolved. That is what constitutes the dialectical law of development of affairs and of phenomena."

Well, what can you say? That planning in China today consists in part of one simple slogan: "More." And that in part it is a process of continual readjustment in the light of production standards that keep changing as the new working class goes through its apprenticeship.

Obviously such a rudimentary economic process is bound to give rise to gigantic errors – gluts and bottlenecks. But they will be corrected in the next revision of the Plan; and, as for the embarrassing surpluses, an effort will be made to direct them into the vast markets of Asia and Africa. Indeed, in China itself takers can be found for almost anything – even if it does require the use of capitalist-style advertising posters!

This, we conclude, is not the tidy planning taught in the great faculties of economics. But is it not the awkward, befuddled awakening of a formidable industrial giant?

No answer. For sleep has long since invaded the railway car as it rolls peacefully along beside the legendary River of Pearls.

FRIDAY, 14 OCTOBER

Six o'clock in the morning. A reception committee is waiting for us.

Canton was one of the most active revolutionary centres, and it was here that Mao trained the peasant leaders, without whom the revolution might never have taken place. Our hosts plunge us into the right atmosphere at once by taking us to see the famous school where Mao used to teach. Founded in 1924, it was an official school in the beginning; at that period relations between the Kuomintang and the Communist Party had not yet been broken off.

We meet the director, and drink tea amidst a dreamlike décor: a sort of patio, full of tropical plants and heavy furniture of carved wood.

We are accompanied by a pretty young Chinese, her too-solemn face framed in thick black braids, no doubt a secretary in the local Cultural Association. She is very graceful in her simple cotton print, white with big green polka-dots; the skirt reaches below her knees, in the style of 1947. Is she twenty? Anyway she is too serious for her age: our most improbable jests draw from her no more smiles than are called for in "the general plan."

Together we tour the school, which is now a museum, a shrine, a place of pilgrimage. "That is the bedroom occupied by the principal of the Revolutionary School," says the director, with emotion. A minute's silence. "This was the teachers' common-room." Mr Hou raises his cap. "And the dining-hall . . ." Tables and benches of rough wood. And finally: "There is Mao's modest bedroom." Emotion is at its height. We gaze silently on the camp-bed, the desk, the chair . . .

Back to the Hotel Aichun ("Love the Masses"), which is rather dismal and desperately empty. But the view makes up for everything; from our ninth-storey window the River of Pearls is a pure marvel; from here, one would never suspect its foul stench.

The scene has an unreal quality, especially at night. The junks look like great butterflies, their black wings folded on their long brown bodies; the sampans suggest fireflies, carrying their little lamps along with the current. They glide by in their hundreds, noiselessly and irresistibly, like spruce logs on our rivers. These boats are so loaded down with rice, or rusty metal, or human manure, so encumbered with passengers and crew, that if the helmsman made one false move they would be swallowed up in the muddy waters.

Whole families live on these sampans, four feet wide and fifteen feet long. The babies are attached to ropes that give them enough play but allow them to be fished out whenever they fall in the river. As soon as they have the strength, they will learn to work the steering-oar. Here is one kind of Chinese that is still remote from the day-nursery and the communal restaurant. Are they to be envied?

In Canton – with its three million inhabitants the largest city of the south – we rediscover something of the poverty-stricken China of yesterday, where men had learned to die of hunger without complaint, or to live on nothing – a pair of trousers, a shirt, a mat to unroll on the family sampan at night, a bowl of rice, a morsel of fish. Mr Hou has told us nothing about it, but it is clear that at least on the River of Pearls there are still Chinese who work more than eight hours a day; at least in Canton there are still coolies, pushing or pulling enormous loads, bodies running with sweat, faces haggard.

We spend part of the evening in the Park of Culture, which was set up as far back as 1951. Exhibitions of art, of flowers, and of Chinese lanterns; theatres, open-air concerts, films, marionettes. A room for chess-players, a basketball field floodlit at night, a skating-rink, ping-pong, badminton; all this scattered through a park full of trees and flowers.

The huge crowd mills about noiselessly, as if it were walking on tiptoe, stopping for an hour at the open-air theatre before going on to admire the acrobats or listen to the symphony orchestra. They hold the children up above their heads to give them a good view of the musicians.

Our hosts are determined to show us an exhibition of the works of the students of the Canton School of Fine Arts – which, it must be said, attracts a smaller crowd than the acrobats. Our guide draws to our attention – though it actually hits you smack in the eye! – that the young artists of China have abandoned "flowers and butterflies" for tractors, blast-furnaces, muscular workers, and peasant women plant-ing red flags in the rice-paddies.

But then how can you explain the popularity of old Chi Pai-shih, the modern painter who just died at nearly a hundred years old? This great artist – born, it is true, in the same village as Mao – painted only flies, grasshoppers, flowers, fruits, and, above all, crabs and rats, with the traditional simplicity and economy of Chinese art, but also with the freshness and clarity of modern art. As far as we know, Chi Pai-shih never conformed to Moscow-inspired socialist realism. And he stayed in favour with the régime until his death.

On leaving the park Hébert and Trudeau, deciding to go for a walk in Canton, take leave of the group. Mr Hou points out that tomorrow's program is very full and we'll have to get up early. We insist. Our Cantonese hosts look disconcerted, but Mr Hou is accustomed by now to our escapades (which are relatively rare, after all), and just gives us an imploring look. All it takes is a little firmness: shake hands with every-body and off we go. Before our hosts recover from their surprise we are far away, lost in the crowd under the ill-lit arcades.

It's ten-thirty. We are in a hot country, and no doubt that's why people stay up later than in the north. Also, the people are more talka-tive and relaxed. Scandalous! – there are cafés where young couples are quietly sipping orangeade. In a confectionery, girls wrapping up toffee explode with laughter under their surgical masks. We peer into a day-nursery and see babies in very clean beds, dreaming of angels – well, at least they're too young to be dreaming about Mao.

For the first time in China we see women and children pursuing the wretched little trades of the streets: urchins of ten or twelve are shining shoes, women sitting on the sidewalks are offering a few fruits for sale, or a dozen red peppers laid out on a handkerchief. At least there is no soliciting, and there are no longer any beggars, as there used to be; evidently the professionals have been mercilessly com-pelled to work . . .

Western travellers who visited Canton four or five years ago still spoke of small prostitutes whose mothers offered them to passers-by, or who offered themselves with little animal-like cries. That is now a memory of the past. The former prostitutes are being re-educated into shock-troops of labour and "excellent Marxists."

It is as mild as a July night. We don't get tired of walking, sniffing at the shops and stalls, watching people as they argue and buy and eat ice cream and read the newspaper. This is a hot city, where clothing is sketchy and at night you see people asleep on the pavement in front of the open doors of their shops.

Why did Mr Hou want to deny us this pleasure? Was it to keep us from witnessing the excrement-collection that takes place at this hour? (Hence the name "night-soil.") We are quite bright enough to realize that the régime couldn't in eleven years bestow a complete sewage system on a country of 650 million people which had done without one from the beginning of time.

In fact in the little streets in the heart of Canton we can't help meeting the excrement collectors and their travelling cesspits. Carrying wooden buckets, they go into every house and work in silence as if they were performing a shameful act. Yet, it is thanks to this manure, eventually dumped in the garden, that the cabbages and lettuces of China are so fine.

But that is another example of the vicious circles that have always kept the Chinese in misery. The soil was poor, so the townsman had to send something to fertilize it. But he was sending at the same time the causes of typhoid and other diseases. In defence, the food, and the water to be used for tea had to be carefully sterilized. Fires perpetually alight for that purpose used up as fuel the wood and other vegetable matter that would otherwise have fertilized the soil with their humus. So the manure had to come from man, and this brought epidemics *unless* the humus was burned up . . . So the devilish cycle grew worse from century to century. There are some things, it seems, that cannot be changed short of a revolution.

Our walk had taken us as far as the river. Trudeau wanted to revisit the Isle of Sha-mun, the erstwhile strictly exclusive retreat of the con-sular corps and of wealthy foreigners – Chinese came to it only as domestics. The traveller of '49 described the peaceful "green" at the centre of the island, and magnificent houses around the edge. He also summoned up the recollection of certain dives where it had not been hard to console oneself with what Chiang had made dangerous – visits to opium dens.

Tonight everything is different. The houses and apartments are populated by Chinese exclusively. Through wide-open windows we see humble interiors, with clotheslines and rows of pallets. Along the boardwalk are Chinese lovers holding hands, and squatting men playing chess. And moored to the shore are evil-smelling sampans.

SUNDAY, 16 OCTOBER

Mr Hou had not foreseen that we would want to go to mass this morning. When we mention it to him, he gives a little frown, but assures us that he finds our request perfectly legitimate. It's agreed. Pi will go with us.

There are about forty of the faithful, and among them we notice a few young people, and some family groups. There is no sermon. After mass we head for the sacristy to greet the priest, a man in his sixties. Pi, who was waiting for us at the door with the polka-dot girl, runs up, visibly alarmed. "Where are you going like that?" he asks.

"To shake the priest's hand —"

"But – but —"

"To have a little chat with him."

"One moment, I'll go and find out if he can see you."

Pi comes back after two minutes. "Unfortunately the priest who speaks French is out of town."

"That's all right. We'll say hullo – in Latin if necessary – to the one who just said mass."

"No, really, he's very busy, he can't see you." Pi is dancing about – he takes our arms to drag us out of the church. Just a moment, young man!

We are still parleying when the priest, who has understood exactly what was going on, comes to meet us. A magnificent head, with gentle, deepset eyes. How we would like to talk at leisure with this man. But that is clearly not on the program; to insist would land him squarely in a delicate situation vis-à-vis the authorities. We content ourselves with shaking his hand and saying a few unimportant words. *He speaks impeccable French.*

For the first time since we have been in China, there is no question of "having a little tea."

In Mr Hou's absence, Pi decides that he will have to make the best of this unforeseen incident. He introduces to us a pale young man whom he has unearthed in the sacristy: "The secretary of the Catholic parish association." It is clear that with this unusual sacristan present we can go ahead. "He will answer all your questions."

Well, let's see. The conversation is taking place in the street, in front of the church door. We bombard the "answerable" one with questions. Passersby gather round us, all the more interested since our remarks are ironical to say the least. Pi loses his head; he doesn't know which way to turn. The crowd grows. "Come on," says Pi, furious, "the secretary will go to the hotel with us. It'll be a better place for discussion." Why not?

We get the strong impression that the secretary is the man imposed by the party on the parish to steer the study groups in the "right" direction, and to make brief reports, not to the priest, but to the government. At all events, he seems poorly grounded in religious questions, contenting himself with vague, stammering answers and contradicting himself without turning a hair. Furthermore, he has been in Canton for only ten years. (It's noticeable, by the way, that most of the "cadres" we have met in Canton come from other regions, and they don't even speak Cantonese. Can it be that there is less enthusiasm here?) When we ask the "sacristan" if there are still seminaries in Canton, he answers that Cantonese seminarists go to Shanghai. We know, of course, that there are no seminaries there. Nothing embarrasses him, though, and he contradicts the evidence with disarming innocence. As was to be expected, he gives us the party line on foreign missionaries – "spies in the pay of the capitalists" and "Chiang's men." Clearly we are dealing with an impostor, and we let him see that we know it. Pi is simply beside himself throughout the interview. Innocently, we ask him questions about the state of his soul.

Of course there is no doubt at all that many foreign missionaries believed that the fate of the Catholic Church was bound up with that of the Kuomintang. In Formosa many of them are still preparing themselves to return to China in the wake of Chiang Kai-shek's armies. This astonishing attitude suggests that some of them, in all good faith, took sides politically when they were in China.

We are not naive enough to believe that the Church would have been tolerated by the régime for long, even if it had never made a mistake. All the same, wouldn't the Christians have resisted Communist seduction more vigorously if the missionaries had not supplied ready arguments for anti-Catholic propaganda? Would the Chinese Church have been transformed so quickly into a national church, separated from Rome, if the missionaries had relied less on the protection of foreign powers whose presence in China, which was anything but a Christian presence, constituted an offence against *all* Chinese? If the missionaries had lived in greater poverty – closer, that is, to the hungry people to whom they were teaching the Gospel of the Poor? Finally, if the hierarchy had become Chinese sooner than it did?

Because of a few errors, it was possible to ruin the reputation of all missionaries very quickly, to the point where relatively few Chinese Catholics could be found to defend them.

Once the missionaries were either expelled from China or imprisoned, the hierarchy found itself partly decapitated. It was easy then to attack the Pope as being under the tutelage of the imperialists. Next, the laity and lower clergy were set in opposition to the Chinese bishops under the pretext of "democratizing the Church." This sapping operation was helped by the Marxist experts who infiltrated into the "patriotic study groups" imposed on all Catholic parishes. In discussions with often ill-prepared Christians, the Marxists had it all their own way.

The Chinese constitution guarantees freedom of religion, but the terribly effective methods used by the State to destroy the Catholic Church make this guarantee totally meaningless. A young Chinese is free to go to mass. But if he does, how can he pass the examination in

Marxism that will determine his admission to university, his promotion, or his increase in salary?

Whatever our hosts may say, a Catholic in the New China cannot be anything but a pariah.

Two Innocents in Red China
(Toronto: Oxford University
Press, 1968)
Translation by I.M. Owen

Economic Rights

>‹

I – The Past

Traditionally, the law was more concerned with civil rights than with economic rights, and understandably so. Since the sixteenth century, western civilization had been evolving in a context of boundless opportunity, provided by expanding markets, inexhaustible resources and technological progress. The aim of the legal machinery was to free man from the fetters left over by medieval institutions, in order that each person might be at liberty to make the most out of the existing environment. Hence the legislators and lawyers were constantly called upon to fashion and to use legal instruments for the protection and development of civil rights and liberties.

Within such a legal framework, western man reached standards of living undreamed of four centuries previously. But in the process, he had set up institutions wherein the principle of maximum self-assertion by all was eventually to lead to maximum insecurity for many. Economic Darwinism produced a great increment in the wants and needs of industrial man, but not always the means to fulfill them adequately. More and more people began to realize that the concept of civil rights availed them little against such realities as economic exploitation or massive unemployment.

Lawyers were reminded that civil rights were only one aspect of human rights, and that they were living in times when they could ill afford to neglect that other aspect, called economic rights. If the law was to be, as Dean Pound put it, "a continually more efficacious social engineering," it would have to provide a framework from which many of the existing causes of social friction and economic waste would be eradicated, and within which many economic "necessities" would acquire the dignity and authority of "rights." Before this could be done, however, lawyers would have to become aware of the new economic structure of society. It is hoped that the present article might help in inducing such an awareness.

II – The Case

In considering economic rights, it is convenient to distinguish between the consumer and the producer. There may come a time when it will be sufficient to protect the rights of the consumer; but in the present state of economic affairs, consumption depends largely on wages and salaries, and the right of most men to consume cannot be adequately protected without guaranteeing their right to produce at fair remuneration.

The case for economic rights might then be stated as follows: Since economic goods are necessary to satisfy the needs of mankind, and since these goods – to become serviceable – must in some way be produced, it follows that every social order should guarantee the rights of man, as a consumer and as a producer. As a producer, man has a right to demand from society that it offer him a market for his useful labour or produce. As a consumer, man has a right to a share of the total production of society, sufficient to enable him to develop his personality to the fullest extent possible.

The present article will briefly examine whether the rights of the Canadian people, as consumers and as producers, are fully respected.

III – The Consumer

Consumer rights, as stated above, imply that no one in the society should be entitled to superfluous or luxury goods until the essentials of life are made available to everyone.

At first glance, that distribution would appear to obtain in Canada. Thanks to our abundant natural wealth and to the techniques of the industrial era, it no longer seems necessary to trample on one another in the scramble for riches. Consequently, most people take it for granted that every Canadian is assured of a reasonable standard of living.

Unfortunately, that is not the case, as is exemplified in the five following instances:

1 – By the figures of the 1951 census, 72 per cent of all wage-earners, and 56 per cent of all heads-of-family wage-earners were making an annual income of less than $2,500, whereas – according to the Toronto Welfare Council – the average Canadian family then needed $2,678 a year to maintain a decent standard of living.

2 – Depressed areas and sub-marginal groups continue to exist: consider the condition of slum-dwellers in large cities, and of the Eskimo and Indian populations.

3 – There does not exist in Canada a comprehensive scheme of social insurance which guarantees – regardless of origin – a decent standard of living to every person who is prevented from earning a living wage by sickness, age, loss of breadwinner, disability, or other cause of unemployment beyond his control. (It would be illogical to think that such hardships could be met through personal savings, at least in the cases referred to in the two preceding paragraphs.)

4 – The present private enterprise economy is geared to the satisfaction of individual needs, but not to that of collective needs.

Consequently there is a gigantic lag in the provision of educational facilities, hospitals, slum-clearance projects, recreational opportunities, highways, and other public services.

5 – The existence of the above-mentioned shortcomings makes it impossible for many citizens to exercise their human rights in non-economic fields. For instance, the cost of education and of medical and dental services prevents all citizens from having an equal chance of developing their intellectual and physical capacities. The high cost of litigation, in the absence of a universal system of legal aid, makes a farce out of the right of equality before the law. And the cost of conducting elections nullifies high-sounding platitudes about political equality.

IV – The Producer
If the modern age in Canada has brought on a vastly increased supply of consumer goods, it has been accompanied by grave encroachments upon the rights of man as a producer, that is to say upon his right to work. That statement can be supported by a quick glance at the condition of (*inter alia*) industrial workers, from four points of view:

1 – The most apparent of the present economic evils is unemployment. For the first nine months of 1961, the unemployed in Canada averaged 7.8 per cent of the labour force: in the face of that fact, it is hardly necessary to dwell upon the reality of cyclical unemployment. But it is important to think a moment about the problem of technological unemployment. Inability to prevent foreseeable disasters such as the mining tragedy in Springhill a few years ago is proof enough that this society has no plan for supplying alternative employment to men whose past occupations either no longer exist, or have become fraught with the risk of sudden death. Consequently, it may well be asked how this economy will manage to deal with the gigantic

upheaval of workers which will presently be brought about by
the third industrial revolution, based on automation, cybernet-
ics and thermo-nuclear energy.

2 – Concerning their right to obtain fair wages, reasonable conditions of work and protection against employer discrimination,
industrial workers have gone a long way towards helping themselves by uniting into trade unions. That such a movement had
to exist for some generations in opposition to the law is of course
no tribute to the progressiveness of the members of the legal
profession. Nor is it a tribute to their vigilance that, at the
present time, union busting in its various forms can continue to
be practised without penalty in this country, where the right of
association is supposed to be firmly entrenched.

3 – Even when they do respect trade-unionism, a large part of
the Canadian population – including most of the legislators and
industrial leaders – do not agree to its full implication. It is a
mistake to believe that the mere existence of unions is sufficient
to create equality between the employer and the employee.
Without the right to strike, there is no equality of status
between labour and management, and consequently labour
agreements between them cannot be based on justice.* In the
same way that Capital can say: "Unless we make a sufficient
profit in a given area, we will withdraw our investment, and
there will be no more employment," likewise Labour must be
able to say: "Unless we enjoy reasonable working terms in such
and such a firm, we will withdraw and *there will be no more
operations*." In other words, the right to strike must include the
right for workers to protect their strike, against strikebreakers
and court injunctions. No group of shareholders can break a

---

* Justice Holmes considered that liberty of contract could not begin until "the equality of position between the parties" had been established. *Coppage v. Kansas*, 236 U.S.
1, 28 (1915).

lock-out by opening up part of a firm where a lock-out is in progress; and likewise no group of workers should be able to operate a firm while a strike is in progress.

4 – But even full recognition of trade-unionism in its present form will not be a sufficient guarantee of producer rights in the industrial age. In the political sphere, men fought for centuries to prove that there is no substitute for self-government. In the economic sphere, it is inevitable that – sooner or later – the same struggle be fought and won. Man does not live by bread alone, and he will never be content until the dichotomy between those who may arbitrarily command and those who must humbly obey is abolished, even in the economic sphere. Industrial democracy will not be reached any more easily than political democracy was, but it must be reached. Even today men are labouring to lay the foundations of a society of equals; and the sooner such problems as price arbitration, and cooperative management or ownership of industry can be seriously discussed, the better this society will be equipped to prevent the industrial revolution from turning into a violent one.

V – The Future

The foregoing statement of economic rights obviously constitutes a large order. But in such matters the service is slow, so it is not unwise to get orders in early.

As long ago as 1793, the Declaration of Rights voted by *La Convention* stated that "society owes subsistence to unfortunate citizens, either by procuring them work or by guaranteeing the livelihood of those who are unable to work." The French constitution of 1848 also affirmed the right to work. And by that time, Proudhon had long been preaching the need of "a 1789" in the economic sphere. Yet nearly a hundred years elapsed between Louis Blanc's demand for "social workshops" and F.D.R.'s Public Works Administration.

So progress is slow, and any group of men who foregather to discuss

"Social Justice" would be failing in their duty if they failed to affirm the rights of man to the fullest extent. Governments must contend with questions of "how, when and where." But in a Law Journal, it is possible to reach for the ultimate goal.

That goal is not the mere inclusion of certain clauses in a Bill of Rights. For Germany in 1919, Spain in 1931, the U.S.S.R. in 1936 wrote into their constitutions very noble declarations concerning the rights of man. And yet those very rights were soon to be trampled upon by dictators.

It is the minds of men which must be changed, and their philosophies. Economic reform is impossible so long as legislators, lawyers and business men cling to economic concepts which were conceived for another age. The liberal idea of property helped to emancipate the bourgeoisie but it is now hampering the march towards economic democracy. The ancient values of private property have been carried over into the age of corporate wealth. As a result, our laws and our thinking recognize as proprietors of an enterprise men who today hold a few shares which they will sell tomorrow on the stock-market; whereas workers who may have invested the better part of their lives and of their hopes in a job have no proprietary right to that job, and may be expropriated from it *without compensation* whenever a strike or lock-out occurs, whenever they grow old, or whenever Capital decides to disinvest.

That same erroneous concept of property has erected a wall of prejudice against reform, and a wall of money against democratic control. As a consequence, powerful financial interests, monopolies and cartels are in a position to plan large sectors of the national economy for the profit of the few, rather than for the welfare of all. Whereas any serious planning by the State, democratically controlled, is dismissed as a step towards Bolshevism.

Yet if this society does not evolve an entirely new set of values, if it does not set itself urgently to producing those services which private enterprise is failing to produce, if it is not determined to plan its development for the good of all rather than for the luxury of the few, and if every citizen fails to consider himself as the co-insurer of his fellow citizen against all socially engineered economic calamities, it is vain to hope that Canada will ever really reach freedom from fear and freedom from want. Under such circumstances, any claim by lawyers that they have done their bit by upholding civil liberties will be dismissed as a hollow mockery.

McGill Law Journal
8/2 (February 1962)

PART III

On Nationalism

Nationalist Alienation

><

The fact is, from the beginning there has been a tendency at *Cité libre* to consider Quebec nationalists as alienated.

We were painfully aware of the inadequacies of Quebec in all areas: the establishment had to be debunked, civil society to be made secular; politics had to be made democratic, economics to be fully grasped; French had to be relearned, Philistines to be removed from university; the frontiers had to be opened to culture and minds opened to progress.

Instinctively, we felt it was ridiculous for nationalists to claim that just about all of our backwardness was "the fault of 'les Anglais'"; but we didn't particularly want to discuss that forever.

Whether or not the Conquest was the cause of all our woes, whether or not "les Anglais" [English Canadians] were the most perfidious occupying power in the history of mankind, it was still true that the French-Canadian community held in its hands *hic et nunc* the essential instruments of its regeneration: by means of the Canadian Constitution, the Quebec State could exercise far-reaching power over the soul of French Canadians and over the territory which they occupied – the richest and largest of all Canadian provinces.

As a result, what seemed more pressing than discussing the responsibility of "les Autres" [literally Others, meaning English Canadians] in our misadventures was that the community make effective use of the power and resources placed at its disposal by the Act of 1867. Because the community was not doing that.

We grew up, and our fathers before us, and their fathers before them, under a provincial state whose policy consisted in disposing of our best and most accessible natural resources, and abdicating any jurisdiction over the social organization and intellectual direction taken by French Canadians. This policy was not imposed by "les Anglais" (that is, all those who did not belong to our ethnic group), although they figured out how to exploit it to the hilt; this policy was imposed on us by our clerical and bourgeois élites: these élites have always prevented the spread of the idea that the State's role was to intervene actively in the historical process and to direct positively the community's energies towards the common weal.

These élites gave a succession of the most varied names to their antidemocratic spirit: the struggle against liberalism, against modernism, against freemasonry, against socialism. But whatever the case, they were acting only to protect class and caste interests against a civil authority whose exclusive responsibility was the public interest. Obviously, I do not mean to say that priests and the bourgeoisie claimed to be seeking anything other than the common weal; but they believed they were the only ones able to come up with a definition of that weal, and as a result they wanted neither a democratic State that would have some real existence beyond themselves, nor politicians who would exercise any authority that conflicted with their own.

In these circumstances, we considered at *Cité libre* that it was more urgent to blast our own people for their laziness, to restore democracy and to attack our clerical and bourgeois ideologies, than to attribute guilt to "les Anglais." Accordingly, the editorial board at *Cité libre* and our faithful contributors seemed to have a common goal: to bring French Canadians to accept their own responsibilities. Each of us wrote and acted in the area where he felt most useful: education, religion, politics, economics, trade-unionism, journalism, literature, philosophy, and so forth.

The friends of *Cité libre* were suffering – as much as anyone else, I guess – from the humiliations which afflicted our ethnic group. But as great as the external attack on our rights may have been, still greater was our own incapacity to exercise those rights. For example, the contempt shown by "les Anglais" for the French language never seemed to rival either in extent or in stupidity that very contempt shown by our own people in speaking and teaching French in such an abominable way. Or again, the violations of educational rights of French Canadians in other provinces never seemed as blameworthy or odious as the narrow-mindedness, incompetence, and lack of foresight that have always characterized education policy in the province of Quebec, where our rights were all nevertheless respected. The same could be said for areas where we claimed we were being wronged: religion, finance, elections, officialdom, and so forth.

So nationalism seemed to us at *Cité libre* like a form of alienation, since it misdirected into hostility and vindication the very intellectual and physical energy we needed for our national restoration; it misdirected into struggles against "les Autres" the very forces that were needed a thousand times over to stand up to the people ultimately responsible for our own utter poverty: our so-called élites.

And among nationalists, the separatist faction seemed to push this alienation to absurd heights: they were ready to call to the barricades and to civil war a people who had not learned how to use constitutional weapons with courage and clear-headedness; the proof of which is the uninterrupted mediocrity of our representatives in Ottawa. The separatists called on the people for acts of heroism (since the economic and cultural "liberation" of "la Laurentie" would have greatly weakened our material and intellectual standard of living) – on the very people who did not even have the courage to stop reading American comics or to go see French movies. And with a criminal insouciance, the separatists wanted to close the borders, inevitably handing back full sovereign powers to the very élites who were responsible for the abject state from which separatists were boldly offering to free us.

It is true that separatists and nationalists nowadays are beginning to consider themselves socialists; and they would answer back that in their "Laurentie" socialists would be in power, rather than the old élites. But they never succeed in demonstrating how this magic trick would work out in reality. How would a people – who had long been subject to the clerical and bourgeois establishment – succeed in throwing off this establishment simply by creating an alliance with it in order to fight "les Anglais"?

Either nationalists form an alliance with traditional forces to fight against "les Anglais," and thus maintain the forces of reaction in power, or they attack traditional forces, but then will be too busy to take on "les Anglais" at the same time.

This is what has happened to us at *Cité libre*. Because we found it absurd to think that French Canada would be more democratic, more inclined to socialism, more secular and more modern, the day it turned in on itself and faced a hostile world, supported only by its out-of-date traditions and reactionary ideologies.

But refusing to close the borders is not the same as abolishing them. *Cité libre* has never been either centralist or *bonne-ententiste*; it is worth reading our articles approving the direct taxation of Mr. Duplessis, and disapproving federal grants to universities, for example. Indeed, we did not believe that French Canadians could reach political maturity by depending on others for the exercise of their rights.

So if our positions had to be summed up in one paragraph, I would say that we sought to make a reality of the Quebec State; and since the act of Confederation gave us abundant powers to reach this end, we considered that nationalist movements were diversionary in nature: indeed, in order to justify the fact that French Canadians had badly and rarely exercised their constitutional powers, the nationalists were eager to demonstrate that we should have had still more powers! As a result, "les Autres" were invariably found guilty of having restricted the very powers which we had neither the intention, nor the ability or the intelligence, to exercise in any case.

In its January issue, *Cité libre* noted "the remarkable rebirth of Quebec nationalism" and proposed to state its position once again. In February, the magazine published a clear and incriminating piece in which Jean-Marc Léger stated that "when the Left says it is anti-national or a-national, it betrays its vocation."

In the current article, I have tried briefly to demonstrate why, in my opinion, *Cité libre* believed and continues to believe that the best way to serve the French-Canadian community is by distrusting nationalist ideology. "When their adulterated ideology saw the light of day, it produced the rotten fruit of the Union Nationale," wrote Guy Cormier in the first issue of *Cité libre* (June 1950).*

Of course, my oversimplified explanation has not done justice to nationalist thought any more than it has to my own. But I wanted to lay out positions in the midst of a debate which is going to continue. Next month, *Cité libre* will publish an article by Guy Cormier, who will revisit the battery he lined up against nationalism – eleven years later. And in the letters to the editor below, the reader will find an open letter on nationalism signed G.C.

I would like to close with a few remarks about this letter. I know its author, a serious and responsible man. On inquiry, I learned that his comments had the approval of a tightly knit group of separatist intellectuals of the young generation, who reject the nationalism of *Le Devoir* (and of Jean-Marc Léger) as too timid, and the nationalism of the magazine *Laurentie* as too backward.

This time, I was surprised to discover that in the minds of many people, *Cité libre* is not separatist simply because it lacks courage (". . . risks that cannot reasonably be assumed, . . . lack of courage," and so forth).

---

* We don't have to ask what kind of fruit we will get from Jean Drapeau's party: the strongman of today's nationalism told the private bills committee that he preferred the Police State to a State dominated by organized crime. I don't, because in the face of organized crime I have laws on my side to put an end to their hold on society; whereas in the face of the police and the dictatorship it would support, I would only have my quickly vanishing liberty.

For his part, G.C. is so convinced that separatism is a perilous position that he asks to keep his letter anonymous, counting ultimately on the residue of courage he is willing to grant us so that his text reaches our readers.

I am not writing this with any irony, but rather to underline that it is perhaps here that we should seek an explanation of the rebirth of nationalism among the young generation. These young people may believe that Quebec clericalism and traditionalism are fatally afflicted, and they make fun of the cowards at *Cité libre* for insisting on taming old toothless lions. From this perspective, the nationalist struggle would seem to be the only significant one worth taking on: and to gain new adherents, nationalism casts itself as an undertaking threatened by "les Anglais."

In this case, we could congratulate young people for their courage, but surely not for their clearheadedness. In our province, backward-looking traditionalism still has the power to devour a few opponents; and clericalism (even in its secular form) still has sharpened claws. I will give a single, but telling, example.

When writing his letter G.C. says that "the clergy are not preventing Mr. Lesage from providing us with a Ministry of Education." But that means rejecting what Mr. Lesage himself has to say about the matter! In fact, Mr. Lesage stated on television last December that the State had only a supportive role to play in the area of education, which was really a matter for the Church and for parents to deal with. This balderdash is universally accepted in Quebec. And while it is philosophically false, it will doubtless long continue justifying the chaotic development, not to mention the absence of any development, of the entire education sector in Quebec. Meanwhile, every diocese and every community (with the Jesuits leading the pack, and who can blame them?) will use the theology of Mr. Lesage to establish its university; and G.C. will continue to believe that "'les Anglais' are to blame" if French Canadians don't have any educational policy.

Young nationalists not only lack a sense of realism, when they believe that internal enemies are dying off: by resisting "les Anglais," they are logically impelled to join forces with the landed and vested interests in the heart of the French-Canadian community. In other words, the young generation has to become essentially conservative, and I see no more breathtaking proof of this than G.C.'s call to "close the borders."

Twenty-five years ago, nationalism succeeded in draining off all the energies freed up by the economic crisis of the 1930s and pouring them into the service of reaction. Neonationalism has to be prevented from doing the same thing with the forces born in the postwar years and which are exacerbated today by the new unemployment crisis.

Open up the borders, our people are suffocating to death!

Cité libre 12/35 (March 1961)
Translation by George Tombs

New Treason of the Intellectuals

><

The collection Federalism and the French Canadians *includes the following text (which appeared originally in* Cité libre *[April 1962]) and a number of others devoted to Quebec nationalism. In his preface to this collection, John T. Saywell summed up the attitude of the author as follows: "Trudeau is no less concerned about the preservation and enrichment of French culture and values than the most determined separatist, nor any less critical of English-Canadian opposition to the development of a genuine bilingualism and biculturalism in Canada. But in principle, he is adamantly opposed to the organization of any political society – Quebec, Canada or whatever – on an ethnic or 'national' base."*

The men whose function it is to defend all eternal and impartial
values, like justice and reason, and whom I call the intellectuals
(les clercs), have betrayed this function in the interests of expediency....
It has been above all for the benefit of the nation that the
intellectuals have perpetrated this betrayal.
JULIEN BENDA

The Geographic Approach

It is not the concept of *nation* that is retrograde; it is the idea that the nation must necessarily be sovereign.

To which the champions of independence for Quebec retort that there is nothing at all retrograde about a concept that has brought independence to India, Cuba, and a multitude of African states.

This argument postulates the equation: independence equals progress. Independence, they insist, is good in itself. And to confound the enemy they fire back the aphorism "Good government is no substitute for self-government."

Their frequent recourse to this battle-cry (which is invariably misquoted – but do we all have to speak English?) indicates the extent of the Separatists' muddled thinking. Self-government does not mean national self-determination. (This is not a matter of showing off one's linguistic brilliance; we have to know what we are talking about when we raise the cry for Quebec's independence.) Let us not confuse these two ideas.

That self-government is a good thing – or, more precisely, that a trend toward so-called responsible government is in general a trend toward progress – I want to concede at the outset of this article. I have too often denounced Union Nationale autocracy in Quebec and Liberal and Socialist paternalism in Ottawa to be suspect on that score. I have always maintained that the people of Quebec would never approach political maturity and mastery of their future so long as they failed to learn by experience the mechanisms of really responsible government. To this end they must thrust aside both the ideologies that preach blind submission to "the authority delegated by God" and those that have us running to Ottawa every time there is a difficult problem to solve.

But what I was calling for then was "liberty *in* the city," observes G.C. What we must have today, he says, is "liberty *of* the city," that is to say, the absolute independence of the French-Canadian nation, full and complete sovereignty for *la Laurentie*. In short, national self-determination. Marcel Chaput writes:

Since the end of the Second World War, more than thirty countries, formerly colonies, have been freed of foreign tutelage and
have attained national and international sovereignty. In 1960
alone seventeen African colonies, fourteen of them French-
speaking, have obtained their independence. And now today it
is the people of French Canada who are beginning to rouse, and
they, too, will claim their place among free nations.

Indeed, Mr. Chaput hastens to admit that French Canada enjoys
rights these people never did. But it does not have complete independence, and, according to him, "its destiny rests, in very large measure, in
the hands of a nation foreign to it."

The confusion is utter and complete.

Practically all these "thirty countries, formerly colonies" are states
in the same way that Canada is a state. They have acceded to full sovereignty just as Canada did in 1931. In no way are they nations in the sense
that French Canada might be a nation. Consequently, putting the independence of Quebec into this particular historical context is pure
sophistry.

The State of India is a sovereign republic. But there are no fewer
than four languages officially recognized there (which include neither
English nor Chinese nor Tibetan nor the innumerable dialects). There
are eight principal religions, several of which are mutually and
implacably opposed. Which nation are we talking about? And just what
independence should we take as an example?

The State of Ceylon embraces three ethnic groups and four religions. In the Malay Federation there are three more ethnic groups. The
Burmese Union arrays half a dozen nationalities one against the other.
The Indonesian Republic comprises at least twelve national groups, and
twenty-five principal languages are spoken there. In Viet Nam, besides
the Tonkinese, the Annamese, and the Cochinchinese there are eight
important tribes.

In Africa the polyethnic nature of the new states is even more striking. The frontiers of these countries simply retrace lines marked out
years ago by the colonialists, according to the fortunes of conquest,

exploration, and administrative whimsy. Consequently, members of one tribe, speaking the same language and sharing the same traditions, have become citizens of different states, and these states are barely more than conglomerations of distinct and rival groups. A sample of what this can lead to can be seen in the former Belgian Congo. But if we examine Ghana, the Sudan, Nigeria, or almost any other ex-colony, there, too, we find the same kind of ethnic complexity. In French West Africa, for example, the population consisted of ten scattered tribes; nevertheless, France found it convenient to divide them up into eight territories. And the course of history is at present transforming these territories into sovereign states. In vain may we look there for nation-states – that is to say, states whose delineations correspond with ethnic and linguistic entities.

As for Algeria, which our *Indépendantistes* are always holding up as an example, there is no doubt what kind of state she is seeking to become. Besides inhabitants of French, Spanish, Italian, Jewish, Greek, and Levantine origin, in this particular country we must count Berbers, Kabyles, Arabs, Moors, Negroes, Tuaregs, Mazabites, and a number of Cheshire cats. Of the disputes, notably between Kabyles and Arabs, we are far from having heard the end.

Finally, as far as concerns Cuba, endlessly discussed by the Separatists as a pattern to be followed, it's all obviously pure cock-and-bull. This country was sovereign under Batista and it is sovereign under Castro. It was economically dependent before and it still is. Democratic self-government was non-existent there yesterday and it is still non-existent there today. So what does that prove? That Castro is not Batista? To be sure; but Hydro-Québec under René Lévesque is not Hydro under Daniel Johnson. A lot of good that argument does for the Separatists.

What emerges from all this is that promoting independence as an end good in itself, a matter of dignity for all self-respecting peoples, amounts to embroiling the world in a pretty pickle indeed. It has been held that every sincere anti-colonialist who wants to see independence for Algeria ought also to want it for Quebec. This argument assumes that Quebec is a political dependant, which shows very poor knowledge of constitutional history; but even if it were, logically speaking one would then have to say that every Quebec Separatist should advocate independence for the Kabyles, or, to give an even better example, independence for twenty-five million Bengalis included in the State of India. Should the Separatists try to take the wind out of my sails by saying that they would indeed like to see this independence for Bengal, I would ask why they would stop there in the good work; in Bengal ninety different languages are spoken; and then there are still more Bengalis in Pakistan – What a lovely lot of separations that would be!

To finish this particular discussion with the aphorism we started with, I am, in the light of all this, tempted to conclude that "good government is a damned good substitute for national self-determination," if one means by this last term the right of ethnic and linguistic groups to their own absolute sovereignty. It would seem, in fact, a matter of considerable urgency for world peace and the success of the new states that the form of good government known as democratic federalism should be perfected and promoted, in the hope of solving to some extent the world-wide problems of ethnic pluralism. To this end, as I will show later, Canada could be called upon to serve as mentor, provided she has sense enough to conceive her own future on a grand scale. John Conway wrote, of true federalism, "Its successful adoption in Europe would go a long way towards ensuring the survival of traditional western civilization. It would be a pity, if, in Canada, so young, so rich and vigorous and plagued with so few really serious problems, the attempt should fail."

Further on the subject of federalism, it would seem well understood that President Wilson, that great champion of the "principle of nationality," in no way intended to invite nationalist secessions, but sought rather to ensure the right of nationalities to a certain amount of local autonomy within existing states.

Moreover, it is quite wrong to insist, as our advocates of independence often do, that the principle of nationality is an internationally recognized right, and sanctioned by the United Nations. Rather than adopting Wilson's equivocal pronouncements, and finding themselves faced with a new wave of plebiscites and secessions echoing the post-World-War-I period, the U.N. has preferred to talk – citing Article I of the Charter – of the right of "peoples" to self-determination. The term "peoples," however, is far from being identical with "ethnic groups."*

The Historical Approach

If the idea of the nation-state is hard to justify in terms of the evolution of anti-colonialism in recent years, how does it look in the light of history as a whole?

At the threshold of time there was man, and also, no doubt, in keeping with man's very nature, that other undeniable fact called the family. Then, very soon, the tribe appeared, a sort of primitive community founded on common customs and speech.

Now the history of civilization is a chronicle of the subordination of tribal "nationalism" to wider interests. No doubt there were always clan loyalties and regional cohesions. But thought developed, knowledge spread, inventions came to light, and humanity progressed wherever there was intermingling of tribes and exchange between them, gathering impetus through commerce and the division of labour, the heavy hand of conquests (from Egypt and China down to the Holy Roman Empire), and the drive of the militant religions (from Buddhism on through Christianity to Islam).

---

* It is obvious that the language of politics is riddled with pitfalls. The word "nation," or "nationality," from the Latin "nasci" (to be born), denotes most often an ethnic community sharing a common language and customs. The Japanese nation. It is in this sense that we speak of the "principle of nationality" leading to the "national state" or "nation-state." But sometimes the reverse is the case, where the state, originally made up of a number of ethnic communities, comes to think of itself as a nation; then the word is understood to mean a political society occupying a territory and sharing customs in common over a considerable period of time. The Swiss nation. In Canada, as I will explain later, there is, or will be, a Canadian nation in so far as the ethnic communities succeed in exorcising their own respective nationalisms. If, then, a Canadian nationalism does take form, it will have to be exorcised in its turn, and the Canadian nation will be asked to yield a part of its sovereignty to a higher authority, just as is asked, today, of the French-Canadian and English-Canadian nations. (For a discussion of the vocabulary of this subject, see p. 4 of a remarkable essay by E.H. Carr in Carr *et al.*, *Nations ou Fédéralisme* [Paris, 1946].)

Finally, after more than sixty-five centuries of history, with the breaking down of the rigid social structure of the Middle Ages, the decline of Latin as the mark of the learned man, and the birth of the cult of individualism, the modern idea of "nation" began to develop in Europe. The displacement of the Church by national Churches, the rise of the *bourgeoisie*, mercantilism for the protection of territorial economies, outrages committed against certain ethnic groups such as the Poles, the Jacobin Revolution, the relentless fervour of Mazzini, the domination of poor nations by industrialized ones like England: so many factors helped fan the flame of nationalist aspirations, leading to the setting up of one national state after another. The countries of Latin America revolted against Spain. Italy and Germany fought their wars of unification. The Greeks and the Slavs rebelled against the Ottoman Empire. Ireland rose against Great Britain. In short, all of Europe and a great deal of the New World took fire. The era of wars of nationalism, starting in Napoleon's day, reached its peak with the two world wars. And so it is that we have entered a new age, the nations now indulging their vanity in the possession and use of nuclear arms.

Some seven thousand years of history in three paragraphs is, of course, a little short. I will have more to say on the subject later, but for the time being it will suffice to keep three things in mind.

The first is that the nation is not a biological reality – that is, a community that springs from the very nature of man. Except for a very small fraction of his history, man has done very well without nations (this for the benefit of our young bloods, who see the slightest dent in the nation's sovereignty as an earth-shaking catastrophe).

The second is that the tiny portion of history marked by the emergence of the nation-states is also the scene of the most devastating wars, the worst atrocities, and the most degrading collective hatred the world has ever seen. Up until the end of the eighteenth century it was generally the sovereigns, not the nations, who made war; and while their sovereigns made war the civilian populations continued to visit each other: merchants crossed borders, scholars and philosophers went freely from one court to another, and conquering generals would take under their personal protection the learned men of vanquished cities. War killed soldiers, but left the various civilizations unhindered. In our day, however, we have seen nations refusing to listen to Beethoven because they are at war with Germany, others boycotting the Peking Opera because they refuse to recognize China, and still others refusing visas or passports to scholars wishing to attend some scientific or humanitarian congress in a country of differing ideology. Pasternak was not even allowed to go to Stockholm to accept his Nobel Prize. A concept of nation that pays so little honour to science and culture obviously can find no room above itself in its scale of values for truth, liberty, and life itself. It is a concept that corrupts all: in peace time the intellectuals become propagandists for the nation and the propaganda is a lie; in war time the democracies slither toward dictatorship and the dictatorships herd us into concentration camps; and finally after the massacres of Ethiopia come those of London and Hamburg, then of Hiroshima and Nagasaki, and perhaps more and more until the final massacre. I know very well that the nation-state idea is not the sole cause of all the evils born of war; modern technology has a good deal to answer for on that score! But the important thing is that the nation-state idea has caused wars to become more and more total over the last two centuries; and that is the idea I take issue with so vehemently. Besides, each time a state has taken an exclusive and intolerant idea as its cornerstone (religion, nationhood, ideology), this idea has been the very mainspring of war. In days gone by religion had to be displaced as the basis of the state before the frightful religious wars came to an end. And there will be no end to wars between nations until in some similar fashion the nation ceases to be the basis of the state.* As for inter-state wars, they will end only if the states give up that obsession whose very essence makes them exclusive and intolerant: sovereignty. Now – to get back to the subject – what worries me about the fact that five million Canadians of French origin cannot manage to share their national sovereignty with seven million Canadians of British origin, beside whom they live and who they know, in general, have no fleas, is that this leaves me precious little

---

* See Emory Reeves, *A Democratic Manifesto* (London, 1943), p. 43, and also, by the same author, *The Anatomy of Peace* (New York, 1945).

hope that several thousand million Americans, Russians, and Chinese, who have never met and none of whom are sure the others are not flea-ridden, will ever agree to abdicate a piece of their sovereignty in the realm of nuclear arms.

The third observation I would draw from the course of history is that the very idea of the nation-state is absurd. To insist that a partic-ular nationality must have complete sovereign power is to pursue a self-destructive end. Because every national minority will find, at the very moment of liberation, a new minority within its bosom which in turn must be allowed the right to demand its freedom. And on and on would stretch the train of revolutions, until the last-born of nation-states turned to violence to put an end to the very principle that gave it birth. That is why the principle of nationality has brought to the world two centuries of war, and *not one single* final solution. France has always had its Bretons and Alsatians, Britain its Scots and its Welsh, Spain its Catalans and Basques, Yugoslavia its Croats and Macedonians, Finland its Swedes and Lapps, and so on, for Belgium, Hungary, Czechoslovakia, Poland, the Soviet Union, China, the United States, all the Latin American countries, and who knows how many others. As far as the more homogeneous countries are concerned, those that have no problems of secession find themselves problems of accession. Ireland lays claim to the six counties of Ulster; Indonesia wants New Guinea. Mussolini's nationalist Italy, when it was done with the *irredentas*, turned to dreams of reconquering the Roman Empire. Hitler would have been satisfied with nothing less than the conquest of the entire non-Aryan world. Now there is something for Quebec's Separatists to sink their teeth into: if there is any validity to their principles they should carry them to the point of claiming part of Ontario, New Brunswick, Labrador, and New England; on the other hand, though, they would have to relinquish certain border regions around Pontiac and Temiskaming and turn Westmount into the Danzig of the New World.

So the concept of the nation-state, which has managed to cripple the advance of civilization, has managed to solve none of the political problems it has raised, unless by virtue of its sheer absurdity. And, where civilization has pushed ahead in spite of all, it is where the intellectuals have found the strength within themselves to put their faith in mankind before any national prejudice: Pasternak, Oppenheimer, Joliot-Curie, Russell, Einstein, Freud, Casals, and many others who have replied: *E pur si muove* to the *raison d'état*.

"Man," said Renan, "is bound neither to his language nor to his race; he is bound only to himself because he is a free agent, or in other words a moral being."

Listen, too, to what Father Delos has to say:

What we must know is whether Man is intended to fill a predetermined role in history, whether history encompasses Man, or whether Man possesses innate powers which transcend all historical forms of culture and civilization; the question is whether it is not a denial of Man's dignity to reduce him to mere identification with any particular mass of humanity.

The Origin of Nationalism

Absurd in principle and outdated in practice as it may be, the idea of the nation-state has enjoyed extraordinary favour, and still does. How can it be? That is what I would like to explore next.

The birth of the modern state can be fixed near the end of the fourteenth century. Until then the feudal system was sufficient to maintain order in Europe, where the means of communication were limited, economy and trade were essentially local, and where, consequently, political administration could remain very much uncentralized. But as trade spread and diversified, as each political-economic unit demanded a broader base and better protection, and as kings found the means of giving free rein to their ambitions, the *bourgeois* classes allied themselves with their reigning monarchs to supplant the powers of feudal lords and of free cities by strong and unified states. In 1576 Jean Bodin ascertained that the new and essential characteristic of these states was "sovereignty," which he described as the *suprema potestas* over its citizens and subjects, unlimited under the law.

For a few centuries absolute monarchy remained master of these sovereign states. But they were not yet nation-states, because their frontiers remained a family matter, in the sense that their locations were shifted according to the fortunes of marriage and of war between the various reigning families. Nationalities were taken so little into account that Louis XIV, for example, after having annexed Alsace, made no attempt to forbid the continued use of German there, and schools for the teaching of French were introduced only twenty years later.

Individualism, scepticism, rationalism, however, continued to undermine the traditional powers. And the day came when absolute monarchy, in its turn, was obliged to step aside to make way for the *bourgeoisie*, its ally of earlier days. But as the dynasties disappeared, there was already a new cohesive agent at work to fill the vacuum and head off a weakening of the state: popular sovereignty, or democratic power.

Democracy indeed opened the way, first to the *bourgeoisie* and much later to all classes, by which all could participate in the exercise of political power. The state then appeared to be the instrument by which eventually all classes – that is to say, the entire nation – could assure peace and prosperity for themselves. And quite naturally all wished to make that instrument as strong as possible in relation to other states. Thus nationalism was born, the child of liberal democracy and the mystique of equality.

Alas, this nationalism, by a singular paradox, was soon to depart from the ideas that presided at its birth. Because the moment the sovereign state was put at the service of the nation it was the nation that became sovereign – that is to say, beyond the law. It mattered little then that the prosperity of some meant the ruin of others. Nations historically strong, those that were industrialized first, those that had inherited strategic or institutional advantages, soon came to see the advantages of their situation. Here rulers closed ranks with the ruled, the haves with the have-nots, and they set out together as a body, in the name of the nationalism that bound them together, to line their pockets and feed their vanity at the expense of weaker nations.

Expansionist nationalism then began to bestow fancy titles upon itself: political Darwinism, Nietzschean mysticism, the white man's burden, civilizing mission, pan-Slavism, Magyarization, and all the other rubbish by which the strong justify their oppression of the weak.

In all these cases the result was the same. Nations that were dominated, dismembered, exploited, and humiliated conceived an unbounded hatred for their oppressors; and united by this hatred they erected against aggressive nationalism a defensive nationalism. And so a chain of wars was ignited that keeps bursting into flame all over the planet.

It is into the depths of this world-wide nationalist phenomenon that we must delve in examining the sub-sub-species Quebec of the sub-species Canada. The Seven Years' War saw the five great powers of Europe deployed against each other in accordance with a complicated system of alliances and compacts. France and Russia fought on the side of Austria, while England aligned herself with Prussia. But while Louis XV lent support to Marie Thérèse with his armies and his money, in the hope of broadening French influence in Europe, Pitt sent to Frederick II plenty of money and a small number of soldiers. These he sent off with English fleets to vanquish France in India and America, and to lay the foundations of the most formidable empire the world has ever known. We know the rest: by the Treaty of Paris, Canada, among others, became English.

At this period the English were already the most nationalist of nationalists. The whole country, proud of its political and economic superiority, unanimously favoured the planting of the flag in the most far-flung lands. This nationalism was necessarily cultural, too; to English eyes they bestowed a priceless favour on the undeserving countries they colonized: the right to share the Anglo-Saxon language and customs. And then, despite having so effectively and admirably built up the cult of civil liberties at home in England, they gave not the slightest thought to the protection of minority rights for others.

From the moment of delivery of the Royal Proclamation of 1763, the intention was obvious: the French Canadian was to be completely assimilated. In 1840 Durham, while "far from wishing to encourage indiscriminately [these] pretensions to superiority on the part of any particular race," none the less considered that assimilation was simply "a question of time and mode."

Throughout this period, Canadians of British origin would have considered it an indignity to be in any inferior position. So they invented all kinds of stratagems by which democracy was made to mean government by the minority.

Generations passed. Hopes of assimilating the French Canadians dimmed to a flicker (although right up to 1948, immigration laws continued to favour immigrants from the British Isles over those from France). But English-speaking Canadians have never given up their condescending attitude to their French-speaking fellows, even to this day.

At Ottawa and in provinces other than ours, this nationalism could wear the pious mask of democracy. Because, as English-speaking Canadians became proportionately more numerous, they took to hiding their intolerance behind acts of majority rule; that was how they quashed bilingualism in the Manitoba legislature, violated rights acquired by separate schools in various provinces, savagely imposed conscription in 1917, and broke a solemn promise in 1942.[*]

In Quebec, "where they had the money if not the numbers, our Anglo-Canadian fellow-citizens have often yielded to the temptation of using without restraint the means at their command." This was how, in politics, Anglo-Canadian nationalism took on the form of what André Laurendeau has so admirably named the "cannibal-king theory" (*théorie du roi-nègre*). Economically, this nationalism has been expressed essentially in treating the French Canadian as *un cochon de payant*. Sometimes, magnanimously, they would go as far as putting a few straw men on boards of directors. These men invariably had two things in common: first, they were never bright enough or strong enough to rise to the top, and second, they were always sufficiently

---

[*]   André Laurendeau has just written with great clarity an account of how, with the plebiscite of 1942, the state became the tool of Anglo-Canadian nationalism, and of how that state took advantage of French-Canadian numerical weakness to divest itself of pledges it had made (*La Crise de la conscription* [Montreal, 1962]). A tale even more shameful could be told of how, during the same war and with similar inspiration, the vengeful powers of the state were turned against the Japanese-Canadian minority.

"representative" to grovel for the cannibal-king's favours and flatter the vanity of their fellow-tribesmen. Finally, in social and cultural matters, Anglo-Canadian nationalism has expressed itself quite simply by disdain. Generation after generation of Anglo-Saxons have lived in Quebec without getting around to learning three sentences of French. When these insular people insist, with much gravity, that their jaws and ears aren't made for it and can't adapt themselves to French, what they really want to get across to you is that they will not sully these organs, and their small minds, by submitting them to a barbarous idiom.

Anglo-Canadian nationalism produced, inevitably, French-Canadian nationalism. As I have said before, speaking of the roots of our nationalism and the futility of its tendencies:

> Defeated, occupied, leaderless, banished from commercial enterprise, poked away outside the cities, little by little reduced to a minority and left with very little influence in a country which, after all, he discovered, explored and colonized, the French Canadian had little alternative for the frame of mind he would have to assume in order to preserve what remained of his own. So he set up a system of defense-mechanisms which soon assumed such overgrown proportions that he came to regard as priceless anything which distinguished him from other people; and any change whatever (be it for the better or not) he would regard with hostility if it originated from outside.

"Alas," I added, "the nationalists' idealism itself has been their downfall. 'They loved not wisely but too well.'"[*]

The Conflict of Nationalisms in Canada

We must accept the facts of history as they are. However outworn and absurd it may be, the nation-state image spurred the political thinking

---

[*] In *The Asbestos Strike* (Toronto: James, Lewis & Samuel, 1974), p. 7 – Ed.

of the British, and subsequently of Canadians of British descent in the
"Dominion of Canada." Broadly speaking, this meant identifying the
Canadian state with themselves to the greatest degree possible.

Since the French Canadians had the bad grace to decline assimilation, such an identification was beyond being completely realizable. So
the Anglo-Canadians built themselves an illusion of it by fencing off the
French Canadians in their Quebec ghetto and then nibbling at its constitutional powers and carrying them off bit by bit to Ottawa. Outside
Quebec they fought, with staggering ferocity, against anything that
might intrude upon that illusion: the use of French on stamps, money,
cheques, in the civil service, the railroads, and the whole works.

In the face of such aggressive nationalism, what choice lay before
the French Canadians over, say, the last century? On the one hand they
could respond to the vision of an overbearing Anglo-Canadian nation-
state with a rival vision of a French-Canadian nation-state; on the other
hand they could scrap the very idea of nation-state once and for all and
lead the way toward making Canada a multi-national state.

The first choice was, and is, that of the Separatists or advocates of
independence; an emotional and prejudiced choice essentially – which
goes for their antagonists too, for that matter – and I could never see
any sense in it. Because either it is destined to succeed by achieving
independence, which would prove that the nationalism of Anglo-
Canadians is neither intransigent, nor armed to the teeth, nor so very
dangerous for us; and in that case I wonder why we are so afraid to face
these people in the bosom of a pluralistic state and why we are prepared
to renounce our right to consider Canada our home *a mari usque ad
mare*. Or else the attempt at independence is doomed to failure and the
plight of the French Canadians will be worse than ever; not because a
victorious and vindictive enemy will deport part of the population and
leave the rest with dwindled rights and a ruined heritage – this eventuality seems most unlikely; but because once again French Canadians
will have poured all their vital energies into a (hypothetically) fruitless
struggle, energies that should have been used to match in excellence,
efficacy, and persistence a (hypothetically) fearsome enemy.

The second choice, for the multi-national state, was, and is, that of the Constitutionalists. It would reject the bellicose and self-destructive idea of nation-state in favour of the more civilized goal of polyethnic pluralism. I grant that in certain countries and at certain periods of history this may have been impossible, notably where aggressive nationalism has enjoyed a crushing predominance and refused all compromise with national minorities. Was this the case in the time of Papineau and the *patriotes*? I doubt it; but the fact remains that the upshot of this "separatist" uprising was an Act of Union which marked a step backward for minority rights from the Constitutional Act of 1791.

As a matter of fact, this second choice was, and is, possible for French Canadians. In a sense the multi-national state was dreamed about by Lafontaine, realized under Cartier, perfected by Laurier, and humanized with Bourassa. Anglo-Canadian nationalism has never enjoyed a crushing predominance and has never been in a position to refuse all compromise with the country's principal national minority; consequently, it has been unable to follow the policy perhaps most gratifying to its arrogance, and has had to resign itself to the situation as imposed by the course of events.

The first of such events was the Quebec Act, passed under the shadow of the American Revolution. Then there were the terrible dark days – three-quarters of a century of them – when Canadians of British origin knew there were fewer of them than of French Canadians. As Mason Wade says of the Loyalists: "They were badly scared men, who had lived through one revolution in America and dreaded another in Canada." Eventually, it was the constant threat of American domination that – like it or not – obliged Anglo-Canadian nationalism to take cognizance of the French-Canadian nation; it would have been virtually impossible otherwise to reunite the remaining colonies of British North America.

In actual fact, Anglo-Canadian nationalism has never had much of an edge. Those among French Canadians who have had the acumen to realize it – the Constitutionalists, as I call them – have naturally wagered on the multi-national state, and have exhorted their compatriots to work for it boldly and eagerly. But those who could not see it have never ceased in their fear of a largely imaginary adversary. Among these are, first, the assimilated converts and boot-lickers who have given in to the idea that French Canada is already dead, and that the Anglo-Canadian nation-state is rising triumphant over its remains; these, though, are insignificant in number and even more so in influence, so I am writing them off as a force to be reckoned with. Secondly, there are Separatists and nationalists of all shapes and sizes baying after independence, who devote all their courage and capabilities to stirring up French-Canadian nationalism in defiance of the Anglo-Canadian variety. These are incessantly promoting what Gérard Pelletier has very aptly called "the state-of-siege mentality." Now, recalling something I once wrote, "the siege was lifted long ago and humanity has marched ever onward, while we remain stewing steadily in our own juice without daring even once to peek over the edge of the pot."

If Canada as a state has had so little room for French Canadians it is above all because we have failed to make ourselves indispensable to its future. Today, for example, it would seem that a Sévigny or a Dorion could perfectly well leave the federal cabinet, as a Courtemanche did, without causing irreparable damage to the machinery of government or the prestige of the country. And, with the sole exception of Laurier, I fail to see a single French Canadian in more than three-quarters of a century whose presence in the federal cabinet might be considered indispensable to the history of Canada as written – except at election time, of course, when the tribe always invokes the aid of its witch-doctors. Similarly, in the ranks of senior civil servants, there is probably not one who could be said to have decisively and beneficially influenced the development of our administration as has, for example, an O.D. Skelton, a Graham Towers, or a Norman Robertson.

Consequently, an examination of the few nationalist "victories" carried off at Ottawa after years of wrangling in high places will reveal probably none that could not have been won in the course of a single cabinet meeting by a French Canadian of the calibre of C.D. Howe. All our cabinet ministers put together would scarcely match the weight of a bilingual cheque or the name of a hotel.

To sum up, the Anglo-Canadians have been strong by virtue only of our weakness. This is true not only at Ottawa, but even at Quebec, a veritable charnel-house where half our rights have been wasted by decay and decrepitude and the rest devoured by the maggots of political cynicism and the pestilence of corruption. Under the circumstances, can there be any wonder that Anglo-Canadians have not wanted the face of this country to bear any French features? And why would they want to learn a language that we have been at such pains to reduce to mediocrity at all levels of our educational system?

No doubt, had English-speaking Canadians applied themselves to learning French with a quarter the diligence they have shown in refusing to do so, Canada would have been effectively bilingual long ago. For here is demonstrated one of the laws of nationalism, whereby more energy is consumed in combating disagreeable but irrevocable realities than in contriving some satisfactory compromise. It stands to reason that this law works to greatest ill effect in respect to minority nationalisms: namely, us.

Let me explain.

The Sorry Tale of French-Canadian Nationalism

We have expended a great deal of time and energy proclaiming the rights due our nationality, invoking our divine mission, trumpeting our virtues, bewailing our misfortunes, denouncing our enemies, and avowing our independence; and for all that not one of our workmen is the more skilled, nor a civil servant the more efficient, a financier the richer, a doctor the more advanced, a bishop the more learned, nor a single solitary politician the less ignorant. Now, except for a few stubborn eccentrics, there is probably not one French-Canadian intellectual who has not spent at least four hours a week over the last year discussing separatism. That makes how many thousand times two hundred hours spent just flapping our arms? And can any one of them honestly say he has heard a single argument not already expounded *ad nauseam* twenty, forty, and even sixty years ago? I am not even sure we have exorcized any of our original bogey men in sixty years. The

Separatists of 1962 that I have met really are, in general, genuinely earnest and nice people; but the few times I have had the opportunity of talking with them at any length, I have almost always been astounded by the totalitarian outlook of some, the anti-Semitism of others, and the complete ignorance of basic economics of all of them.

This is what I call *la nouvelle trahison des clercs*: this self-deluding passion of a large segment of our thinking population for throwing themselves headlong – intellectually and spiritually – into purely escapist pursuits.

Several years ago I tried to show that the devotees of the nationalist school of thought among French Canadians, despite their good intentions and courage, were for all practical purposes trying to swim upstream against the course of progress. Over more than half a century "they have laid down a pattern of social thinking impossible to realize and which, from all practical points of view, has left the people without any effective intellectual direction."

I have discovered that several people who thought as I did at that time are today talking separatism. Because their social thinking is to the left, because they are campaigning for secular schools, because they may be active in trade union movements, because they are open-minded culturally, they think that their nationalism is the path to progress. What they fail to see is that they have become reactionary *politically*.

Reactionary, in the first place, by reason of circumstances. A count, even a rough one, of institutions, organizations, and individuals dedicated to nationalism, from the village notary to the Ordre de Jacques Cartier, from the small businessman to the Ligues du Sacré-Coeur, would show beyond question that an alliance between nationalists of the right and of the left would work in favour of the former, by sheer weight of numbers. And when the leftists say they will not make such an alliance until it is they who are in the majority, I venture to suggest once again that they will never be so as long as they continue to waste their meagre resources as they do now. Any effort aimed at strengthening the nation must avoid dividing it; otherwise such an effort loses all effectiveness so far as social reform is concerned, and for that matter can only lead to consolidation of the *status quo*. In this sense the alliance is already working against the left, even before being concluded.

In the second place, the nationalists – even those of the left – are politically reactionary because, in attaching such importance to the idea of nation, they are surely led to a definition of the common good as a function of an ethnic group, rather than of all the people, regardless of characteristics. This is why a nationalistic movement is by nature intolerant, discriminatory, and, when all is said and done, totalitarian.* A truly democratic government cannot be "nationalist," because it must pursue the good of all its citizens, without prejudice to ethnic origin. The democratic government, then, stands for and encourages good citizenship, never nationalism. Certainly, such a government will make laws by which ethnic groups will benefit, and the majority group will benefit proportionately to its number; but that follows naturally from the principle of equality for all, not from any right due the strongest. In this sense one may well say that educational policy in Quebec has always been democratic rather than nationalistic; I would not say the same for all the other provinces. If, on the other hand, Hydro-Québec were to expropriate the province's hydro-electric industries for nationalistic rather than economic reasons, we would already be on the road to fascism. The right can nationalize; it is the left that socializes and controls for the common good.

In the third place, any thinking that calls for full sovereign powers for the nation is politically reactionary because it would put complete and perfect power in the hands of a community which is incapable of realizing a complete and perfect society. In 1962 it is unlikely that any nation-state – or for that matter any multi-national state either – however strong, could realize a complete and perfect society; economic,

---

*   As early as 1862, Lord Acton was already writing thus: "The nation is here an ideal unit founded on the race. . . . It overrules the rights and wishes of the inhabitants, absorbing their divergent interests in a fictitious unity; sacrifices their several inclinations and duties to the higher claim of nationality, and crushes all natural rights and all established liberties for the purpose of vindicating itself. Whenever a single definite object is made the supreme end of the State – the State becomes for the time being inevitably absolute." John Dalberg-Acton, *Essays on Freedom and Power* (Glencoe, 1948), p. 184.

military, and cultural interdependence is a *sine qua non* for states of the twentieth century, to the extent that none is really self-sufficient. Treaties, trade alliances, common markets, free trade areas, cultural and scientific agreements, all these are as indispensable for the world's states as is interchange between citizens within them; and just as each citizen must recognize the submission of his own sovereignty to the laws of the state – by which, for example, he must fulfil the contracts he makes – so the states will know no real peace and prosperity until they accept the submission of their relations with each other to a higher order. In truth, the very concept of sovereignty must be surmounted, and those who proclaim it for the nation of French Canada are not only reactionary, they are preposterous. French Canadians could no more constitute a perfect society than could the five million Sikhs of the Punjab. We are not well enough educated, nor rich enough, nor, above all, numerous enough, to man and finance a government possessing all the necessary means for both war and peace. The fixed per-capita cost would ruin us. But I shall not try to explain all this to people who feel something other than dismay at seeing *la Laurentie* already opening embassies in various parts of the world, "for the diffusion of our culture abroad." Particularly when these same people, a year ago, seemed to be arguing that we were too poor to finance a second university – a Jesuit one – in Montreal.

To this third contention, that sovereignty is unworkable and contradictory, the Separatists will sometimes argue that, once independent, Quebec could very well afford to give up part of her sovereignty on, for instance, re-entering a Canadian Confederation, because then her choice would be her own, a free one. That abstraction covers a multitude of sins! It is a serious thing to ask French Canadians to embark on several decades of privation and sacrifice, just so that they can indulge themselves in the luxury of choosing "freely" a destiny more or less identical to the one they have rejected. But the ultimate tragedy would be in not realizing that French Canada is too culturally anaemic, too economically destitute, too intellectually retarded, too spiritually paralysed, to be able to survive more than a couple of decades of stagnation, emptying herself of all her vitality into nothing but a cesspit, the mirror of her nationalistic vanity and "dignity."

The Younger Generation

What French Canadians now in their twenties will find hard to forgive in people of my generation a few years from now is the complacency with which we have watched the rebirth of separatism and nationalism. Because by then they will have realized how appallingly backward French Canada is in all fields of endeavour. What! they will say to the intellectuals, you did so little writing and so little thinking and yet you had time to ruminate over separatism? What! they will say to the sociologists and political scientists, in the very year that men were first put into orbit you were replying gravely to inquiries on separatism that in your opinion, perhaps, yes, one day, no doubt, possibly.... What! they will say to the economists, with the western world in its age of mass production striving, by all kinds of economic unions, to reproduce market conditions already enjoyed within such large political unions as the United States and the Soviet Union, how could you, in Quebec, have looked on with satisfaction at a movement whose aims would have reduced to nil any common market for Quebec industry? What! they will say to the engineers, you could not even manage to build a highway that would survive two Canadian winters and you were pipe-dreaming of a Great Wall all the way around Quebec? What! they will say to the judges and lawyers, civil liberties having survived in the province of Quebec thanks only to the Communists, the trade unions, and the Jehovah's Witnesses, and to English and Jewish lawyers and the judges of the Supreme Court in Ottawa,[*] you had nothing better to do than cheer on the coming of a sovereign state for French Canadians? Finally they will come to the party politicians. What! they will say, you, the Liberals, spent twenty-five years growing fat on sovereignty filched from the

---

[*] Seven times in the last decade alone, beginning in 1951, the Supreme Court in Ottawa has reversed the decisions of the Court of Appeal of the Province of Quebec, decisions which would have spelled disaster for civil liberties: the Boucher case (seditious libel); the Alliance case (loss of union certification); the Saumur case (distribution of pamphlets); the Chaput case (religious assembly); the Birks case (compulsory religious holidays); the Switzman case (padlock law); the Roncarelli case (administrative discretion). At the moment of going to press we learn that yet an eighth case can now be added to this list: the case of *Lady Chatterley's Lover*.

provinces; you, the Conservatives, alias Union Nationale, subjected Quebec to two decades of retroactive, vindictive, discriminatory, and stultifying laws; and you, of the Social-Democratic-cum-New-Democratic Party, in the name of some obscure sort of federal *raison d'État*, had sabotaged the *Union des forces démocratiques* and thereby snuffed out any glimmer of hope for Quebec's radicals; and you all discovered, all of a sudden, that Quebec must have more independence, some of you to the point of becoming avowed Separatists?

I venture to predict that among these young people of such acid criticism there will be one called Luc Racine, who will be a little sorry that he once wrote as follows in *Cité libre*: "If today's youth has turned to separatism, it is not from indifference to the great problems facing humanity, but from the desire to concentrate its efforts on conditions that are within its power to change." Because by then he will understand that a given people, at a given moment in their history, possess only a given amount of intellectual energy; and that if a whole generation devotes the greater part of that energy to imbecilities, that generation, for all practical purposes, will indeed have shown its "indifference to the great problems facing humanity." (I would lend a word of advice to Racine, however: that in 1972 he not take it into his head to talk about nationalism as a form of alienation, because my friend André Laurendeau will once again feel compelled to fly to the defence of his forebears, protesting that in 1922 Abbé Groulx deserved our complete respect.)*

So much for that. But how does it happen that separatism enjoys such a following *today* among the younger generation? How is it, for example, that so many young people, responding to *Cité libre*'s editorial "Un certain silence," have declared themselves for separatism?

---

* An emotional allusion to an emotional rejoinder by Laurendeau, *Le Devoir*, March 3, 1961. This soul of refinement, one of the fairest-minded men I know, who shares with Bourassa the privilege of being the favourite target of the Separatists (who, logically enough, will not allow that nationalism could be anything but separatist), rarely speaks of nationalism without betraying, in some little detail, a blind spot. Thus it was that in an otherwise excellent editorial (*Le Devoir*, January 30, 1962), he put forth the ridiculous idea of a "moral conscription of French Canadians." What! Mr. Laurendeau? Conscription!?

Pelletier has pointed out that, having preached – through *Cité libre* – systematic scepticism in the face of established dogmatism, and having practised it as regards most of our traditional institutions, we should hardly be surprised if a new generation should turn it against one of the establishments we ourselves have spared: the Canadian state.

This has some validity at the psychological level; but it fails to explain the reactionary direction of their dissension.

For my part, I would think there would be some analogy to be found in the democratic impetus that gave birth to the various nationalisms in Europe a century or two ago. The death of Duplessis marked the end of a dynasty and of the oligarchy it had fostered. The advent of liberal democracy to the province bore promise of power for all classes henceforth. But in practice the newly self-conscious classes have found most roads to a better life blocked: the clergy clings to its grip on education, the English continue to dominate our finances, and the Americans intrude upon our culture. Only Quebec as a state would appear to belong unquestionably to French Canadians; and the fullest power for that state is therefore highly desirable. Democracy having declared all men equal within the nation, so all nations should enjoy equality one to another, meaning in particular that ours should be sovereign and independent. It is predicted that the realization of our nation-state will release a thousand unsuspected energies, and that, thus endowed, French Canadians will at last take possession of their rightful heritage. In other words, there is supposed to be some sort of creative energy that will bestow genius on people who have none and give courage and learning to a lazy and ignorant nation.

This is the faith that takes the place of reason for those who are unable to find a basis for their convictions in history, or economics, or the constitution, or sociology. "Independence," writes Chaput, "is much more a matter of disposition than of logic. . . . More than reason, we must have pride." That is the way all those dear little girls and young ladies feel, who like to put it in a nutshell thus: "Independence is a matter of dignity. You don't argue about it; you feel it." Isn't that the sort of thing that many poets and artists say? Jean-Guy Pilon writes:

When the day comes that this cultural minority, hitherto only tolerated in this country, becomes a nation unto itself within its own borders, our literature will take a tremendous leap ahead. Because the writer, like everyone else in this society, will feel free. And a free man can do great things.

Now it would seem that Chaput is an excellent chemist. What I would like to know, though, is how the energies set in motion by independence are going to make him a better one; he need show us nothing else in order to woo us into separatism. As for his book, it bears the mark of an honest and dedicated man, but it destroys itself with one of its own sentences: "To hope that one day, by some sort of magic, the French-Canadian people will suddenly reform and become as one body respectful of the law, correct in its speech, devoted to culture and high achievement, without first becoming imbued with some inspiring ideal: this is a dangerous aberration." So Chaput rejects magic, but counts on an inspiring ideal as the way of salvation for our people. As if reform, correctness of speech, culture, and high achievement – *all of which are already accessible to us under the existing Canadian constitution* – were not in themselves inspiring ideals! And in what way is the other ideal he proposes – the nation-state – any more than a kind of magic called forth to fill in for our lack of discipline in pursuing the true ideals?

It would seem, too, that Pilon is a good poet. I would like him to tell me – in prose, if he likes – how national sovereignty is going to make him "a free man" and "capable of doing great things." If he fails to find within himself, in the world about him and in the stars above, the dignity, pride and other well-springs of poetry, I wonder why and how he will find them in a "free" Quebec.

No doubt bilingualism is attainable only with some difficulty. But I will not admit that this should be any insurmountable hurdle to men who call themselves intellectuals, particularly when the language they carp over is one of the principal vehicles of twentieth-century civilization. The day of language barriers is finished, at least as far as science and culture are concerned; and if Quebec's intellectuals refuse to master another language than their own, if they will recognize no loyalty but to their nation, then they may be renouncing forever their place among the world's intellectual élite.

For men of intellect the talk about energy set in motion by national independence means nothing. Their function, particularly if they come from a milieu where sentiment takes the place of reason and prejudice the place of understanding, is to think, and then think some more. If their intellectual pursuits have led to a dead end, there is only one thing to do: turn around and go back. Any attempt at escaping through intellectual hocus-pocus is contemptible; as Arthur Miller has said in *L'Express*, "The task of the real intellectual consists of analyzing illusions in order to discover their causes."

True enough, but for people in general it is another matter. Nationalism, as an emotional stimulus directed at an entire community, can indeed let loose unforeseen powers. History is full of this, called variously chauvinism, racism, jingoism, and all manner of crusades, where right reasoning and thought are reduced to rudimentary proportions. It could be that in certain historical situations, where oppression was intolerable, misery unspeakable, and all alternative escape routes blocked, it was nationalism that sparked the subsequent break for freedom. But the arousing of such a passion as a last resort has always had its drawbacks, and the bad has invariably gone hand in hand with the good. This bad has almost always included a certain amount of despotism, because people who win their freedom with passion rather than with reason are generally disappointed to find themselves just as poor and deprived as ever; and strong governments are necessary to put an end to their unrest.

I was in Ghana during the first months of her independence. The poets were no better, the chemists no more numerous, and, on a more tangible level, salaries were no higher. Since the intellectuals were unable to explain to the people why this should be, they distracted their attention to some obscure island in the Gulf of Guinea which needed to be "reconquered." To this end a large slice of this economically destitute state's budget was earmarked for the army – which ultimately served to put the parliamentary opposition in jail.

A similar thing has happened in Indonesia. This former-colony-turned-state, which is only barely succeeding in governing itself and has yet to achieve prosperity, has called its people to arms to liberate its territories in New Guinea. Now these territories do not belong to it for any reason whatever, neither of race, nor language, nor geography. Nevertheless, I have met, in Quebec, men of radical convictions who – through inability to reason in any terms other than of national sovereignty – consider the operation justified. The State of Quebec can count on these men one day, when, unable to improve social conditions for her people, she sends them off to win "her islands" in Hudson Bay. Already the Honourable Mr. Arsenault is preparing us for this glorious epic. And Lesage stands ready with his applause.

Most fortunately, the backbone of our people entertain fewer illusions on such subjects, and show more common sense, than do our intellectuals and *bourgeoisie*. The province's large trade unions have pronounced themselves categorically against separatism. They are well aware of the powers latent in mob passion; but, rightly, they shrink from setting in motion a vehicle with faulty steering and unsound brakes.

In short, those who expect to "release energies" by independence (or the feeling of independence) are playing the sorcerer's apprentice. They are resolving not one single problem by the exercise of reason; and in stirring up collective passions they are engaging an unpredictable, uncontrollable, and ineffective mechanism. (It will be noted that I am talking here primarily of energies supposedly to be released *by* independence; about the energies behind the *origins* of today's separatism, I had something to say in *Cité libre* of March 1961, p. 5. But on that, Messrs. Albert and Raymond Breton offer in the present issue by far the most serious study ever made on the subject.)

As a final argument, certain young people justify their flirtation with separatism as a matter of tactics: "If the English get scared enough we'll get what we want without going as far as independence." This tactic has already provoked concessions of purely symbolic value for French Canadians: one slogan ('The French Canadians deserve a New Deal'), two flags (Pearson–Pickersgill), a few new names for old companies (e.g., La Compagnie d'électricité Shawinigan), several appointments to boards of directors, and a multitude of bilingual cheques (Diefenbaker). *De minimis non curat praetor*, but all the same I must confess that the flap among English-speaking politicians and businessmen is funny to see. It bears witness certainly to a guilty conscience for their own nationalistic sins. But that could have its repercussions, too. There is nothing meaner than the coward recovered from his fright. And I would like to think that then French Canada would be bolstered by a younger generation endowed with richer assets than their nationalistic passion.

The Future

If, in my opinion, the nation were of purely negative value, I would not be at such pains to discredit a movement that promises to lead the French-Canadian nation to its ruin.

The nation is, in fact, the guardian of certain very positive qualities: a cultural heritage, common traditions, a community awareness, historical continuity, a set of mores; all of which, at this juncture in history, go to make a man what he is. Certainly, these qualities are more private than public, more introverted than extroverted, more instinctive and primitive than intelligent and civilized, more self-centred and impulsive than generous and reasonable. They belong to a transitional period in world history. But they are a reality of our time, probably useful, and in any event considered indispensable by all national communities.

Except to pinpoint ourselves in the right historical perspective, then, there is not much to be gained in brushing them aside on the ground that the nation of French Canadians will some day fade from view and that Canada itself will undoubtedly not exist forever. Benda points out that it is to the lasting greatness of Thucydides that he was able to visualize a world in which Athens would be no more.

But the future with which we should concern ourselves here is the one we are building from day to day. The problem we must face squarely is this: without backsliding to the ridiculous and reactionary idea of national sovereignty, how can we protect our French-Canadian national qualities?

As I have already said earlier in this article, we must separate once and for all the concepts of state and of nation, and make Canada a truly pluralistic and polyethnic society. Now in order for this to come about, the different regions within the country must be assured of a wide range of local autonomy, such that each national group, with an increasing background of experience in self-government, may be able to develop the body of laws and institutions essential to the fullest expression and development of their national characteristics. At the same time, the English Canadians, with their own nationalism, will have to retire gracefully to their proper place, consenting to modify their own precious image of what Canada ought to be. If they care to protect and realize their own special ethnic qualities, they should do it within this framework of regional and local autonomy rather than a pan-Canadian one.

For the incorporation of these diverse aspirations the Canadian constitution is an admirable vehicle. Under the British North America Act, the jurisdiction of the federal State of Canada concerns itself with all the things that have no specific ethnic implications, but that have to do with the welfare of the entire Canadian society: foreign affairs, the broader aspects of economic stability, foreign trade, navigation, postal services, money and banking, and so on. The provinces, on the other hand, have jurisdiction over matters of a purely local and private nature and those that affect ethnic peculiarities: education, municipal and parochial affairs, the administration of justice, the celebration of marriage, property and civil rights, and so forth. Nevertheless, in keeping with the fact that none of the provincial borders coincides perfectly with ethnic or linguistic delineations, no provincial government is encouraged to legislate exclusively for the benefit of a particular ethnic group in such a way as to foster a nation-state mentality at the provincial level. On this point the record of Quebec's treatment of its minorities can well stand as an example to other provinces with large French, German, Ukrainian, and other minorities.

I have no intention of closing my eyes to how much Canadians of British origin have to do – or rather, undo – before a pluralist state can become a reality in Canada. But I am inclined to add that that is *their* problem. The die is cast in Canada: there are two main ethnic and linguistic groups; each is too strong and too deeply rooted in the past, too firmly bound to a mother-culture, to be able to engulf the other. But if the two will collaborate at the hub of a truly pluralistic state, Canada could become the envied seat of a form of federalism that belongs to tomorrow's world. Better than the American melting-pot, Canada could offer an example to all those new Asian and African states already discussed at the beginning of this article, who must discover how to govern their polyethnic populations with proper regard for justice and liberty. What better reason for cold-shouldering the lure of annexation to the United States? Canadian federalism is an experiment of major proportions; it could become a brilliant prototype for the moulding of tomorrow's civilization.

If English Canadians cannot see it, again I say so much the worse for them; they will be subsiding into a backward, short-sighted, and despotic nationalism. Lord Acton, one of the great thinkers of the nineteenth century, described, with extraordinarily prophetic insight, the error of the various nationalisms and the future they were preparing. Exactly a century ago he wrote:

> A great democracy must either sacrifice self-government to unity or preserve it by federalism. . . . The co-existence of several nations under the same State is a test, as well as the best security of its freedom. It is also one of the chief instruments of civilization. . . . The combination of different nations in one State is as necessary a condition of civilized life as the combination of men in society. . . . Where political and national boundaries coincide, society ceases to advance, and nations relapse into a condition corresponding to that of men who renounce intercourse with their fellow-men. . . . A State which is incompetent to satisfy different races condemns itself; a State which labours to neutralize, to absorb, or to expel them is

destitute of the chief basis of self-government. The theory of nationality, then, is a retrograde step in history.

It goes without saying that if, in the face of Anglo-Canadian nationalism, French Canadians retreat into their own nationalistic shell, they will condemn themselves to the same stagnation. And Canada will become a sterile soil for the minds of her people, a barren waste prey to every wandering host and conquering horde.

I will say it once again: the die is cast in Canada. Neither of our two language groups can force assimilation on the other. But one or the other, or even both, could lose by default, destroying itself from within, and dying of suffocation. And accordingly, by the same law of retribution and in just reward for faith in humanity, victory is promised to the nation that rejects its nationalistic obsessions and, with the full support of its members, applies all the powers at its command to the pursuit of the most far-reaching and human ideal.

By the terms of the existing Canadian constitution, that of 1867,[*] French Canadians have all the powers they need to make Quebec a political society affording due respect for nationalist aspirations and at the same time giving unprecedented scope for human potential in the broadest sense. (On pages 98–9 of his book, Mr. Chaput proposes sixteen items of economic reform which could be undertaken by an independent Quebec. Except for the first, which would abolish taxes levied by Ottawa, all these reforms could be undertaken under the present constitution! On pages 123–4, Mr. Chaput outlines, in seven items, the measures by which an independent Quebec could ensure the protection of French-Canadian minorities outside Quebec. None of these, except the declaration of sovereignty itself, would be any more accessible to an independent Quebec than it is to present-day Quebec.)

If Quebec became such a shining example, if to live there were to partake of freedom and progress, if culture enjoyed a place of honour

---

[*]   This was what I had in mind when I wrote – referring to the younger Separatists – something that annoyed a great many people: "They . . . are tilting headlong at problems which already had their solution a century ago" (*Cité libre*, December 1961, p. 3).

there, if the universities commanded respect and renown from afar, if the administration of public affairs were the best in the land (and none of this presupposes any declaration of independence!) French Canadians would no longer need to do battle for bilingualism; the ability to speak French would become a status symbol, even an open sesame in business and public life. Even in Ottawa, superior competence on the part of our politicians and civil servants would bring spectacular changes.

Such an undertaking, though immensely difficult, would be possible; it would take more guts than jaw. And therein, it would seem to me, is an "ideal" not a whit less "inspiring" than that other one that has been in vogue for a couple of years in our little part of the world.

For those who would put their shoulders to the wheel, who would pin their hopes for the future on the fully developed man of intellect, and who would refuse to be party to *la nouvelle trahison des clercs*, I close with a final word from the great Lord Acton:

Nationalism does not aim either at liberty or prosperity, both of which it sacrifices to the imperative necessity of making the nation the mould and measure of the State. Its course will be marked with material as well as moral ruin, in order that a new invention may prevail over the works of God and the interests of mankind.

John T. Saywell, ed., *Federalism and the French Canadians* (Toronto: Macmillan, 1968)
Translation by Patricia Claxton

Federalism, Nationalism, and Reason*

State and Nation

The concept of federalism with which I will deal in this paper is that of a particular system of government applicable within a sovereign state; it flows from my understanding of state and nation. Hence I find it necessary to discuss these two notions in part I of this paper, but I need only do so from the point of view of territory and population. Essentially, the question to which I would seek an answer is: what section of the world's population occupying what segment of the world's surface should fall under the authority of a given state?

Until the middle of the eighteenth century, the answer was largely arrived at without regard to the people themselves. Of course in much earlier times, population pressures guided by accidents of geography and climate had determined the course of the migrations which were to

---

* I wish to thank my friends Albert Breton, Fernand Cadieux, Pierre Carignan, Eugene Forsey, and James Mallory, who read the manuscript and helped me clarify several ideas. Since the paper was read, on June 11, 1964, other friends have been very helpful with their comments; I dare not acknowledge them by name until I have had time to work their suggestions into this paper.

spill across the earth's surface. But by the end of the Middle Ages, such migrations had run their course in most of Europe. The existence of certain peoples inhabiting certain land areas, speaking certain languages or dialects, and practising certain customs, was generally taken as data – *choses données* – by the European states which arose to establish their authority over them.

It was not the population who decided by what states they would be governed; it was the states which, by wars (but not "people's wars"), by alliances, by dynastic arrangements, by marriages, by inheritance, and by chance, determined the area of territory over which they would govern. And for that reason they could be called territorial states. Except in the particular case of newly discovered lands, the population came with the territory; and except in the unusual case of deportations, very little was to be done about it.

Political philosophers, asking questions about the authority of the state, did not inquire why a certain population fell within the territorial jurisdiction of a certain state rather than of another; for the philosophers, too, territory and population were just data; their philosophies were mainly concerned with discovering the foundations of authority over a *given* territory and the sources of obedience of a *given* population.

In other words, the purpose of Locke and Rousseau, not unlike that of the medieval philosophers and of the ancient Stoics, was to explain the origins and justify the existence of political authority *per se*; the theories of contract which they derived from natural law or reason were meant to ensure that within a given state bad governments could readily be replaced by good ones, but not that one territorial state could be superseded by another.

Such then was the significance of social contract and popular sovereignty in the minds of the men who made the Glorious Revolution, and such it was in the minds of those who prepared the events of 1776 in America and 1789 in France. As things went, however, the two latter "events" turned out to be momentous revolutions, and the ideas which had been put into them emerged with an immensely enhanced significance.

In America, it became necessary for the people not merely to replace a poor government by a better one, but to switch their allegiance from one territorial state to another, and in their own words, to

> declare, that these United Colonies, are, and of right ought to be, free and independent states; that they are absolved from all allegiance to the British crown, and that all political connection, between them and the state of Great Britain, is and ought to be totally dissolved; and that, as free and independent states, they have full power to levy war, conclude peace, contract alliances, establish commerce, and to do all other acts and things which independent states may of right do.

Here then was a theory of government by consent which took on a radically new meaning. Since sovereignty belonged to the people, it appeared to follow that any given body of people could at will transfer their allegiance from one existing state to another, or indeed to a completely new state of their own creation. In other words, the consent of the population was required not merely for a social contract, which was to be the foundation of civil society, or for a choice of responsible rulers, which was the essence of self-government; consent was also required for adherence to one territorial state rather than to another, which was the beginning of national self-determination.

Why the theory of consent underwent such a transformation at this particular time is no doubt a matter for historical and philosophical conjecture. Perhaps the prerequisites had never been brought together before: a population (1) whose political traditions were sufficiently advanced to include the ideology of consent, (2) subject to a modern unitary state the centre of which was very remote, and (3) inhabiting a territory which was reasonably self-contained.

Be that as it may, it appears to be at this juncture in history that the word "nation" became charged with a new potential. In the past, the *word* had meant many things, from Machiavelli's "Ghibelline nation" to Montesquieu's "pietistic nation"; its broadest meaning seems to have been reached by the *Encyclopédistes*, who understood thereby, "une quantité considérable de peuple, qui habite une certaine étendue de pays, renfermée dans de certaines limites, et qui obéit au même gouvernement" [a considerable number of people who inhabit a certain expanse of territory, enclosed in certain limits, and obey the same government]. The *idea* of nation also had roots which plunged deep in history; and a sentiment akin to nationalism had sometimes inspired political action, as when French rulers reacted against Italian popes. But the idea, like the word, only took on its modern meaning during the last quarter of the eighteenth century.

Consequently, it might be said that in the past the (territorial) state had defined its territorial limits which had defined the people or nation living within. But henceforth it was to be the people who first defined themselves as a nation, who then declared which territory belonged to them as of right, and who finally proceeded to give their allegiance to a state of their own choosing or invention which would exercise authority over that nation and that territory. Hence the expression "nation-state." As I see it, the important transition was from the *territorial state* to the *nation-state*. But once the latter was born, the idea of the *national state* was bound to follow, it being little more than a nation-state with an ethnic flavour added. With it the idea of self-determination became the principle of nationalities.

Self-determination did not necessarily proceed from or lead to self-government. Whereas self-government was based on reason and proposed to introduce liberal forms of government into existing states, self-determination was based on will and proposed to challenge the legitimacy and the very existence of the territorial states.

Self-determination, or the principle of nationalities (I am talking of the doctrine, for the expressions became current only later), was bound to dissolve whatever order and balance existed in the society of states prevailing towards the end of the eighteenth century. But no matter; for it was surmised that a new order would arise, free from wars and inequities. As each of the peoples of the world became conscious of its identity as a collectivity bound together by natural affinities, it would define itself as a nation and govern itself as a state. An international order of nation-states, since it would be founded on the free will of free people, would necessarily be more lasting and just than one which rested on a hodge-podge of despotic empires, dynastic kingdoms, and aristocratic republics. In May 1790, the Constituent Assembly had proclaimed: "La nation française renonce à entreprendre aucune guerre dans un but de conquête et n'emploiera jamais de forces contre la liberté d'aucun peuple." [The French nation abandons the idea of launching any war of conquest and shall never resort to force against the freedom of any people.]

Unfortunately, things did not work out quite that way. The French Revolution, which had begun as an attempt to replace a bad government by a good one, soon overreached itself by replacing a territorial state by a nation-state, whose territory incidentally was considerably enlarged. In 1789, the *Déclaration des droits de l'homme et du citoyen* had stated: "Le principe de toute souveraineté réside essentiellement dans la Nation. Nul corps, nul individu ne peut exercer d'autorité qui n'en émane expressément." [The source of all sovereignty resides essentially in the Nation. No corporate body, no individual can exercise any authority not expressly emanating from the Nation.] But who was to be included in the nation? Danton having pointed out in 1793 that the frontiers of France were designated by Nature, the French nation willed itself into possession of that part of Europe which spread between the Rhine, the Pyrenees, the Atlantic Ocean, and the Alps.

France was indeed fortunate, in that her natural frontiers thus enabled her to correct the disadvantage which might have arisen in Alsace, for example, from a will based on linguistic frontiers. Fortunately for German-speaking peoples, however, Fichte was soon to discover that the natural frontiers were in reality the linguistic ones; thus the German nation could will itself towards its proper size, provided of course that the language principle be sometimes corrected by that of historical possession, in order for instance to include Bohemia. Other nations, such as Poland, enlightened their will by greater reliance on the historical principle, corrected when necessary by the linguistic one. Then finally there were nations who, spurning such frivolous guide-lines as geography, history, and language, were favoured by direct communication with the Holy Ghost; such was the privilege of the United States of America, who saw the annexation of Texas, California, and eventually Canada as – in the words of O'Sullivan – "the fulfillment of our manifest destiny to overspread the continent alloted by Providence for the free development of our yearly multiplying millions."

The political history of Europe and of the Americas in the nineteenth century and that of Asia and Africa in the twentieth are histories of nations labouring, conspiring, blackmailing, warring, revolutionizing, and generally willing their way towards statehood. It is, of course, impossible to know whether there has ensued therefrom for humanity more peace and justice than would have been the case if some other principle than self-determination had held sway. In theory, the arrangement of boundaries in such a way that no important national group be included by force in the territorial limits of a state which was mainly the expression of the will of another group, was to be conducive to peaceful international order. In practice, state boundaries continued to be established and maintained largely by the threat of or the use of force. The concept of right in international relations became, if anything, even more a function of might. And the question whether a national minority was "important" enough to be entitled to independence remained unanswerable except in terms of the political and physical power that could be wielded in its favour. Why did Libya become a country in 1951 and not the Saar in 1935, with a population almost as great? Why should Norway be independent and not Brittany? Why Ireland and not Scotland? Why Nicaragua and not Quebec?

As we ask ourselves these questions, it becomes apparent that more than language and culture, more than history and geography, even more than force and power, the foundation of the nation is will. For there is no power without will. The Rocky Mountains are higher than the Pyrenees, but they are not a watershed between countries. The Irish Sea and the Straits of Florida are much narrower than the Pacific Ocean between Hawaii and California, yet they are more important factors in determining nationhood. Language or race do not provide, in

Switzerland or Brazil, the divisive force they are at present providing in Belgium or the United States.

Looking at the foregoing examples, and at many others, we are bound to conclude that the frontiers of nation-states are in reality nearly as arbitrary as those of the former territorial states. For all their anthropologists, linguists, geographers, and historians, the nations of today cannot justify their frontiers with noticeably more rationality than the kings of two centuries ago; a greater reliance on general staffs than on princesses' dowries does not necessarily spell a triumph of reason. Consequently, a present-day definition of the word "nation" in its juristic sense would fit quite readily upon the population of the territorial states which existed before the French and American revolutions. A nation (as in the expressions: the French nation, the Swiss nation, the United Nations, the President's speech to the nation) is no more and no less than the entire population of a sovereign state. (Except when otherwise obvious, I shall try to adhere to that juristic sense in the rest of this paper.) Because no country has an absolutely homogeneous population, all the so-called nation-states of today are also territorial states. And the converse is probably also true. The distinction between a nation-state, a multi-national state, and a territorial state may well be valid in reference to historical origins; but it has very little foundation in law or fact today and is mainly indicative of political value judgments.

Of course, the word "nation" can also be used in a sociological sense, as when we speak of the Scottish nation, or the Jewish nation. As Humpty Dumpty once told Alice, a word means just what one chooses it to mean. It would indeed be helpful if we could make up our minds. Either the juristic sense would be rejected, and the word "people" used instead (the people of the Soviet Union, the people of the United States; but what word would replace "national"? People's? Popular?); in that case "nation" would be restricted to its sociological meaning, which is also closer to its etymological and historical ones. Or the latter sense would be rejected, and words like "linguistic," "ethnic," or "cultural group" be used instead. But lawyers and political scientists cannot remake the language to suit their convenience; they will just have to hope that "the context makes it tolerably clear which of the two [senses] we mean."*

However, for some people one meaning is meant to flow into the other. The ambiguity is intentional and the user is conveying something which is at the back of his mind – and sometimes not very far back. In such cases the use of the word "nation" is not only confusing, it is disruptive of political stability. Thus, when a tightly knit minority within a state begins to define itself forcefully and consistently as a nation, it is triggering a mechanism which will tend to propel it towards full statehood.[†]

That, of course, is not merely due to the magic of words, but to a much more dynamic process which I will now attempt to explain. When the erstwhile territorial state, held together by divine right, tradition, and force, gave way to the nation-state, based on the will of the people, a new glue had to be invented which would bind the nation together on a durable basis. For very few nations – if any – could rely on a cohesiveness based entirely on "natural" identity, and so most of them were faced with a terrible paradox: the principle of national self-determination which had justified their birth could just as easily justify their death. Nationhood being little more than a state of mind, and every sociologically distinct group within the nation having a contingent right of secession, the will of the people was in constant danger of dividing up – unless it were transformed into a lasting consensus.

The formation of such a consensus is a mysterious process which takes in many elements, such as language, communication, association, geographical proximity, tribal origins, common interests and history,

---

* Eugene Forsey, "Canada: Two Nations or One?" *Canadian Journal of Economics and Political Science*, Vol. XXVIII (November 1962), p. 488. Mr. Forsey's discussion is as usual thorough and convincing.

† *Cf.* Max Weber, *Essays in Sociology* (London, 1948), p. 176: "A nation is a community of sentiment which would adequately manifest itself in a state of its own; hence, a nation is a community which normally tends to produce a state of its own." And R. MacIver, *Society* (New York, 1937), p. 155: "There are nations then which do not rule themselves politically, but we call them nations only if they seek for political autonomy."

external pressures, and even foreign intervention, none of which, however, is a determinant by itself. A consensus can be said to exist when no group within the nation feels that its vital interests and particular characteristics could be better preserved by withdrawing from the nation than by remaining within.

A (modern) state needs to develop and preserve this consensus as its very life. It must continually persuade the generality of the people that it is in their best interest to continue as a state. And since it is physically and intellectually difficult to persuade continually through reason alone, the state is tempted to reach out for whatever emotional support it can find. Ever since history fell under the ideological shadow of the nation-state, the most convenient support has obviously been the idea of nationalism. It becomes morally "right," a matter of "dignity and honour," to preserve the integrity of the nation. Hence, from the emotional appeal called nationalism is derived a psychological inclination to obey the constitution of the state.

To say that the state uses nationalism to preserve its identity is not to say that the state is the inventor of nationalism. The feeling called nationalism is secreted by the nation (in whatever sense we use the word) in much the same way as the family engenders family ties, and the clan generates clannishness. And just like clannishness, tribalism, and even feudalism, nationalism will probably fade away by itself at whatever time in history the nation has outworn its utility: that is to say, when the particular values protected by the idea of nation are no longer counted as important, or when those values no longer need to be embodied in a nation to survive.

But that time is not yet; we have not yet emerged from the era of the nation-state when it seemed perfectly normal for the state to rely heavily, for the preservation of the national consensus, on the gum called nationalism, a natural secretion of the nation. In so doing, the state (or the political agents who desired a state) transformed the feeling into a political doctrine or principle of government. Nationalism, as defined by history, is a doctrine which claims to supply a formula for determining what section of the world's population occupying what segment of the world's surface *should* fall under the authority of a given state; briefly stated, the formula holds that the optimum size of the sovereign state (in terms of authority and territory) is derived from the size of the nation (in terms of language, history, destiny, law, and so forth).[*]

It might be remarked here that history is not always logic; and in the case of nationalism it has embarked upon a type of circular reasoning which leaves the mind uneasy. The idea of nation which is at the origin of a new type of state does not refer to a "biological" reality (as does, for instance, the family); consequently the nation has constantly and artificially to be reborn from the very state to which it gave birth! In other words, the nation first decides what the state should be; but then the state has to decide what the nation should remain.

I should add that some people who call themselves nationalists would not accept this line of reasoning. Nationalism to them has remained a mere feeling of belonging to the nation (in a sociological or cultural sense); they liken it to a dream which inspires the individual and motivates his actions, perhaps irrationally but not necessarily negatively. I cannot, of course, quarrel with people merely because they wish to drain two centuries of history out of a definition. I can only say that it is not about *their* nationalism that I am writing in this paper; it is only fair to remind them, however, that their "dreams" are being converted by others into a principle of government.

Let us then proceed to see what happens when the state relies on nationalism to develop and preserve the consensus on which it rests.

Nationalism and Federalism

Many of the nations which were formed into states over the past century or two included peoples who were set apart geographically (like East and West Pakistan, or Great Britain and Northern Ireland), historically (like the United States or Czechoslovakia), linguistically (like Switzerland or Belgium), racially (like the Soviet Union or Algeria). Half of the aforesaid countries undertook to form the national consensus

---

[*] *Cf.* Kedourie, *Nationalism*, p. 1: "The doctrine [of nationalism] holds that . . . the only legitimate type of government is national self-government."

within the framework of a unitary state; the other half found it expedi-
ent to develop a system of government called federalism. The process
of consensus-formation is not the same in both cases.

It is obviously impossible, as well as undesirable, to reach unanimity on all things. Even unitary states find it wise to respect elements of
diversity, for instance by administrative decentralization as in Great
Britain,* or by language guarantees as in Belgium; but such limited
securities having been given, a consensus is obtained which recognizes
the state as the sole source of coercive authority within the national
boundaries. The federal state proceeds differently; it deliberately reduces
the national consensus to the greatest common denominator between
the various groups composing the nation. Coercive authority over the
entire territory remains a monopoly of the (central) state, but this
authority is limited to certain subjects of jurisdiction; on other subjects, and within well-defined territorial regions, other coercive authorities exist. In other words, the exercise of sovereignty is divided between
a central government and regional ones.

Federalism is by its very essence a compromise and a pact. It is a
compromise in the sense that when national consensus on *all* things is
not desirable or cannot readily obtain, the area of consensus is reduced
in order that consensus on *some* things be reached. It is a pact or quasi-
treaty in the sense that the terms of that compromise cannot be
changed unilaterally. That is not to say that the terms are fixed forever;
but only that in changing them, every effort must be made not to
destroy the consensus on which the federated nation rests. For what
Ernest Renan said about the nation is even truer about the federated
nation: "L'existence d'une nation est . . . un plébiscite de tous les jours."
[The existence of a nation is . . . a daily plebiscite.] This obviously did
not mean that such a plebiscite could or should be held every day, the
result of which could only be total anarchy; the real implication is clear:
the nation is based on a social contract, the terms of which each new
generation of citizens is free to accept tacitly, or to reject openly.

---

*   Since the Government of Ireland Act, 1920, it might be more exact to think of Great
Britain and Northern Ireland as forming a quasi-unitary state.

Federalism was an inescapable product of an age which recognized the principle of self-determination. For on the one hand, a sense of national identity and singularity was bound to be generated in a great many groups of people, who would insist on their right to distinct statehood. But on the other hand, the insuperable difficulties of living alone and the practical necessity of sharing the state with neighbouring groups were in many cases such as to make distinct statehood unattractive or unattainable. For those who recognized that the first law of politics is to start from the facts rather than from historical "might-have-been's," the federal compromise thus became imperative.

But by a paradox I have already noted in regard to the nation-state, the principle of self-determination which makes federalism necessary makes it also rather unstable. If the heavy paste of nationalism is relied upon to keep a unitary nation-state together, much more nationalism would appear to be required in the case of a federal nation-state. Yet if nationalism is encouraged as a rightful doctrine and noble passion, what is to prevent it from being used by some group, region, or province within the nation? If "nation algérienne" was a valid battle cry against France, how can the Algerian Arabs object to the cry of "nation kabyle" now being used against them?

The answer, of course, is that no amount of logic can prevent such an escalation. The only way out of the dilemma is to render what is logically defensible actually undesirable. The advantages *to the minority group* of staying integrated in the whole must on balance be greater than the gain to be reaped from separating. This can easily be the case when there is no real alternative for the separatists, either because they are met with force (as in the case of the U.S. Civil War), or because they are met with laughter (as in the case of the *Bretons bretonnants*). But when there is a real alternative, it is not so easy. And the greater the advantages and possibilities of separatism, the more difficult it is to maintain an unwavering consensus within the whole state.

One way of offsetting the appeal of separatism is by investing tremendous amounts of time, energy, and money in nationalism, *at the federal level*. A national image must be created that will have such an appeal as to make any image of a separatist group unattractive.

Resources must be diverted into such things as national flags, anthems, education, arts councils, broadcasting corporations, film boards; the territory must be bound together by a network of railways, highways, airlines; the national culture and the national economy must be protected by taxes and tariffs; ownership of resources and industry by nationals must be made a matter of policy. In short, the whole of the citizenry must be made to feel that it is only within the framework of the federal state that their language, culture, institutions, sacred traditions, and standard of living can be protected from external attack and internal strife.

It is, of course, obvious that a national consensus will be developed in this way only if the nationalism is emotionally acceptable to all important groups within the nation. Only blind men could expect a consensus to be lasting if the national flag or the national image is merely the reflection of one part of the nation, if the sum of values to be protected is not defined so as to include the language or the cultural heritage of some very large and tightly knit minority, if the identity to be arrived at is shattered by a colour-bar. The advantage as well as the peril of federalism is that it permits the development of a regional consensus based on regional values; so federalism is ultimately bound to fail if the nationalism it cultivates is unable to generate a national image which has immensely more appeal than the regional ones.

Moreover, this national consensus – to be lasting – must be a living thing. There is no greater pitfall for federal nations than to take the consensus for granted, as though it were reached once and for all. The compromise of federalism is generally reached under a very particular set of circumstances. As time goes by these circumstances change; the external menace recedes, the economy flourishes, mobility increases, industrialization and urbanization proceed; and also the federated groups grow, sometimes at uneven paces, their cultures mature, sometimes in divergent directions. To meet these changes, the terms of the federative pact must be altered, and this is done as smoothly as possible by administrative practice, by judicial decision, and by constitutional amendment, giving a little more regional autonomy here, a bit more centralization there, but at all times taking great care to preserve the delicate balance upon which the national consensus rests.

Such care must increase in direct proportion to the strength of the alternatives which present themselves to the federated groups. Thus, when a large cohesive minority believes it can transfer its allegiance to a neighbouring state, or make a go of total independence, it will be inclined to dissociate itself from a consensus the terms of which have been altered in its disfavour. On the other hand, such a minority may be tempted to use its bargaining strength to obtain advantages which are so costly to the majority as to reduce to naught the advantages to the latter of remaining federated. Thus, a critical point can be reached in either direction beyond which separatism takes place, or a civil war is fought.

When such a critical point has been reached or is in sight, no amount, however great, of nationalism can save the federation. Any expenditure of emotional appeal (flags, professions of faith, calls to dignity, expressions of brotherly love) at the national level will only serve to justify similar appeals at the regional level, where they are just as likely to be effective. Thus the great moment of truth arrives when it is realized that *in the last resort* the mainspring of federalism cannot be emotion but must be reason.

To be sure, federalism found its greatest development in the time of the nation-states, founded on the principle of self-determination, and cemented together by the emotion of nationalism. Federal states have themselves made use of this nationalism over periods long enough to make its inner contradictions go unnoticed. Thus, in a neighbouring country, Manifest Destiny, the Monroe Doctrine, the Hun, the Red Scourge, the Yellow Peril, and Senator McCarthy have all provided glue for the American Way of Life; but it is apparent that the Cuban "menace" has not been able to prevent the American Negro from obtaining a renegotiation of the terms of the American national consensus. The Black Muslims were the answer to the argument of the Cuban menace; the only answer to both is the voice of reason.

It is now becoming obvious that federalism has all along been a product of reason in politics. It was born of a decision by pragmatic politicians to face facts as they are, particularly the fact of the hetero-geneity of the world's population. It is an attempt to find a rational compromise between the divergent interest-groups which history has thrown together; but it is a compromise based on the will of the people.

Looking at events in retrospect, it would seem that the French Revolution attempted to delineate national territories according to the will of the people, without reference to rationality; the Congress of Vienna claimed to draw state boundaries according to reason, without reference to the will of the people; and federalism arose as an empirical effort to base a country's frontiers on both reason and the will of the people.

I am not heralding the impending advent of reason as the prime mover in politics, for nationalism is too cheap and too powerful a tool to be soon discarded by politicians of all countries; the rising *bour-geoisies* in particular have too large a vested interest in nationalism to let it die out unattended.* Nor am I arguing that as important an area of human conduct as politics could or should be governed without any reference to human emotions. But I would like to see emotionalism channelled into a less sterile direction than nationalism. And I am saying that within sufficiently advanced federal countries, the auto-destructiveness of nationalism is bound to become more and more apparent, and reason may yet reveal itself even to ambitious politicians as the more assured road to success. This may also be the trend in unitary states, since they all have to deal with some kind of regionalism or other. Simultaneously in the world of international relations, it is becoming more obvious that the Austinian concept of sovereignty could only be thoroughly applied in a world crippled by the ideology of the nation-state and sustained by the heady stimulant of nationalism. In the world of today, when whole groups of so-called sovereign states are experimenting with rational forms of integration, the exercise of sovereignty will not only be divided within federal states; it will have to

---

* On the use of nationalism by the middle classes, see Cobban, *Dictatorship*, p. 140. And for a striking and original approach, see Albert Breton, "The Economics of Nationalism," *Journal of Political Economy*, August 1964.

be further divided between the states and the communities of states. If this tendency is accentuated the very idea of national sovereignty will recede and, with it, the need for an emotional justification such as nationalism. International law will no longer be explained away as so much "positive international morality," it will be recognized as true law, a "coercive order . . . for the promotion of peace."*

Thus there is some hope that in advanced societies, the glue of nationalism will become as obsolete as the divine right of kings; the title of the state to govern and the extent of its authority will be conditional upon rational justification; a people's consensus based on reason will supply the cohesive force that societies require; and politics both within and without the state will follow a much more functional approach to the problems of government. If politicians must bring emotions into the act, let them get emotional about functionalism!

The rise of reason in politics is an advance of law; for is not law an attempt to regulate the conduct of men in society rationally rather than emotionally? It appears then that a political order based on federalism is an order based on law. And there will flow more good than evil from the present tribulations of federalism if they serve to equip lawyers, social scientists, and politicians with the tools required to build societies of men ordered by reason.

Who knows? Humanity may yet be spared the ignominy of seeing its destinies guided by some new and broader emotion based, for example, on continentalism.

Canadian Federalism: The Past and the Present

Earlier in this paper, when discussing the concept of national consensus, I pointed out that it was not something to be forever taken for granted. In present-day Canada, an observation such as that need not proceed from very great insight. Still, I will start from there to examine some aspects of Canadian federalism.

---

* Hans Kelsen, *Law and Peace* (Cambridge, 1948), pp. 1 and 7.

Though, technically speaking, national self-determination only became a reality in Canada in 1931, it is no distortion of political reality to say that the Canadian nation dates from 1867, give or take a few years. The consensus of what is known today as the Canadian nation took shape in those years; and it is the will of that nation which is the foundation of the state that today exercises its jurisdiction over the whole of the Canadian territory.

Of course, the will of the Canadian nation was subjected to certain constraints, not least of which was the reality of the British Empire. But, except once again in a technical sense, this did not mean very much more than that Canada, like every other nation, was not born in a vacuum, but had to recognize the historical as well as all other data which surrounded its birth.

I suppose we can safely assume that the men who drew up the terms of the Canadian federal compromise had heard something of the ideology of nationalism which had been spreading revolutions for seventy-five years. It is likely too that they knew about the Civil War in the United States, the rebellions of 1837–8 in Canada, the Annexation Manifesto, and the unsatisfactory results of double majorities. Certainly they assessed the centrifugal forces that the constitution would have to overcome if the Canadian state was to be a durable one: first, the linguistic and other cultural differences between the two major founding groups, and, secondly, the attraction of regionalisms, which were not likely to decrease in a country the size of Canada.

Given these data, I am inclined to believe that the authors of the Canadian federation arrived at as wise a compromise and drew up as sensible a constitution as any group of men anywhere could have done. Reading that document today, one is struck by its absence of principles, ideals, or other frills; even the regional safeguards and minority guarantees are pragmatically presented, here and there, rather than proclaimed as a thrilling bill of rights. It has been said that the binding force of the United States of America was the idea of liberty, and certainly none of the relevant constitutional documents lets us forget it. By comparison, the Canadian nation seems founded on the common sense of empirical politicians who had wanted to establish some law and order over a disjointed half-continent. If reason be the governing virtue of federalism, it would seem that Canada got off to a good start.

Like everything else, the Canadian nation had to move with the times. Many of the necessary adjustments were guided by rational deliberation: such was the case, for instance, with most of our constitutional amendments, and with the general direction imparted to Canadian law by the Privy Council decisions. It has long been a custom in English Canada to denounce the Privy Council for its provincial bias; but it should perhaps be considered that if the law lords had not leaned in that direction, Quebec separatism might not be a threat today: it might be an accomplished fact. From the point of view of the damage done to Quebec's understanding of the original federal compromise, there were certainly some disappointing – even if legally sound – judgments (like the New Brunswick, Manitoba, and Ontario separate school cases) and some unwise amendments (like the B.N.A. No. 2 Act, 1949); but on balance, it would seem that constitutional amendment and judicial interpretation would not by themselves have permanently damaged the fabric of the Canadian consensus if they had not been compounded with a certain type of adjustment through administrative centralization.

Faced with provinces at very different stages of economic and political development, it was natural for the central government to assume as much power as it could to make the country as a whole a going concern. Whether this centralization was always necessary, or whether it was not sometimes the product of bureaucratic and political empire-builders acting beyond the call of duty,* are no doubt debatable questions, but they are irrelevant to the present inquiry. The point is that over the years the central administrative functions tended to develop rather more rapidly than the provincial ones; and if the national consensus was to be preserved some new factor would have to be thrown into the balance. This was done in three ways.

---

* As an example of unjustifiable centralization, J.R. Mallory mentions the federal government's policy concerning technical schools (Montreal *Star*, February 4, 1964).

First, a countervailing regionalism was allowed and even fostered in matters which were indifferent to Canada's economic growth. For instance, there was no federal action when Manitoba flouted the constitution and abolished the use of the French language in the legislature;* and there was no effective federal intervention** under paragraphs 3 and 4 of Section 93 (B.N.A. Act) or under paragraphs 2 and 3 of Section 22 (Manitoba Act) when New Brunswick, Ontario, and Manitoba legislated in a way which was offensive to the linguistic or religious aspirations of their French-speaking populations.

Second, a representative bureaucracy at the central level was developed in such a way as to make the regions feel that their interests were well represented in Ottawa. A great administrative machine was created, in which "the under-representation of Quebec can be considered an ethnic and educational factor rather than a regional one."† It was this efficient bureaucracy, by the way, which was unable to convert the machinery of government to the production of bilingual cheques and letterheads during the forty years it took to debate the subject in Parliament; then suddenly the reform took place in five minutes without help even from the cabinet. But such are the miracles of automation!

Third, tremendous reserves of nationalism were expended, in order to make everyone good, clean, unhyphenated Canadians. Riel was neatly hanged, as an example to all who would exploit petty regional differences. The Boer War was fought, as proof that Canadians could overlook their narrow provincialisms when the fate of the Empire was

---

* The French language was also abolished in the territories. See F.R. Scott, *Civil Liberties and Canadian Federalism* (Toronto, 1959), p. 32.

** The operative word here is "effective." It will be remembered that Bowell's government in Ottawa did try to remedy the situation, first by order-in-council – the dispositions of which Manitoba refused to obey – and then by a bill in the House of Commons; which was obstructed by Laurier's Liberals, who went on to win the 1896 election.

† John Porter, "Higher Public Servants and the Bureaucratic Elite in Canada," *Canadian Journal of Economics and Political Science*, Vol. XXIV (November 1958), p. 942.

at stake. Conscription was imposed in two world wars, to show that in the face of death all Canadians were on an equal footing. And lest nationalism be in danger of waning, during the intervals between the above events Union Jacks were waved, Royalty was shown around, and immigration laws were loaded in favour of the British Isles.

Need I point out that in those three new factors, French Canadians found little to reconcile themselves with centralization? First, regionalism as condoned by Ottawa meant that the French Canadians could feel at home in no province save Quebec. Second, representative bureaucracy for the central government meant that regional safeguards would be entrusted to a civil service somewhat dominated by white Anglo-Saxon Protestants. And third, nationalism as conceived in Ottawa was essentially predicated on the desirability of uniting the various parts of the nation around one language (English) and one flag (the Union Jack).

I readily admit that there are elements of oversimplification in the four preceding paragraphs. But I am prepared to defend quite strenuously the implications which are contained therein: that the rational compromise upon which the nation rested in 1867 was gradually replaced by an emotional sop; and that this sop calmly assumed away the existence of one-third of the nation. In other words, the French-Canadian denizens of a Quebec ghetto, stripped of power by centralization, were expected to recognize themselves in a national image which had hardly any French traits, and were asked to have the utmost confidence in a central state where French Canada's influence was mainly measured by its not inconsiderable nuisance value.

Under such circumstances, Canadian nationalism – even after it ceased looking towards the Empire, which took quite some time – could hardly provide the basis for a lasting consensus. So time and time again, counter-nationalist movements arose in Quebec which quite logically argued that if Canada was to be the nation-state of the English-speaking Canadians, Quebec should be the nation-state of the French Canadians. But these warning signals were never taken seriously; for they were hoisted in years when Quebec had nowhere to go, and it obviously could not form an independent state of its own. But a time was bound to come – "Je suis un chien qui ronge l'os" [I am a dog that gnaws the bone] – when French-Canadian national self-determination could no longer be laughed out of court; a time when the frightened Quebec and Ottawa governments (albeit in obvious contempt of their respective constitutional mandates) found sense in making "scientific" studies of separatism.*

In short, during several generations, the stability of the Canadian consensus was due to Quebec's inability to do anything about it. Ottawa took advantage of Quebec's backwardness to centralize; and because of its backwardness that province was unable to participate adequately in the benefits of centralization. The vicious circle could only be broken if Quebec managed to become a modern society. But how could this be done? The very ideology which was marshalled to preserve Quebec's integrity, French-Canadian nationalism, was setting up defence mechanisms the effect of which was to turn Quebec res-olutely inward and backwards. It befell the generation of French Canadians who came of age during the Second World War to break out of the dilemma; instead of bucking the rising tides of industrialization and modernization in a vain effort to preserve traditional values, they threw the flood-gates open to forces of change. And if ever proof be required that nationalism is a sterile force, let it be considered that fifteen years of systematic non-nationalism and sometimes ruthless anti-nationalism at a few key points of the society were enough to help Quebec to pass from a feudal into a modern era.

Technological factors could, practically alone, explain the sudden transformation of Quebec. But many agents from within were at work, eschewing nationalism and preparing their society to adapt itself to modern times. Typical amongst such agents were the three following. Laval's *Faculté des sciences sociales* began turning out graduates who were sufficiently well equipped to be respected members of the central representative bureaucracy. The *Confédération des travailleurs catholiques du Canada* came squarely to grips with economic reality and helped transform Quebec's working classes into active participants

---

* *La Presse*, May 12, 1964. Montreal *Gazette*, May 21, 1964.

in the process of industrialization. The little magazine *Cité libre* became a rallying point for progressive action and writing; moreover it understood that a modern Quebec would very soon call into question the imbalance towards which the original federal compromise had drifted, and it warned that English-Canadian nationalism was headed for a rude awakening; upholding provincial autonomy and proposing certain constitutional guarantees, it sought to re-establish the Canadian consensus on a rational basis.

The warnings went unheeded; Ottawa did not change.[*] But Quebec did: bossism collapsed, blind traditionalism crumbled, the Church was challenged, new forces were unleashed. When in Europe the dynasties and traditions had been toppled, the new societies quickly found a new cohesive agent in nationalism; and no sooner had privilege within the nation given way to internal equality than privilege *between* nations fell under attack; external equality was pursued by way of national self-determination. In Quebec today the same forces are at work: a new and modern society is being glued together by nationalism, it is discovering its potentialities as a nation, and is demanding equality with all other nations. This in turn is causing a backlash in other provinces, and Canada suddenly finds herself wondering whether she has a future. What is to be done?

If my premises are correct, nationalism cannot provide the answer. Even if massive investments in flags, dignity, protectionism, and Canadian content of television managed to hold the country together a few more years, separatism would remain a recurrent phenomenon, and very soon again new generations of Canadians and Quebeckers would be expected to pour their intellectual energies down the drain of emotionalism. If, for instance, it is going to remain *morally wrong* for Wall Street to assume control of Canada's economy, how will it become

---

[*] Who would have thought it possible, five years ago, that a prime minister of Canada, after giving into various provincial ultimata, would go on to say: "I believe that the provinces and their governments will play an increasingly important role in our national development. I for one welcome that as a healthy decentralization . . ." (Montreal *Star*, May 27, 1964.) Too much, too late. . . .

morally right for Bay Street to dominate Quebec's or – for that matter – Nova Scotia's?

It is possible that nationalism may still have a role to play in backward societies where the *status quo* is upheld by irrational and brutal forces; in such circumstances, *because there is no other way*, perhaps the nationalist passions will still be found useful to unleash revolutions, upset colonialism, and lay the foundations of welfare states; in such cases, the undesirable consequences will have to be accepted along with the good.

But in the advanced societies, where the interplay of social forces can be regulated by law, where the centres of political power can be made responsible to the people, where the economic victories are a function of education and automation, where cultural differentiation is submitted to ruthless competition, and where the road to progress lies in the direction of international integration, nationalism will have to be discarded as a rustic and clumsy tool.

No doubt, at the level of individual action, emotions and dreams will still play a part; even in modern man, superstition remains a powerful motivation. But magic, no less than totems and taboos, has long since ceased to play an important role in the normal governing of states. And likewise, nationalism will eventually have to be rejected as a principle of sound government. In the world of tomorrow, the expression "banana republic" will not refer to independent fruit-growing nations but to countries where formal independence has been given priority over the cybernetic revolution. In such a world, the state – if it is not to be outdistanced by its rivals – will need political instruments which are sharper, stronger, and more finely controlled than anything based on mere emotionalism: such tools will be made up of advanced technology and scientific investigation, as applied to the fields of law, economics, social psychology, international affairs, and other areas of human relations; in short, if not a pure product of reason, the political tools of the future will be designed and appraised by more rational standards than anything we are currently using in Canada today.

Let me hasten to add that I am not predicting which way Canada will turn. But because it seems obvious to me that nationalism – and of course I mean the Canadian as well as the Quebec variety – has put her on a collision course, I am suggesting that cold, unemotional rationality can still save the ship. Acton's prophecy, one hundred years ago, is now in danger of being fulfilled in Canada. "Its course," he stated of nationality, "will be marked with material as well as moral ruin, in order that a new invention may prevail over the works of God and the interests of mankind." This new invention may well be functionalism in politics; and perhaps it will prove to be inseparable from any workable concept of federalism.

This article was read to a joint meeting of the Canadian Political Science Association and the Association of Canadian Law Teachers in June 1964, and was subsequently published in P.A. Crepeau and C.B. Macpherson, eds., *The Future of Canadian Federalism* (Toronto: University of Toronto Press, 1965).

PART IV

On the Constitution

In 1964, Trudeau considered constitutional reform to be one of the least pressing kinds of reforms. But circumstances would later force him to take a much more active interest in it. Here are the most important articles and essays he devoted to constitutional reform, some of which led to the patriation of the Canadian Constitution in 1982.

Comparative Federalism

><

To misquote Clemenceau, I am sometimes tempted to say that politics is too serious to be left to the politicians.

After all, look at them, listen to them. The idea of the sovereign means nothing more to them than kings and queens. They take the Privy Council for a judicial body. They write "state" when they should be writing "State." They say that laws are adopted by the executive, or even by the government. They believe the police are part of the judiciary – or are quite simply "an instrument of society." They mix up administration and Parliament, which explains how they logically end up speaking of municipal laws. They sometimes think of themselves as democrats – which they use as an argument to claim that senior civil servants should be answerable to the people. Some of them ignore the fact that Quebec is a State, and has been one for a long time; as a result, they campaign long and hard for the State of Quebec, without imagining that the words they use evoke the legal status of Wyoming more than that of France or Cuba.

Three times out of four these politicians are lawyers; they are supposed to have studied constitutional law. So they are in fact more extraordinary than the Bourbons: not only have they learned nothing, but they have also forgotten everything they picked up in university.

"Forgotten everything" doesn't amount to much; in this respect students are all much the same: generally they consider constitutional law to be a subject of no importance, possibly because it won't earn them much money.

Even so, the miracle is that politicians like these manage not only to do politics, but also to make policy. By which I mean: governing the citizens. Laws are made, the wheels of the administration keep turning, judgements are handed down, taxes are collected, public works are executed, the guilty are punished; order prevails. How can it be explained that men of so little talent manage to do something requiring so much talent: running a country, a city, a society? Could it be that politics is neither an art nor a science but simply an instinct? Could it be that intelligence has nothing to do with it, and a knowledge of constitutional law even less? Men organize themselves a little like bees or ants; whatever one does and whatever happens, society will be governed, politics will happen. So, let's move on to more important things . . .

It is true that societies will end up being governed whatever happens. But the weakness of this reasoning is to consider it a matter of indifference whether societies are well or poorly governed, whereas in fact it makes a huge difference. In times past, the difference showed up slowly: consider that the gradual impoverishment of Spain took many centuries. But in the technological age, decades can make a huge difference: consider Israel and the Transjordan; or Ontario and Quebec . . .

Which brings me to my topic. Our politicians (which is to say, once again, our lawyers) urgently need to understand how the State of Canada actually works. And they should also urgently stop imagining that Canadian federalism is afflicted with unique and intractable problems; they should study how other countries find solutions to comparable problems. A book has recently come out that will help our politicians to do just that, as long as they are able to read English. It is *Comparative Federalism* by Professor Edward McWhinney, at Osgoode Hall Law School in Toronto.*

---

*   Edward McWhinney, *Comparative Federalism* (Toronto: University of Toronto Press, 1962).

Political science consists, above all, of constitutional law. No matter how indispensable the works of Canadian political scientists may be, they will never fill the void left by the intellectual laziness and mediocrity of lawyers. Fortunately, at distant intervals the honour of the legal profession is saved by an original thinker. Professor McWhinney is just such a thinker: and his method is admirable.

Comparative Federalism is no dry analysis of constitutional texts. Professor McWhinney is not interested in the way fundamental laws are written, but rather in the way they work and the way they are applied. In the first pages of the book (p. viii), the author raises the most serious objections to federal systems: he devotes three chapters (4, 5, 6) to studying the most serious problems a country with a federal Constitution has to resolve. Then, he offers with admirable clarity responses to these objections, solutions to these problems, drawing from constitutional practice in the United States, West Germany, and Canada.

Naturally, the special role played by the Supreme Court in each of these three countries is the focus of particular attention. Clearly, Canadians would learn a few lessons if they took the trouble to examine other situations. For example, the Supreme Court of Canada seems to be a court with too little familiarity with public law, and its members are recruited without having any real breadth of vision (pp. 26 and 27). Another example is that the sociological perspective that guided the Supreme Court of the United States in the question of integrating Blacks (p. 72) could be profitably examined by Canadian politicians who would like to know how to give Canada a truly bilingual character.

The author also underlines (p. 98) the tendency to burden the Supreme Court with political responsibilities which, according to the letter of the Constitution, are assumed by the executive (in the case of disallowance) or by the legislative branch (the role of the Senate).

This evolution is just one more reason why public-law specialists in Canada should give some serious thought to the problems raised by the way the Supreme Court is currently set up. Personally, I am increasingly coming to believe that Canadian federalism will reach full maturity only if we entrench in our Constitution a declaration of human rights and freedoms. Among other things, the existence of such a declaration would make it possible to restrict the actions of the Supreme Court to the area of public law. In this way, provinces could exercise their autonomy with all the more freedom, since this freedom would come within certain civilizing and democratic standards guaranteed by the declaration of rights and applied by the Supreme Court.

In other words, I think that jurists should borrow the idea of equalization from economists; because if it is important to guarantee minimum living standards to the citizens of all provinces, shouldn't there also be a way of ensuring the enjoyment of minimum rights, for example, in the area of freedom of association, of separate schools, and so forth?

No doubt, these suggestions take us far from *Comparative Federalism*. But unless I am mistaken, they are inspired by the philosophy of federalism which Professor McWhinney articulates so well (see the first two chapters of the book). As for the way this philosophy is applied, Professor McWhinney quotes the example of a judgement by the Supreme Court of the United States, which seems to be "the most important contemporary statement as to the affirmative duties of cooperation and of mutual self-restraint existing among members of the ... federal system; for it establishes what amounts, almost, to a code of intergovernmental good faith or good manners, to be enforced if necessary by the courts as norms of federal constitutional law" (p. 83). Another similar example is drawn from German practice (p. 86).

As a matter of fact, the whole book is worthwhile. Does it have any weaknesses? None come to mind. It is important to understand at the outset that, when Professor McWhinney speaks of the nation, he means the Canadian nation (pp. 7, 13, 14, 50, and so on), but by nationalism he means the English-Canadian variety (p. 21). French-Canadian nationalism, meanwhile, is a local value (pp. 19, 65), a special position (p. 13). But none of that really matters, and if I pushed my criticism too far, I would prove only that I haven't understood much of Professor McWhinney's lessons. Because what he is teaching above all is that "the key to the working practice of federal government in a plural society is, in fact, the spirit of moderation" (p. 99). From this point of view,

English-speaking Canadians also have a lot to learn from Professor McWhinney's book.

Reading *Comparative Federalism* should be a requirement for anyone running as a candidate in Canadian elections. Everyone discussing Canada's constitutional future should read it. The quality of discussions would be vastly improved as a result.

Revue du notariat 65/9
(April 1963)
Translation by George Tombs

We Need a Bill of Rights (1)

>‹

Of all the institutional changes which I believe to be desirable in Canada, I would rank constitutional reform among the least pressing; and consequently I tend to consider much of the present discussion of the BNA Act as processes of alienation or politics of diversion. Of course, if I had the power to alter the constitution tomorrow, I dare say I could improve upon that document considerably. But such also is the belief of every other citizen of this country, each one holding *his own* project to be the best. And that is the point: we could waste months and years in vainly seeking compromise and agreement, as indeed happened when Mr. St. Laurent and then Mr. Diefenbaker convened their federal–provincial conferences on constitutional amendment. The present fad for constitutional change is keeping most politicians and opinion-makers busy, especially those whose knowledge of the constitution borders closest on ignorance. In the meantime, remarkably little is done to remedy the real disorders which plague the Canadian people, even though most of them could be righted under the present constitution.

Unless Canadians wish to embark upon the perilous course of making a new constitution every few years, they should not at this time undertake to rewrite the BNA Act. New *rapports de force* are perhaps beginning to emerge between the central and the regional governments in Canada, and they must be given time to work themselves out before any attempt is made to translate them into the basic law of the country.

On the one hand, Quebec, having only just now discovered the interventionist theory of the state, is naturally still very poorly equipped in men and in ideas equal to the tasks at hand; consequently the current clamor for vastly enlarged provincial powers can only appear as a sorry excuse for the inefficient exercise of the present powers.

On the other hand, the Ottawa government is showing such a lack of leadership in national affairs that it can hardly be trusted with working out a new philosophy of federalism; before sitting down to rewrite the constitution, one must have some idea of what kind of society it is intended to govern. The manipulation of legal symbols and of global ideas by the central government has all the appearances of a device to disguise the absence of a true polity for Canada. One well remembers how the constitutional ploy served in the past to impede real reform. For instance, the fight for an entrenched bill of rights in Canada was gaining ground all during the Forties. Implementation of the bill, which would have entailed amendment by traditional constitutional means, was delayed until the much more complicated question of amending the constitution in Canada was solved. (Mr. St. Laurent, *Hansard*, May 21, 1951.) That meant nothing was accomplished on either score.

I believe that the whole procedure should be reversed. First, a clearer perception of goals by the central and regional governments. Secondly, an attempt to fulfill those goals on an *ad hoc* basis, under the present distribution of powers. Only thirdly, consideration of individual constitutional amendments.

The only important instance where the third stage appears to have been reached by the Canadians seems to me to be precisely in the area of a bill of rights. Since 1946, four provinces and the central government have given themselves statutory bills of rights. Numerous parliamentary committees have enquired into the matter. Many public bodies, including the Canadian Bar, have reported on the subject. Much writing has been published by historians and other concerned persons.

And, what is more important in the present context, a constitutionally entrenched bill of rights seems to be the best tool for breaking the ever-recurring deadlock between Quebec and the rest of Canada. If certain language and educational rights were written into the constitution, along with other basic liberties, in such a way that *no* government – federal or provincial – could legislate against them, French Canadians would cease to feel confined to their Quebec ghetto, and the Spirit of Separatism would be laid forever.

At a time when many Canadians are toying with the idea of abolishing "the forms to which they are accustomed," they might be well advised to consider first whether their evils are insufferable, and second whether they can be redressed under the present constitution. Amateur revolutionaries could do worse than take some advice from the professionals who declared Independence on July 4, 1776:

"Prudence, indeed, will dictate, that governments long established should not be changed for light and transient causes."

Maclean's (February 8, 1964)

We Need a Bill of Rights (2)

⊁⊰

I have been asked what need there is in Canada for a bill of rights. My answer is that our need may not be so great as is that of persons in some other countries. But my answer as well is that we should not overemphasize our righteousness. We are not in this country innocent of book-burning or -banning legislation, or deprivations by law of previously guaranteed minority-language rights, of legal expropriation which at times appears to be more akin to confiscation, of persons arrested in the night and held incommunicado for days. We have no reason to be complacent. How many Canadians know that Canadian law permits evidence to be introduced by the police in criminal trials no matter how illegally that evidence may have been obtained? Apart from confessions, for which there are elaborate rules to ensure that they are voluntary, incriminating evidence is admissible in our courts no matter how obtained. It may have been gained by fraud; the law-enforcement agencies may have stolen it; they may have obtained it without a search warrant, or by means of breaking-and-entering private premises. To the great credit of the police forces of this country, these tactics are seldom employed. But do we wish to live in a country where they may be employed? And where, on occasion, they are employed? Where one standard of conduct is expected of citizens and another permitted of government agencies?

I do not, and it is my guess that the great number of Canadians do not.

Constitutional Conference,
Ottawa, February 5–7, 1968

Quebec and the Constitutional Problem[*]

✦

Essentially, a constitution is designed to last a long time. Legal author-ity derives entirely from it; and if it is binding only for a short period it is not binding at all. A citizen – to say nothing of a power group – will not feel obliged to respect laws or governments he considers unfavourable to him if he thinks that they can easily be replaced: if the rules of the constitutional game are to be changed in any case, why not right now? A country where this mentality is prevalent oscillates between revolution and dictatorship. France, once it had started down the slippery path, gave itself eighteen constitutions in 180 years.

I do not believe that Quebec is powerful enough to afford such waste. Our province must have a long period of constitutional stability if it is to establish a sound basis for the great economic, social, and cultural development it wishes to achieve. Furthermore, the rest of the country

---

[*] This essay was written during February, March, and April of 1965, while I was at the Institut de recherche en droit public at the University of Montreal. It was meant as a working document for some private organizations that wanted to submit a brief to the Constitution Committee of the Quebec Legislative Assembly. As this essay has already been widely circulated, I have decided to publish it under my name. It goes without saying that my opinions are not necessarily those of the Institut de recherche en droit public or the private organizations I have mentioned above.

would refuse to negotiate seriously with us if it had reason to suspect that any constitutional concession granted to Quebec would merely lead to new and greater demands. This means that the "revision of the Canadian constitution" mentioned in the mandate of the Legislative Assembly's Constitution Committee must be interpreted as taking place over several generations.

All the evidence seems to indicate that at the moment Quebec is not ready to say precisely what constitutional system of government it would like to have during the next half-century. When it comes to constitutional matters, political thinking in Quebec tends on the whole to be vague and self-contradictory. For example, our public opinion has long maintained that provincial unanimity should be required for any constitutional amendment; now that the idea of unanimity is embodied in the Fulton–Favreau formula,* however, it is rejected as an obstacle to Quebec's "special status"! One need only glance at the briefs presented to the Constitution Committee to realize just how various and fluctuating our public opinion can be. It is now fashionable to be for change – but for *what* change, exactly? That, alas, is where there is a complete lack of consensus.

To my mind, this only goes to prove that we must not meddle with the constitution just yet. The real danger is that all these constitutional debates will provide an escape valve for our energies, and useful diversionary tactics for those who fear the profound social reforms advocated by the progressive element in our province. Worse still, if we did succeed at this stage in imposing a new constitutional framework, we would merely fetter this progressive element instead of giving it greater freedom of action.

If it is indeed true that Quebec is on the march, let us first find out just where it wishes to go, and where it in fact *can* go. There will still be

---

* The Fulton–Favreau formula, named after two successive federal ministers of justice, provided for the amendment of the Canadian Constitution by Canadian political authorities. It was put forward in 1964 by the government of Canada. The Quebec government of Jean Lesage was at first favourable to that initiative but later reversed itself and finally rejected the formula – Ed.

ample time for lawyers to incorporate both what is desirable and what is feasible into the law.

All these reasons, taken together, lead me to exercise great restraint in suggesting constitutional reforms; and they account for the fact that in recent years I have appeared as a supporter of the constitutional *status quo*. As I have demonstrated in previous sections [of this document], the constitution has very little to do with the state of economic, technical, and demographic inferiority in which the French Canadians of Quebec find themselves today. I am not in a frantic hurry to change the constitution, simply because I *am* in a frantic hurry to change reality. And I refuse to give the ruling classes the chance of postponing the solving of *real* problems until after the constitution has been revised. We have seen only too often how, in the past, discussions centering on ideas such as the form of the state, nationhood, provincial autonomy, and independence have served to conceal the impotence of the ruling classes when faced with the profound transformation of our society by the industrial revolution. All I ask of our present ruling classes is that they stop being so preoccupied with the hypothetical powers an independent Quebec might have, and start using the powers the real Quebec does have a bit more often and a bit more wisely.

In the economic field, it is infinitely less important to dream up new constitutional phrasing that would allow Quebec to recoup a larger percentage of federal taxes (this is already happening under our present constitution) than it is to move our province to the forefront of industrial progress (the result of which would be to increase substantially the very basis of provincial taxation).

Similarly, in the social and cultural fields, it is infinitely less important for Quebec to modify the constitution so as to acquire an international judicial identity, than to invest immense energy in agrarian reform and better urban planning, and concentrate all the strength it can muster upon educational reforms.

It should not be concluded from what I am saying that I am less aware than others of imperfections in the B.N.A. Act and the rules of federalism embodied in it. There is nothing easier than proposing constitutional reforms, and I could very easily outline several points that would some day have to be taken into account by a new constitution. For example:

a) A Bill of Rights could be incorporated into the constitution, to limit the powers that legal authorities have over human rights in Canada. In addition to protecting traditional political and social rights, such a bill would specifically put the French and English languages on an equal basis before the law.

b) The protection of basic rights having thus been ensured, there would be no danger in reducing the central government's predominance in certain areas (for example, by abolishing the right of reservation and disallowance); at the same time, this would have the advantage of getting rid of some of the constitution's imperial phraseology.

c) The organic law relating to the central government could be revised in order to give it a more authentically federal character. In particular, conflicts in jurisdiction between federal and provincial levels could be judged by an independent body deriving its authority directly from the constitution. The Senate could also be reformed so that it represented the provinces more directly. Far from diminishing the authority of Parliament, such a measure would increase provincial confidence in the legislation that emanates from Ottawa (for example, in matters of tariffs or macro-economic policy).

These points are certainly important, and no doubt Canadians will have to face them some day – perhaps following the repatriation of the constitution. But I refuse to propose them formally at the moment, for the reasons I have already given, which I would like to summarize briefly once again:

Natural forces are presently favouring provincial autonomy. It is the centralizers who should be pressing for constitutional changes. If Quebec negotiators were cannier, they would affect supreme indifference, saying blandly: "Oh, the constitution isn't all that bad after all. . . . We are so busy trying to change the social and economic *status quo* that we simply haven't time for constitutional reforms just at the moment. . . . But if you are really keen about it, of course we are prepared to discuss revisions with you – say, in a few months' time, or perhaps next year?"

Meanwhile, decentralization would have continued apace, the strong provinces would have established competent administrations which would be difficult to dislodge, and Quebec would have found several allies in its struggle for an improved federal system. Better still, our progress in the province would have raised the prestige of Canada's entire French-speaking population.

And so when constitutional negotiations finally began – at the instigation of other provinces! – Quebec could concentrate all its bargaining power on the most crucial point, which I have called in section V [of this paper] "a very small constitutional modification." In conclusion I should like to make a few comments on this modification.

It is obvious that most of Canada's constitutional crises, like the present one, arise from ethnic problems, and more precisely from the question of the rights pertaining to the French language. As I have said earlier (in section III), the French language will be able to express progressive values only if North Americans who speak it are themselves in the forefront of progress, that is to say if they compete on an equal basis with English-speaking Canadians.

But the competition *must* be on an equal basis. Otherwise, the French population is in danger of becoming paralysed by an excess of defensive mechanisms. We shall develop the mentality of a beleaguered people, withdrawing into Quebec the better to sustain the siege. In other words, French Canadians may be forced by *English*-Canadian nationalism to push Quebec nearer to a national state and sooner or later to independence.

On this matter as on many others, the Fathers of Confederation showed great wisdom. Although they may have suspected that French Canadians would *in fact* always remain a linguistic minority, it seems that they wished to avoid making them feel a minority as far as *rights* were concerned. To put it in another way, while recognizing that French

Canadians might always feel more at home in Quebec, they attempted to prevent the law from fostering in them a sense of inferiority or from giving them any excuse to feel like aliens in other parts of Canada.

According to Section 92 of the constitution, education became the responsibility of the provinces, as French Canadians had wished. The first paragraph, however, made it unconstitutional for provinces to interfere with confessional schools; and it is mainly through these, as is well known, that French Canadians develop and transmit their particular cultural values. Moreover, the last two paragraphs gave the central government power to rectify infringements upon "any right or privilege," including linguistic rights, of the (religious) group that includes almost all French Canadians.

Section 133 gave the French language official status for the exercise of the following political rights:

a) At the federal level, the two languages were placed on an absolutely equal basis for all legislative as well as judicial functions. There was no mention of executive functions, but very likely this was due partly to the fact that in 1867 there was a much smaller number of people involved in the military and civil services, and partly to the fact that the cabinet was not defined by the constitution, but by custom; and in practice custom has gradually ensured that the number of French Canadians in the cabinet is more or less proportionate to their population. In so far as federal political institutions are concerned, then, the intention seems to have been to place English and French on an equal basis throughout Canada, and consequently to give the central government a genuinely bilingual character.

b) In so far as provincial political institutions are concerned, the French language obtained equal rights only in those provinces where there was a considerable number of French Canadians. In practice, this meant Quebec; but the future was left open – for, according to Section 92, paragraph 1, each province could give the French language a position corresponding to the size of the French-Canadian population in that province. The spirit in which this was intended is evident if one considers that three years later, when the central government created Manitoba, whose population contained a large percentage of French-speaking people, French was placed on a par with English in this province.

In substance, then, the Canadian constitution created a country where French Canadians could compete on an equal basis with English Canadians; both groups were invited to consider the whole of Canada their country and field of endeavour.

Unfortunately, for reasons that I cannot go into here, but that on the whole reflect less credit on English than on French Canadians, the rules of the "constitutional game" were not always upheld. In the matter of education, as well as political rights, the safeguards so dear to French Canadians were nearly always disregarded throughout the country, so that they came to believe themselves secure only in Quebec.

Worse still, in those areas not specifically covered by the constitution, the English-speaking majority used its size and wealth to impose a set of social rules humiliating to French Canadians. In the federal civil service, for example, and even more so in the Canadian armed forces, a French Canadian started off with an enormous handicap – if indeed he managed to start at all. This was true also in finance, business, and at all levels of industry. And that is how English became the working language, even in Quebec, and at all levels from foreman to bank president.

These social "rules of the game" do not lie within the mandate of the Constitution Committee. But a complete transformation of these rules is most urgently needed. And I have already described, especially in section IV, the conditions that are necessary if French Canadians are to revise these rules so that they operate in their favour.

The Constitution Committee, however, must propose amendments to the constitutional rules. The constitution must be so worded that any

French-speaking community, anywhere in Canada, can fully enjoy its linguistic rights. In practice, this means that for the purpose of education, wherever there is a sufficient number of French-speaking people to form a school (or a university), these people must have the same rights as English Canadians in the matter of taxes, subsidies, and legislation on education. Of course, the concepts "sufficient number" and "equal rights" will often have to be defined judicially or administratively; but both judges and administrators have as a guide the fact that these concepts have been applied for the past hundred years in remote areas of Quebec wherever there lived a "sufficient number" of English-speaking Canadians.

(a) At the federal level, the two languages must have absolute equality. With regard to legislative and judicial functions, this is already theoretically the case, according to Section 133 of the constitution; but the theory must be completely incorporated into actual practice so that, for example, any law or ruling is invalid if the English and French texts are not published side by side. Like the United States, we must move beyond "separate but equal" to "complete integration."

With regard to the executive functions, innovation is clearly required. Of course, it would be difficult to test the bilingualism of ministers of the Crown, and no doubt the whole thing will rest upon which men the voters decide to elect. (But it might also be decided by the fact that unilingual ministers would become frustrated when decisions were sometimes taken in French, and sometimes in English within the cabinet.) Everywhere else, and notably in the civil service and the armed forces, the two languages must be on a basis of absolute equality. This concept of equality must also be put into effect by management and by the courts. A simple, fair way of doing this might be to institute reciprocal rules: for example, if an infantry corporal or a minor Post Office official is exempted from knowing French because his functions bring him into contact with only a small percentage of French-speaking people, the same rule should apply to English when English-speaking people constitute the same small percentage. Or, to take another example, if a knowledge of English is required in the higher echelons of the civil service, then the same should be true of French. It is obvious that if such rules were applied overnight, they would result in a great many injustices and might indeed bring the state machinery grinding to a halt. But the introduction of such reforms must nevertheless be carried out according to a fixed schedule set by law (we could take the example of the Supreme Court of the United States, which, in matters of racial integration, bases its decisions on the spirit, the general tendency, and to some extent the chronological intentions of the legislation brought before it).

(b) At the provincial level, similar reciprocal rules must be applied. In principle, the language of the majority will be the only official one. However, when a province contains a French or English minority larger than, say, 15 per cent, or half a million inhabitants, legislative and judicial functions must be exercised in such a way that the two languages are given absolute equality. It is very doubtful whether the same rule could be applied to the executive function; regardless of the size of its minorities, a province will therefore be able to remain unilingual on this point, provided of course that any citizen has the right to an English–French interpreter in his dealings with officials. (In practice, this could lead to the establishment of a bilingual civil service in those provinces where there was a sufficiently large and concentrated French or English minority.)

Such reforms must certainly be incorporated into constitutional law. It would not be very realistic to rely upon goodwill or purely political action. For example, in a province containing a greater number of Canadians of Ukrainian origin than of French origin, it would be rash to think that an elected provincial legislature would risk giving French schools privileges that Ukrainian schools did not have. Nor is it wise to rely entirely upon federal intervention: the ill-fated "remedial legislation" of 1896, relating to Manitoba schools, taught us to be cautious on this score.

The reforms I am proposing must therefore be written into the constitution itself, and must be irrevocably binding upon both the federal and provincial governments. As I suggested earlier, the guarantees contained in Sections 93 and 133 of the constitution must be extended and incorporated into a clear, imperative text which could be worded more or less along these lines: "Any law passed by the Parliament of Canada and relating to its executive, legislative, and judicial functions, as well as any law on matters of education passed by a provincial Legislature, or any constitutional text, will be invalid if it does not place the English and French languages on a basis of absolute judicial equality." And also: "In any province where there is a French or English minority exceeding 15 per cent or one-half million inhabitants, no law relating to legislative or judicial functions will be valid if it does not place the English and French languages on a basis of absolute judicial equality; however, a number will not be considered to exceed 15 per cent or one-half million inhabitants, unless it has been so established at two successive decennial censuses." And lastly: "It will be the right of every citizen to have an English–French interpreter in his dealings with any level of authority either in the central or the provincial governments."

Those are more or less the comments I wished to make about the constitution. The reforms I am proposing may seem quite modest in comparison with the vast upheaval favoured by so many Quebeckers these days; but this is because I want to keep to what I consider to be the absolute essential. This essential, however modest, implies an immense transformation of attitudes and of what I have called the social rules of the game. If this is achieved, sterile chauvinism will disappear from our Canadian way of life, and other useful constitutional reforms will follow suit without too much difficulty. If, on the other hand, the essential is not achieved, there is really no point in carrying the discussion any further; for this will mean that Canada will continue to be swept periodically by the storms of ethnic dispute, and will gradually become a spiritually sterile land, from which both peace and greatness have been banished.

John T. Saywell, ed., *Federalism and the French Canadians* (Toronto: Macmillan, 1968) Translated by Joanne L'Heureux

The Meech Lake Accord (1)

><-

We have in our country the patriotism of Ontarians, the patriotism of Quebecers and the patriotism of westerners: but there is no Canadian patriotism, and there will not be a Canadian nation as long as we do not have a Canadian patriotism.

HENRI BOURASSA

The real question to be asked is whether the French Canadians living in Quebec need a provincial government with more powers than the other provinces.

I believe it is insulting to us to claim that we do. The new generation of business executives, scientists, writers, film-makers and artists of every description has no use for the siege mentality in which the elites of bygone days used to cower. The members of this new generation know that the true opportunities of the future extend beyond the boundaries of Quebec, indeed beyond the boundaries of Canada itself. They don't suffer from any inferiority complex, and they say good riddance to the times when we didn't dare to measure ourselves against "others" without fear and trembling. In short, they need no crutches.

Quite the contrary, they know that Quebecers are capable of playing a leading role within Canada and that – if we wish it – the entire country can provide us with a powerful springboard. In this, today's leaders have finally caught up to the rest of the population, which never paid much heed to inward-looking nationalism – that escape from reality in which only the privileged could afford to indulge.

Unfortunately, the politicians are the exception to the rule. And yet one would have thought that those who want to engage in politics in our province would have learned at least one lesson from the history of the last 100 years: Quebecers like strong governments, in Quebec and in Ottawa. And our most recent history seems to establish beyond question that if Quebecers feel well represented in Ottawa, they have only mistrust for special status, sovereignty-association and other forms of separatism. They know instinctively that they cannot hope to wield more power within their province, without agreeing to wield less in our nation as a whole.

How, then, could 10 provincial premiers and a federal prime minister agree to designate Quebec as a "distinct society"?

It's because they all, each in his own way, saw in it some political advantage to themselves:

1: Those who have never wanted a bilingual Canada – Quebec separatists and western separatists – get their wish right in the first paragraphs of the accord, with recognition of "the existence of French-speaking Canada . . . and English-speaking Canada."

Those Canadians who fought for a single Canada, bilingual and multicultural, can say goodbye to their dream: We are henceforth to have two Canadas, each defined in terms of its language. And because the Meech Lake accord states in the same breath that "Quebec constitutes, within Canada, a distinct society" and that "the role of the legislature and government to preserve and promote [this] distinct identity . . . is affirmed," it is easy to predict what future awaits anglophones living in Quebec and what treatment will continue to be accorded to francophones living in provinces where they are fewer in number than Canadians of Ukrainian or German origin.

Indeed, the text of the accord spells it out: In the other provinces, where bilingualism still has an enormously long way to go, the only requirement is to "protect" the status quo, while Quebec is to "promote" the distinct character of Quebec society.

In other words, the government of Quebec must take measures and the legislature must pass laws aimed at promoting the uniqueness of Quebec. And the text of the accord specifies at least one aspect of this uniqueness. "French-speaking Canada" is "centred" in that province.

Thus Quebec acquires a new constitutional jurisdiction that the rest of Canada does not have: promoting the concentration of French in Quebec. It is easy to see the consequences for French and English minorities in the country, as well as for foreign policy, for education, for the economy, for social legislation, and so on.

2: Those who never wanted a Charter of Rights entrenched in the Constitution can also claim victory. Because "the Constitution of Canada shall be interpreted in a manner consistent with . . . [Quebec's] role to preserve and promote the distinct identity" of Quebec society, it follows that the courts will have to interpret the Charter in a way that does not interfere with Quebec's "distinct society" as defined by Quebec laws.

For those Canadians who dreamed of the Charter as a new beginning for Canada, where everyone would be on an equal footing and where citizenship would finally be founded on a set of commonly shared values, there is to be nothing left but tears.

3: Those who want to prevent the Canadian nation from being built on such a community of values are not content merely to weaken the Charter: They are getting a constitutionalized – that is, irreversible – agreement "which will commit Canada to withdrawing from all services . . . regarding the reception and the integration (including linguistic and cultural integration)" of immigrants. We can guess what ideas of Canada will be conveyed to immigrants in the various provinces, with Canada undertaking to foot the bill for its own balkanization, "such withdrawal to be accompanied by fair compensation."

What's more, this principle of withdrawal accompanied by "fair compensation" is to be applied to all "new shared-cost programs." That will enable the provinces to finish off the balkanization of languages and cultures with the balkanization of social services. After all, what provincial politician will not insist on distributing in his own way (what remains, really, of "national objectives"?) and to the advantage of his constituents, the money he'll be getting painlessly from the federal treasury?

4: For those who – despite all the Canadian government's largesse with power and with funds – might still have been hesitant to sign the Meech Lake accord, the Prime Minister had two more surprises up his sleeve. From now on, the Canadian government won't be able to appoint anyone to the Supreme Court and the Senate except people designated by the provinces! And from now on, any province that doesn't like an important constitutional amendment will have the power to either block the passage of that amendment or to opt out of it, with "reasonable compensation" as a reward!

This second surprise gives each of the provinces a constitutional veto. And the first surprise gives them an absolute right of veto over Parliament, since the Senate will eventually be composed entirely of persons who owe their appointments to the provinces.

It also transfers supreme judicial power to the provinces, since Canada's highest court will eventually be composed entirely of persons put forward by the provinces.

What a magician this Mr. [Brian] Mulroney is, and what a sly fox! Having forced Mr. Bourassa [Quebec premier Robert Bourassa] to take up his responsibilities on the world stage, having obliged him to sit alongside the Prime Minister of Canada at summit conferences where francophone heads of state and heads of government discuss international economics and politics, he also succeeds in obliging him to pass laws promoting the "distinct character" of Quebec.

Likewise having enjoined Mr. Peckford [Newfoundland premier Brian Peckford] to preside over the management of Canadian seabeds, having compelled Mr. Getty [Alberta premier Don Getty] to accept the dismantling of Canadian energy policy, having convinced Mr. Peterson [Ontario premier David Peterson] to take up his responsibilities in the negotiation of an international free trade treaty, having promised jurisdiction over fisheries to the East and reform of the Senate to the West, Mr. Mulroney also succeeds in imposing on all these fine folks the heavy burden of choosing senators and Supreme Court justices! And all this without even having to take on the slightest extra task for the Canadian government, be it national regulation of securities markets, be it the power to strengthen the Canadian common market, be it even the repeal of the overriding ("notwithstanding") clause of the Charter.

In a single master stroke, this clever negotiator has thus managed to approve the call for Special Status (Jean Lesage and Claude Ryan), the call for Two Nations (Robert Stanfield), the call for a Canadian Board of Directors made up of 11 first ministers (Allan Blakeney and Marcel Faribeault), and the call for a Community of Communities (Joe Clark).

He has not quite succeeded in achieving sovereignty-association, but he has put Canada on the fast track for getting there. It doesn't take a great thinker to predict that the political dynamic will draw the best people to the provincial capitals, where the real power will reside, while the federal capital will become a backwater for political and bureaucratic rejects.

What a dark day for Canada was this April 30, 1987! In addition to surrendering to the provinces important parts of its jurisdiction (the spending power, immigration), in addition to weakening the Charter of Rights, the Canadian state made subordinate to the provinces its legislative power (Senate) and its judicial power (Supreme Court); it did this without hope of ever getting any of it back (a constitutional veto granted to each province). It even committed itself to a constitutional "second round" at which the demands of the provinces will dominate the agenda.

All this was done under the pretext of "permitting Quebec to fully participate in Canada's constitutional evolution." As if Quebec had not, right from the beginning, fully participated in Canada's constitutional evolution!

More than a half-dozen times since 1927, Quebec and the other provinces tried together with the Canadian government to "repatriate" our Constitution and to agree on an amending formula.

"Constitutional evolution" presupposed precisely that Canada would have its Constitution and would be able to amend it. Almost invariably, it was the Quebec provincial government that blocked the process. Thus, in 1965, Mr. Lesage and his minister at the time, Mr. René Lévesque, withdrew their support from the Fulton–Favreau formula (a plan to amend the British North America Act) after they had accepted

and defended it. And Mr. Bourassa, who in Victoria in 1971 had proposed a formula which gave Quebec a right of absolute veto over all
constitutional amendments, withdrew his own endorsement 10 days
after the conference. In both cases, the reason for backing off was the
same: Quebec would "permit" Canada to Canadianize the colonial document we had instead of a Constitution, only if the rest of Canada
granted Quebec a certain "special status."

The result was that 10 years later, when the Canadian government
tried once again to restart the process of constitutional evolution, it
faced the roadblock of 10 provinces which all wanted their own "special
status"; inevitably, they had enrolled in the school of blackmail of
which Quebec was the founder and top-ranking graduate.

The rest of the story is well known. The Canadian government
declared that it would bypass the provinces and present its constitutional
resolution in London. The Supreme Court acknowledged that this would
be legal but that it wouldn't be nice. The Canadian government made an
effort at niceness that won the support of nine provinces out of 10. Mr.
Lévesque, knowing that a constitutional deal would interfere with the
progress of separatism, played for broke, refused to negotiate and turned
again to the Supreme Court to block "the process of constitutional evolution." He lost his gamble. The court declared not only that Quebec had no
right of veto (Mr. Bourassa had in any event rejected it in Victoria, and
Mr. Lévesque had lost it somewhere in the west of the country), but also
that Quebec was fully a party to "Canada's constitutional evolution."

A gamble lost, a gamble won – big deal! Quebec public opinion,
with its usual maturity, applauded the players and then, yawning,
turned to other matters.

But not the nationalists! Imagine: They had tried to blackmail once
again, but Canada had refused to pay. It was more than a lost gamble, it
was "an attack in force" (Law professor Léon Dion and many others), it
was "an affront to Quebec" (Paul-André Comeau, assistant editor of *Le
Devoir*). Because in addition to being perpetual losers, the nationalists
are sore losers. For example, they didn't lose the 1980 referendum: The
people made a mistake, or were fooled by the federal government.
Likewise, after Robert Bourassa and René Lévesque had foolishly passed

up a right of veto for Quebec, it was necessary to somehow blame it on the federal government: attack in force, affront!

The provincialist politicians, whether they sit in Ottawa or in Quebec, are also perpetual losers; they don't have the stature or the vision to dominate the Canadian stage, so they need a Quebec ghetto as their lair. If they didn't have the sacred rights of French Canadians to defend against the rest of the world, if we could count on the Charter and the courts for that, they would lose their reason for being. That is why they are once again making common cause with the nationalists to demand special status for Quebec.

That bunch of snivellers should simply have been sent packing and been told to stop having tantrums like spoiled adolescents. But our current political leaders lack courage. By rushing to the rescue of the unhappy losers, they hope to gain votes in Quebec; in reality, they are only flaunting their political stupidity and their ignorance of the demographic data regarding nationalism.

It would be difficult to imagine a more total bungle.

Mr. Bourassa, who had been elected to improve the economic and political climate in the province, chose to open combat on the one battlefield where the Péquistes have the advantage: that of the nationalist bidding war. Instead of turning the page on Mr. Lévesque's misadventures, he wanted to make them his own. Instead of explaining to people that, thanks to the ineptitude of the Péquistes we were fully bound by the Constitution of 1982, Mr. Bourassa preferred to espouse the cause of the "moderate" nationalists.

A lot of good it does him now! The Péquistes will never stop demonstrating that the Meech Lake accord enshrines the betrayal of Quebec's interests. And a person as well-informed as [newspaper columnist] Lysiane Gagnon was able to twit Mr. Bourassa thus: "Quebec didn't achieve even a shadow of special status . . . the other provinces fought tooth and nail for the sacrosanct principle of equality. And they too will have everything Quebec asked for!" (*La Presse*, May 2, 1987). Does not the very nature of immaturity require that "the others" not get the same "trinkets" as we?

The possibility exists, moreover, that in the end Mr. Bourassa, true to form, will wind up repudiating the Meech Lake accord, because Quebec will still not have gotten enough. And that would inevitably clear the way for the real saviors: the separatists.

As for Mulroney, he had inherited a winning hand.

During the earlier attempts to Canadianize the Constitution, prime ministers Mackenzie King, St. Laurent, Diefenbaker, Pearson and Trudeau had acted as if it couldn't be done without the unanimous consent of the provinces. That gave the provinces a considerable advantage in the negotiations and accounted for the concessions that the Canadian prime ministers had to contemplate in each round of negotiations. It is likely, for instance, that if King had been prepared to accept unanimity (Mulroney-style) as the amending formula, the Constitution could have been repatriated as early as 1927.

But since 1982, Canada had its Constitution, including a Charter which was binding on the provinces as well as the federal government. From then on, the advantage was on the Canadian government's side; it no longer had anything very urgent to seek from the provinces; it was they who had become the supplicants. From then on, "Canada's constitutional evolution" could have taken place without preconditions and without blackmail, on the basis of give and take among equals. Even a united front of the 10 provinces could not have forced the federal government to give ground: With the assurance of a creative equilibrium between the provinces and the central government, the federation was set to last a thousand years!

Alas, only one eventuality hadn't been foreseen: that one day the government of Canada might fall into the hands of a weakling. It has now happened. And the Right Honorable Brian Mulroney, PC, MP, with the complicity of 10 provincial premiers, has already entered into history as the author of a constitutional document which – if it is accepted by the people and their legislators – will render the Canadian state totally impotent. That would destine it, given the dynamics of power, to eventually be governed by eunuchs.

The Toronto Star (May 27, 1987)

The Meech Lake Accord (2)

>‹

*T*o *the Editor*:

On March 4th, your columnist Marcel Adam simply went too far when he wrote the following words in *La Presse* about the Constitutional Act of 1982:

"Fraud is not too strong a word to describe the political 'coup de force' [power grab] of 1982: an event entirely without precedent in this country and possibly without parallel in other federal democracies, a 'coup de force' designed to impose reforms on Quebec running completely against what was expected from commitments taken to keep Quebec in the federation."

The accusation is therefore that "right after the referendum campaign, Trudeau launched" a constitutional reform "running completely against what was expected from commitments taken. . . ." And then "Trudeau's reform was contemptuous in form and fraudulent in content." And finally: "A fool's bargain that has cost Quebec dearly."

But what is the truth about the matter?

During my nineteen years in political life and my sixteen previous years of writing for *Cité libre* and teaching constitutional law, I was against the notion of "special status" for Quebec.

True enough, during the referendum campaign, I told Quebeckers that if the No side won, I was committed to carry through with the constitutional process begun in 1967, at the time of the Interprovincial Conference held by Premier John Robarts on the suggestion of Premier Daniel Johnson.

During this entire period, my view had not changed. I maintained that any reform had to begin with the patriation of the Constitution, to which would be added an amending formula granting a veto power to Quebec and a Charter of Rights guaranteeing the equality of the French and English languages, among other things. But above all no special status for Quebec.

Where is the fraud? Where is the fool's bargain? For the first time ever, the Constitutional Act of 1982 gave Canada its own Constitution, and it entrenched a Charter of Rights in which articles 16 to 20 established the equality of the French and English languages. It is true that Quebec's veto power was only partially reflected (articles 38[2] and 41), but that was because Premier René Lévesque had preferred the amending formula proposed by Alberta, rather than the absolute veto I had proposed to Mr. Bourassa at the Victoria Conference in 1971 (he rejected it) and again to Mr. Lévesque between 1976 and 1981.

Of course, these reforms were not sought by separatists and nationalists who wanted a special status for Quebec. But by what logic could these people believe that a defeat for the Yes side would be followed by reforms designed to please the Yes side, and against which a good part of the No side had always fought?

Premier Lévesque understood the nature of our reforms perfectly well; four days before the referendum, in an interview published in *Le Devoir* on May 16, 1980, he said that, judging by "the comments Trudeau has made recently, . . . the new formula [would be] as centralist . . . as ever." (Quotation taken from a speech by Mr. Gigantes in the Senate on December 20, 1988. The senator also quoted an interview given by Jean Chrétien a few days before the referendum; the federal minister responsible for constitutional matters maintained that a prior condition of Trudeau's "renewed federalism" was a federal government strong enough to redistribute wealth in Canada, and which would not grant special status to any province.)

Once again, Mr. Adam, where is the fraud? When and where did I ever propose a fool's bargain or make false representations to Quebec voters, before, during, or after the referendum?

And where is the "coup de force" by which a supposedly "contemptuous" reform was imposed on Quebec?

From 1927 right up to 1979, during a long series of federal–provincial conferences, all Canadian prime ministers had sought to replace the British North America Act, which served as a Constitution, with an authentically Canadian Constitution. Each attempt failed because one or more provinces had come out against it.

In 1980, a majority of the Quebec people rejected the separatist option by answering No to a quite convoluted question (which some people could have considered contemptuous and fraudulent . . .). The Canadian government considered that Canada had avoided disintegration and should make a supreme effort to acquire formal sovereignty, by breaking any constitutional link with Great Britain, and by acquiring a charter of human rights which applied to all Canadians.

This led to long negotiations . . . But ultimately, nothing came of them, and in spring 1981 the parties split up into two camps: on the one hand, the Péquiste government plus seven other provinces, and, on the other, the federal government plus Ontario and New Brunswick.

After fifty-four years of failed attempts at patriation, the federal government decided to cut the Gordian knot: 114 years after its creation as a country, Canada declared its independence without the unanimous consent of the provinces.

So was this a "coup de force" or a legal political decision? We would soon find out: three provinces (Quebec among them) put the question to the Supreme Court and got a ruling in September 1981, according to which the operation would be legal, although it offended customary practice.

Everyone then returned to the negotiating table. The Gang of Eight provinces (including Quebec) made several counterproposals, which were accepted in the hopes of reaching unanimity: the "notwithstand-ing" clause reduced the impact of the Charter, Alberta's amending formula replaced the Victoria formula, the provinces would acquire some new jurisdictions relating to indirect taxation and international trade. In spite of all that, we were in a deadlock once again.

At the beginning of November 1981, the federal side made a pro-posal which temporarily got the support of the Government of Quebec, but which displeased the seven provinces in alliance with Quebec. These latter provinces felt betrayed and let it be known they would seek a compromise solution without Quebec. The compromise was found and was offered to the Government of Quebec, which refused to accept it.

Once more, Canada decided to declare independence without the unanimous consent of the provinces.

Was this a "coup de force" or a legal political decision? We would soon find out: Quebec put the question to the Supreme Court and was told that the operation was legal and did not breach customary prac-tice, since no single province had a veto power. The same judgement ruled that Quebec was indeed bound by the Constitution Act of 1982. (As a result, there is no need to use the Meech Lake Accord in order to "bring Quebec into the Constitution"; those who maintain the oppo-site, from Mr. Adam through Mr. Bourassa to Mr. Mulroney, are only talking nonsense.)

Maybe what we have here is a political checkmate. Without doubt it's a bad calculation, an unsuitable alliance. It is surely a failed attempt at blackmail. But a "fool's bargain," Mr. Adam? "A power grab . . . without parallel in other federal democracies?" Name me just one fed-eration where the government of a single constitutive part could con-tinually thwart the general will for independence.

What conclusions should we draw from all this?

"In this affair," concludes Mr. Adam, "Quebec is the victim . . . [of] those who isolated Quebec . . ." and he sees "the Meech Lake Accord [as] a gesture of atonement towards Quebec." It's always somebody else's fault! But wasn't Quebec actually isolated by its own Péquiste government, which sought independence for Quebec while rejecting independence for Canada?

So much for that! Mr. Adam demands atonement: nothing less than the unconditional acceptance by Canadians of the Meech Lake Accord. An accord, however, which he fears "will be bad . . . for Canada in the long term." An accord which he considers has the peculiarity of "never being interpreted the same way, even by the people who negotiated it." An accord – and here he agrees with Mr. Bourassa – "whose failure will hurt Canada more than Quebec."

Finally, Mr. Adam, I recognize a certain honesty underneath the trappings of the outraged nationalist. So, surprise me now: go a step further! Since the Meech Lake Accord is bad for Canada, and since Quebec doesn't care all that much about it, why don't we agree together that Canada will be better off if the Meech Lake monster were to drown at the bottom of the lake from which its hideous head should never have appeared in the first place.

La Presse (March 10, 1989)
Translation by George Tombs

The Meech Lake Accord (3)

><

To the Editor:

Let me reply in a few paragraphs to the six columns published in *La Presse* on March 14th, as a response to my article of March 10th.

In my article, I maintained that my pre-referendum commitments to constitutional renewal could be interpreted in only one way: renewal, the way I had always proposed it from 1968 onwards. So there was no question of "fraud," as Mr. Adam claimed in his column of March 6th.

Then Mr. Claude Morin butted in. Mr. Trudeau, he said in substance, promised renewal to Quebeckers. Therefore, Quebeckers had the right to expect that he would move in the direction Quebec wanted.

(Mr. Morin conveniently left out the part of my commitment concerning the other provinces, which also wanted to block our attempts at constitutional reform. In *La Presse* on March 11th, Mme. Lysiane Gagnon accurately quoted the original text; I thank her for having pre-emptively contradicted what Mr. Morin would write four days later: "I quoted . . . what was really said. There was nothing else.")

However, in Mr. Morin's mind, Quebec is the entity whose political expression is the provincial government. And that is exactly where the sophism lies. For me as well as for all non-separatist Quebeckers, Quebec is also the entity which expresses itself politically by means of the federal government. That is, of the government I had the honour of leading from 1968 to 1984, except for a nine-month interlude. And it is insulting to Quebeckers to suggest that in 1980 they were unable to understand that their federal government had been fighting for constitutional renewal since 1968 – and that this renewal was very different from what the Péquistes were proposing.

But that is exactly the insult Mr. Morin is guilty of. He wants to make a case against me based on assumptions. He reveals what he really thinks, when he maintains that "Mr. [René] Lévesque and other people initiated in the ways of politics knew how to decode" Trudeau's intentions. After claiming that the "uneducated" . . . "for many years had not been able to understand [me]," he concludes that I wanted to mislead these "uneducated people . . . [who] made up a larger and more easily swayed electorate than people initiated in the ways of politics."

(Moreover, Mr. Adam makes the same distinction between "people initiated in constitutional matters," who apparently understood me, and "Quebeckers as a whole, who are not much interested in constitutional debates.")

That in summary is the argument of the people who lost the referendum in 1980. The "uneducated" (Mr. Morin uses the expression three times) were not clever enough to understand that the constitutional reform continually offered by our government since 1968 would be exactly the one we would introduce if the result of the referendum were favourable to us.

So when a majority of the Quebec people voted No, they made a mistake; or more to the point these poor "people who could not be swayed" were misled, victimized by a "fraud" and a "coup de force." In other words, the separatists did not really lose the referendum! And the Meech Lake Accord is a kind of atonement, a kind of compensation owed to Quebeckers, to those good folk whose very survival depends on special status.

What contempt for the Quebec people!

And what contempt for Quebec's elected representatives, because they were apparently not any better equipped to understand what Mr. Morin calls "the perversity of the results of the post-referendum constitutional operation."

Let's just remember that Quebec's federal members of Parliament voted in favour of the 1982 Constitution by a margin of 73 votes to 3 (vote of December 2, 1981). And Quebec's provincial members of the National Assembly voted 70 to 38 against "endorsing the proposed patriation of the Constitution" (vote of December 1, 1981). Unless I am very much mistaken, that comes to a total of 72 deputies who did not endorse the 1982 Constitution, and a total of 111 who did endorse it. Quite the power grab, when you stop to think it was endorsed by 60 per cent of the elected representatives of the Quebec people!

So much, Dear Editor, for Mr. Morin. As for Mr. Adam, in his article of March 11, he writes that he "is entering . . . in the realm of intentions," which he knows "is a little odious." Of course, that doesn't prevent him, in an article on March 14, from building a second case against me based on assumptions, and supporting Mr. Mulroney's position: "Do you believe for a second that Mr. Trudeau and his colleagues would have gone ahead in 1981–82 with the patriation of the Constitution without the consent of Queen's Park [Ontario]?"

Well, I haven't the faintest idea, and neither have Mr. Mulroney and Mr. Adam. I only know that it is despicable to write history in the conditional tense. Especially because, if you write history in the conditional tense, you have to be honest about it.

If the Government of Ontario had blocked every attempt to patriate the Constitution since 1927, if between 1964 and 1971 this government had withdrawn support for a patriation formula it had already proposed or accepted, if it had been told by the Supreme Court that it did not have a veto power, if this government was the one seeking the dismemberment of Canada and had just lost a referendum to this effect, if more than 95 per cent of Ontario's MPs in Ottawa had endorsed the constitutional renewal sought by Quebec and eight other provinces, well sure! I believe we would have gone ahead without the consent of Queen's Park.

But obviously, as they say in Vienna, if my grandmother had wheels she would be a bus. You know perfectly well, Dear Editor, this is not the way history should be written.

La Presse (March 22, 1989)
Translation by George Tombs

Patriation and the Supreme Court

><

Bora Laskin, a brilliant legal scholar who taught law at the University of Toronto and Osgoode Hall, was named Chief Justice of Canada in 1973 and died in office. When the Supreme Court was called upon to determine on what conditions the Canadian Constitution could be patriated in Canada, he wrote a minority judgment which is discussed in the following address by Pierre Elliott Trudeau on the occasion of the opening in Toronto of a library bearing Laskin's name.

I never talked politics with Bora Laskin, and I have no idea how he voted before he was on the bench, nor how he might have voted had he not become a judge.

I suppose he could be called a conservative in that he showed great respect for our laws and established public institutions. Or a liberal because of his faith in the individual as a rational being and a free agent in society. Or a radical, since he tempered freedom with justice and tended to empower the underprivileged.

What drew me to him when I knew nothing of him except his writings was his great intelligence, combined with a concern for human beings and an apparent desire to live in a society which permitted self-fulfilment to all. Those qualities characterized much of his teaching and many of his judicial decisions. In particular, they contributed mightily to the wisdom of the dissent he formulated along with Justices Estey and McIntyre in the *Patriation Reference*.

That dissent, I shall argue in this address, was not only the better law, but the better common sense, and consequently it was also wiser politically. Had it prevailed over the majority view, I believe that Canada's future would have been more assured.

But let me begin with two preliminary remarks.

First it is a pleasure as well as an honour to be associated with the opening of the Bora Laskin law library. After Bora Laskin became Chief Justice, his functions and mine called for frequent meetings on administrative matters concerning the Court, and my admiration soon grew into a strong friendship for Bora and his wife, Peggy. For that reason, I felt I could break the self-imposed rule that I had followed since my retirement, that of never accepting invitations to deliver convocation speeches.

My second remark has to do with timing. The Laskin library was scheduled for an opening on September 6th last, and this address was to have been delivered on that date. That meant I had to choose between shortening my summer vacation – or calling for help. I chose the latter, and consequently I am deeply indebted to my two colleagues Pierre Legrand and Tom Brady for their invaluable assistance in providing me with lengthy notes on the case law concerning conventions as well as on the judgments and commentaries arising out of the *Patriation Reference*.

So now to my topic.

In constitutional societies, the rule of law – to borrow Dicey's well-known expression – applies to the state as well as to the individual; and courts of last resort, when called upon to interpret the constitution, must determine the rights and obligations that governments and people possess in relation to each other. In that sense they become part of the process of empowering people and institutions; that is to say, they become part of the process of politics.

Thus our Supreme Court, when it acts in constitutional matters, is of necessity participating in the governance of Canada. This is not a new development, somehow made necessary by the adoption of the Charter of Rights, and which – as some critics have wrongly alleged – would tend to "Americanize" us. The Supreme Court of Canada, and before it the Judicial Committee of the Privy Council, have been engaged in lawmaking or in adjudicating power for Canada, its people and its provinces since the first constitutional decision rendered after the adoption of the BNA Act.

I have long ceased to be a student of Canadian constitutional law. But I have not quite forgotten all I learned during my political career. It is against that background that I propose to review some aspects of the fateful Supreme Court decision on the patriation of the constitution, arguably the most important decision it ever rendered or ever will render. Indeed, the various judicial opinions that were handed down in the *Patriation Reference* went to the very roots of the constitution, determining at a particular point in time the nature of the constituent power for Canada, and therefore defining – albeit indirectly – the essence of Canadian sovereignty. Because of that, the political consequences flowing from those opinions were of great importance, and they will continue to reverberate into the future, throughout whatever history may yet lie ahead.

At the same time, these momentous judicial opinions have themselves been shaped by past history. It will be remembered that the patriation process began at the federal–provincial conference of 1927 convened by Prime Minister William Lyon Mackenzie King to give effect to the Balfour Declaration of the preceding year. That declaration was to lead in 1931 to the passage of the Statute of Westminster, which allowed certain former colonies of the United Kingdom to achieve full legal independence.

Canada alone within that group of colonies could not lay claim to a constitution of its own, complete with amending process. It was to seek agreement on such a process that the first ministers were meeting in

1927. Professor Ken McNaught puts the issue this way in his *History of Canada*:

> The decade's surge of provincialism was symbolized by a Dominion–Provincial Conference in 1927 at which Tory Premier Ferguson of Ontario and Liberal Premier Taschereau of Québec joined in proclaiming the "compact theory" of Confederation – a position which would give near autonomy to the provinces and which saw federal powers as being merely delegated to Ottawa by the provinces.

In such circumstances, it was inevitable that the first ministers would fail to agree on the amending process. They so failed in 1927, under Mackenzie King's leadership. And since the issue was never put to rest, they failed again under Bennett in 1931, as they would fail under St. Laurent in 1950, under Diefenbaker in 1960, under Pearson in 1964, and under Trudeau in 1971.

The first ministers failed because they could not come to a consensus on the nature of Canadian sovereignty. They could not decide whether that sovereignty ultimately rested with the provinces, who, by coming together, made up a country called Canada, or whether it resided in some undefined combination of federal state and provinces, all existing in their own right and each exercising a share of the overall sovereignty. And it seemed rather obvious – given the unlikelihood at the time that a prime minister of Canada would ever capitulate to the compact theorists – that the first ministers would continue failing forever and Canada would never be a truly sovereign country, unless the problem were somehow resolved.

During the 1980–82 constitutional exercise, the federal government proposed to cut the Gordian knot by arguing that the sovereignty of Canada ultimately resided neither in the provinces nor in the federal government, but in the Canadian people. The provincial governments collectively rejected that view, even objecting to the use of the words "the people of Canada" in a preamble to the constitution and proposing instead a description of Canada as a country made up of "provinces . . . freely united," thus returning to the selfsame concept that had prevented patriation in 1927.

The premiers also unanimously made it abundantly clear, by the so-called Château Consensus, on September 12, 1980, that they would never permit the patriation of the Canadian constitution until jurisdictional powers had been drastically reallocated in favour of the provinces.

The federal government took the position that a reallocation of powers between the two orders of government was a legitimate subject of negotiation, but that the right of Canadians to have a constitution of their own should not be subordinated to the open-ended process of satisfying any premier's insatiable desire for increased provincial powers. Since it was generally recognized that, technically speaking, patriation of the constitution could proceed only from a resolution of the Parliament of Canada addressed to the Parliament at Westminster, and since such a joint address had never been moved, for lack of sufficient provincial support, it appeared that complete sovereignty for Canada – as well as the vesting of that sovereignty in the Canadian people – could forever be held to ransom by one or more provinces. Fifty-three years of failure were there to prove the point.

There were only two ways to solve the conundrum. The government of Canada could accept the "compact theory," recognizing that our country was nothing more than a community of communities, in which fundamental powers (including the power to patriate the constitution) flowed from provinces that had freely united to form a loose confederation. Or the government of Canada, as the sole governing body empowered to act in the name of all Canadians, could reject the compact theory, hold that Canada was something more than and different from the sum of its parts, and proceed to patriate the constitution unilaterally.

We chose the latter course when, as prime minister, I rejected the Château Consensus and announced that the federal government would initiate the process of patriation by laying a joint address before Parliament. Twelve years had elapsed since I had begun negotiating patriation with the premiers, and fifty-three years had gone by since Mackenzie King had first attempted to patriate with provincial consent.

In Parliament, Mr. Joe Clark proved to be a very effective Leader of the Opposition, holding up and prolonging debate on the patriation address for some six months, during which time the federal initiative had gained the acceptance of two provinces and the opposition of eight, three of which referred the matter to their respective appellate courts, and thence to the Supreme Court of Canada.

One final point concerning the historical context: in spite of decades of political tension and acrimonious debate between the federal government and the provinces, the several judgments on the provincial references were to be formulated in an intellectual vacuum. There existed no contemporary body of doctrine pertaining to the *locus* of Canadian sovereignty or to the nature of the constituent power, although individual politicians had expressed their own views. Premier Allan Blakeney of Saskatchewan, for instance, and to a certain extent Mr. Clark as Leader of the Opposition, had formulated positions akin to a compact theory of confederation. And I had repeatedly challenged the Canadian intellectual establishments to fill the gap by participating in the debate on the nature of the Canadian state, which continued to divide the provincial premiers and the federal prime minister during my terms of office. But, as far as I was able to perceive, the academic and legal communities had in the main chosen to remain aloof, while the press tended to view the whole matter as the petty obsession of a quarrelsome prime minister.

It is perhaps for this reason that when the judgments were finally rendered, first by the appellate courts, then by the Supreme Court, they dealt with the law and the conventions, but only obliquely touched on the notions of sovereignty and constituent power. And that is no doubt why one distinctive character of all the judgments went largely unnoticed even by most legal commentators: the majority judgment on the existence of a convention fatally tilted the doctrine of Canadian sovereignty away from the people and towards the several governments, that is to say, towards one form or another of the compact theory of confederation.

The Supreme Court delivered four opinions in the *Patriation Reference* in September 1981. Two of them dealt with the legality of the proposed address to the United Kingdom Parliament. By a seven-to-two majority, the Court held that the Senate and House of Commons had the legal power to make such an address regardless of whether or not the provinces gave their assent.

Two other judgments dealt with the question of whether provincial consent was required for such an address. A majority of six judges found that provincial consent was required by convention, though that convention did not require such consent to be unanimous. Chief Justice Laskin, along with Justices Estey and McIntyre, dissented, finding that unanimous provincial consent was not required by convention; they refused to consider whether any lesser degree of support was required, since the questions under reference were plainly and only asking whether a convention of unanimity existed, and since all but one of the provinces opposing the federal initiative had pleaded in favour of unanimous provincial consent.

What I find most remarkable about the majority judgment is the number of times their Lordships chose to turn a deaf ear and a blind eye to the legal arguments that might have led them in another direction.

First, they had to find that the aspect of the reference dealing with conventions was indeed a matter on which the courts could legally pass judgment. Courts had often in the past refused to answer questions deemed unsuitable for judicial determination. In this case, because conventions are enforceable through the political process, the courts should not even have engaged in declaring their existence. In choosing to answer the question there is little doubt that the Supreme Court allowed itself – in Professor P.W. Hogg's words – "to be manipulated into a purely political role," going beyond the lawmaking functions that modern jurisprudence agrees the Court must necessarily exercise.

Second, having decided to deal with conventions, the majority judges had to determine whether a convention existed or not, that is to say, whether precedents existed in sufficient numbers and had been expressed with sufficient consistency and clarity to constitute a rule which the political actors accepted as binding. The pleadings themselves should have made it obvious that there existed no such conventional rule, since – of the eleven political bodies involved – seven believed in a rule of unanimity, one in a rule of less than unanimity, and the other three believed in no rule whatsoever.

Third, having rejected the political evidence provided by the politicians themselves, the majority judges had to ascertain the beliefs of actors long dead. Since Confederation, the Court counted twenty-two requests by the Canadian Parliament to the United Kingdom for constitutional amendments. Fifteen of the amendments can be considered important, and of these fifteen, ten were requested by joint address and enacted by the United Kingdom without prior consultation with the provinces. Here again, it can hardly be said that consultation with the provinces, let alone consent of the provinces, constituted a general rule accepted and practised by the political players, living or dead.

Fourth, setting aside the historical evidence as a whole, the Court decided to concentrate only on those amendments which affected provincial powers directly. If one includes among such amendments the ones that affected provincial powers indirectly as well as directly, one finds a range of consents that extends from all provinces to none, hardly evidence of a firm rule.

Fifth, having arbitrarily assumed that the words "affects federal–provincial relations" in the reference should be amended to read "*directly* affects federal–provincial relations," the Court chose to consider only those amendments which affected provincial powers directly. Among the twenty-two amendments, the Court counted five such instances (1930, 1931, 1940, 1951, and 1964), only the last three of which constituted a transfer of jurisdiction from the provinces to the federal state. Having thus set aside the history of constitutional amendments during the first sixty-three years of Confederation, and having dismissed the precedents in seventeen out of twenty-two instances of amendments, the Court chose to consider only those cases where unanimous consent of the provinces had been obtained, and thus backed itself into a position where it could only be looking at a convention of unanimous provincial consent.

Sixth, having probably realized that the rule of unanimity emerging from their selection of evidence could only lead to the continuation of fifty-four years of constitutional deadlock – a situation that was patently repugnant to common sense – their Lordships nonetheless refused to seek refuge in the nature of the joint address before them. Yet this address was obviously a case apart, since no prior constitutional amendment remotely resembled the Charter of Rights and Freedoms or the amending formula included in the "patriation package." The Charter, though limiting federal and provincial powers, did not do so by disturbing the existing balance between the federal and provincial governments; its impact on the distribution of powers was at most indirect, and therefore should not have been associated with the constitutional precedents of 1930, 1940, 1951, and 1964. As for the amending formula, it involved, if anything, a surrender of *federal* power, since it precluded any further constitutional amendment by way of unilateral joint address of Parliament.

Seventh, having ignored the uniqueness of the joint address before them, the majority judges had to find some other way of breaking out of the box of unanimity in which their selection of evidence had put them. So they decided blatantly to *invent* a convention calling for "a substantial degree of provincial consent." Despite saying that conventions, unlike the common law, cannot be discovered by a court, the majority did just that, since by their own showing, the precedents for the "substantial measure of provincial consent" convention simply did not exist. Neither therefore did the convention which the majority purported to find. Indeed, out of the eleven political players only one – Saskatchewan – had pleaded that such a convention existed. And another would go on to claim that whatever "substantial" meant, Quebec had to be included, a claim that was to be negated in a necessary "clarification" by the Supreme Court in December 1982. How can a clear and firm rule be said to exist when "substantial" turned out to mean some unstated number between two and ten? As the late Senator Eugene Forsey vividly put it:

The Prime Minister of Canada, confronted by the Court's decision, could not know whether he was conventionally bound, on the Court's showing, to get the consent of six provinces, or seven, or eight, or nine; or which of them it must include. But let him stray one inch from the path of the convention the six judges professed to have worked out for him and his action would be branded "unconstitutional," even "immoral," "morally wrong."

Eighth, having created a vague convention *ex nihilo*, their Lordships could still have sidestepped the purely political role that beckoned. There is compelling case law to the effect that even when a clear convention does exist, it is not the business of the courts to state that the convention somehow invalidates an action acknowledged to be legal. In the case of *Madzimbuto* v. *Lardner-Burke and George* (1969), the Privy Council was willing to note, as a fact, the existence of convention, but that convention was treated as in essence irrelevant to the resolution of the legal dispute before it. As Lord Reid put it: "Their Lordships in declaring the law are not concerned with conventions. They are only concerned with the legal power of Parliament." In Canada, too, the courts had previously made it clear that conventions can never be legally binding, and that they cannot have any effect on legal powers either. As C.J. Duff put it in the *Disallowance Reference*: "We are not concerned with constitutional usage . . . or constitutional practice. . . . We are concerned with questions of law." And for one fleeting moment, it looked as if the majority judges were going to escape undue politicization of the Court; in the *Patriation Reference* itself, they observe that conventions "are generally in conflict with the legal rules which they postulate and the courts are bound to enforce the legal rules. . . . This conflict . . . prevents the courts from enforcing conventions." But alas! this court was intent on pressing the political players to accept as binding a rule that only politicians can create and that only the political process should sanction. For it went on to state that some conventions "may be more important than laws," and that consequently their breach or observance had to do with a fundamental issue of "constitutionality and legitimacy." In holding that the federal action, though legal, was unconstitutional and illegitimate, the Court made it effectively impossible for the federal government to proceed to Westminster with any hope of success.

On the basis of all the foregoing eight points, there seems to be little doubt that the majority judges had set their minds to delivering a judgment that would force the federal and provincial governments to seek a political compromise. No doubt believing in good faith that a political agreement would be better for Canada than unilateral legal patriation, they blatantly manipulated the evidence before them so as to arrive at the desired result. They then wrote a judgment which tried to lend a fig-leaf of legality to their preconceived conclusion.

It has often been remarked by commentators – to the point of having become, so to speak, conventional wisdom, echoed as usual by the media – that in taking their stand the majority judges provided the framework within which a political settlement eventually became possible. Having rejected unilateralism and unanimity, the Court embraced the "Canadian way," supporting both sides and forcing a political compromise. In the socio-political context that prevailed in 1981, say those commentators, it would have been quite irresponsible for the Supreme Court to decline jurisdiction over constitutional conventions. It had to play a role, while still respecting the part to be played by the political actors – which it did by leaving the contents of the convention suitably vague.

Some of you may remember that I have always been wary of conventional wisdom. After fifty-four years of failure to patriate the constitution through compromise, it seemed to me that Canadians had a right to expect a legal decision from their Supreme Court, rather than some well-meaning admonitions about what was politically proper. And my purpose in returning to the *Patriation Reference* today is to point out, with the benefit of hindsight, that the minority judgment, couched in what Professor Edward McWhinney has described as Chief Justice Laskin's "clearly identifiable drafting style," was not only the better law but also the wiser counsel.

Better law, in the sense that, on most of the eight points that I detailed above, the minority's decision is based on much sounder legal reasoning. The minority's interpretation of the questions asked seems the more natural one, particularly since the three provinces that had submitted those questions to their appellate courts had themselves argued that *unanimous* provincial consent was required, not some undetermined "substantial degree of provincial consent." The minority's examination of the precedents regarding amendments to the BNA Act is also more convincing: it ranges over all previous amendments and avoids excessively narrow concentration on those amendments which had specifically transferred powers to or from the provinces. Furthermore, the argument that amendments *indirectly* affecting the provinces also had to be considered is a sound one, considering the nature of the joint address under examination.

The minority also avoids the wrenching manipulation of the legal tests to which the majority had to resort in order to be able to ascertain the existence of a convention. The minority found that the precedents did not support the existence of a convention of unanimous provincial consent, that the political actors had not recognized one, and that such a convention was not inherent in the nature of Canadian federalism. Therefore, said the minority, the federal resolution was not in breach of convention because the one alleged satisfied none of the constitutional tests.

The minority judgment also avoided the excessive measure of what might be called judicial lawmaking in which the majority engaged, first to find the convention, and second to declare it to have been breached. The minority's emphasis on conventions as political phenomena to be created, modified, terminated, and sanctioned by political players is more consistent with the purely political nature of conventions.

This in turn shows a better sense of a court's institutional capacity than does the majority decision. Courts deal with disputes which they must resolve on an either/or basis: the plaintiff wins or he loses. The majority tried to say "maybe" instead of "yes" or "no" and did so in regard to a highly politicized issue. The minority's ruling, in contrast, does resolve a dispute in a justiciable form: it answered "no" to the

factual question of whether or not a convention of unanimous provincial consent to constitutional amendments existed. This is the type of
ruling that the legal community, indeed the people at large, legitimately expect a court of justice to make, and for which it is equipped.
By refraining from interventions in the process by which conventions
are created, modified, or enforced, it leaves these to the politicians,
who by admission of both majority and minority are in sole charge of
conventions.

Finally, the minority's more strictly legal approach lends itself far
less to political manipulation of the courts than does the majority's.
By refusing to go beyond its role as interpreter of the law, the minority avoided the temptation to which the majority succumbed, that of
trying to act as political arbiter at a time of political crisis. While there
are no doubt differing views of how well the court performed this
role in the *Patriation Reference*, it is not a role to which a court of law
striving to remain above the day-to-day currents of political life
should aspire.

By way of conclusion, permit me to state my own view of the
Court's performance as political arbiter: I am profoundly convinced
that the minority judgment was based on a much sounder understanding of the political reality.

It seems clear to me that the provinces had put the questions on the
convention in case they lost on the legal question. In other words, they
were using the courts to strengthen their political position in bargaining with the federal government. And Canadians today are certainly
justified in wondering whether the majority, in accepting to be so used,
were not totally mistaken as to the political impact of their decision.
When all is said and done, were not Chief Justice Laskin and his two
dissenting colleagues more prescient in confining their enterprise to a
search for the proper legal result? The *Patriation Reference* decision
produced two sets of problems, which the Court's adoption of Chief
Justice Laskin's position would have neatly avoided.

First, the way in which the majority opinion strengthened the
provinces' hand is – to quote with approval from Professor Hogg's
well-known text on constitutional law – "probably the reason why the

provinces were able to secure the insertion of the override clause in the Charter of Rights and the substitution of the opting-out amending formula – the two major concessions made by the federal government to achieve the agreement of November 5, 1981." I need hardly add that one may surely be forgiven for thinking that these were less than happy developments, as was the forced abandonment by the federal government of its attempt to include a referendum provision in the amendment formula.

Second, to quote Professor Peter Russell, because "it cast a heavy mantle of political illegitimacy over the constitutional changes that would result from . . . a procedure" that had not secured provincial consent, the Court was placing any one of the provinces in the privileged position of being able to hold out and, as patriation went ahead without it, of being able to pose as a political martyr as soon as the memory of historical events had begun to fade.

Wasn't the risk of this sequence of events unfolding particularly acute, given the well-known political allegiance of the party then in power in Quebec? It is surely arguable that Chief Justice Laskin and his two colleagues were wise enough to realize that the separatist government of Quebec would always refuse to endorse any Canadian constitutional reform short of sovereignty-association, and that in such circumstances it would be better for the Court not to interpose itself as a mediator in a political battle between a government that had decided to proceed with patriation by all legal means and one that had decided to stop legal patriation by all political means. Is it not conceivable that the dissenting justices understood that a Supreme Court decision which sent back to the bargaining table nine provinces that were prepared to bargain and one that was not would grant that latter province a lever to pry itself out of the Canadian constitutional family? Of course, that is exactly what happened, with the result that the provincial government which early on had set its mind to deliberately frustrate the patriation process was put in the position of being able to cry foul and to claim that it had been singled out as a victim by the rest of Canada, when the rest of Canada had merely followed the rules resulting from a reference made to the Supreme Court by that very same province.

No doubt it can be argued, with hindsight, that the constitution would have been better left alone rather than brought to such a dismal destination. Indeed, I am on record since the mid-sixties as having pointed out the dangers of embarking on a constitutional voyage when the virus of constitutionitis had begun to infect the ship of state. But the provinces took matters into their own hands in 1967 by assembling at the "Confederation for Tomorrow" Conference. Surely the federal government had no choice but to accept the challenge and sail on.

And once the provinces had appealed to the Supreme Court as the arbiter of conventions, surely those provinces had no choice but to accept that there would be winners and losers. How then can politicians and academics argue, as they do today, that one loser had been unfairly treated by the Fates he himself had conjured?

Indeed, was not the unkindest fate of all the one meted out to the government of Canada, which, as a consequence of the Supreme Court decision, was faced with the choice of either patriating the constitution according to the legal and conventional rules set down by Canada's highest tribunal or backing down in front of a provincial government whose avowed purpose was nothing less than the destruction of Canada?

If we had done the latter, Canada would have ceased to be governed by the rule of law, having recognized that now and forever more the highest law in the land could only evolve and be determined through a process of political blackmail manipulated by one province.

Not surprisingly, the federal government and nine provincial governments chose to proceed, supported in that course by 71 out of the 75 members of Parliament elected from Quebec, and by 38 of the 108 deputies elected to Quebec's National Assembly, for a total weighted support of 65 percent of all elected representatives from "la belle province." In the wake of that support came three public opinion polls taken in Quebec during the months following patriation, showing that the people of Quebec also firmly agreed with the 1982 constitutional amendment. That in turn was followed by the rapid disintegration of the Parti Québécois and the concomitant resurgence of the Quebec economy, which placed well above the Canadian average. One might even add that four of the five judges on the Quebec Court of Appeals had previously legitimized the patriation process (in April 1981).

So much then for the current babble that Quebeckers had felt victimized by the sequence of events beginning with the "No" victory in the 1980 referendum and ending with the patriation of the constitution in 1982.

As to the epilogue, it remains to be written. But it is not too early to observe that, with the passage of time, the fading of memories, the growth of a guilt complex at Queen's Park, plus much falsifying of history in Ottawa, the subsequent allegation – fabricated by many of Quebec's opinion leaders – that their province was humiliated in 1982, gradually took on the appearance of historical fact. In the resulting political situation, the stage was set for an unprecedented abdication of sovereign powers by the federal government, undertaken in order to placate those very politicians who had merely played the game of "loser takes all," and who modestly asked for nothing more than to have their cake and eat it too.

Address, Opening of Bora
Laskin Library (March 21, 1991)
Reprinted under the title
Fatal Tilt in the "Point of View"
series of books (Toronto:
HarperCollins, 1991).

Quebec's Blackmail

>-<

I. Pride and Money

Commenting on Quebec nationalist politics in the first issue of *Cité libre* 42 years ago, I wrote, "The country can't exist without us, we think to ourselves. So watch out you don't hurt our feelings.... We depend on our power of blackmail in order to face the future.... We are getting to be a sleazy bunch of master blackmailers."

Things have changed a lot since then, but for the worse. Four decades ago, all Duplessis was asking for his province was that it be left in peace to go its own slow pace. His rejection of proposals for constitutional reform was intended mostly to block an updating of Canada's economic and social institutions. And Quebec's "no" was formulated by a relatively small political class. In today's Quebec, however, the official blackmail refrain gets backup from a whole choir of those who like to think they are thinking people: "If English Canada won't accept Quebec's traditional, minimum demands, we'll leave...."

Leave for where? What for?

Consider that in the past 22 years the province of Quebec has been governed by two premiers. The first was the one who coined the phrase "profitable federalism." We'll stay in Canada if Canada gives us enough money, he argued. However, adds the Allaire report that he commissioned, the rest of Canada must hand over nearly all its constitutional powers, except of course the power to give us lots of money. And to put a bit more kick in the blackmail, no opportunity is missed to point out that Quebec's (alleged) right of self-determination is written into this premier's party program. This is the premier who prides himself in not practising "federalism on bended knee."

The other premier was the one who invented "sovereignty-association." He demanded all the powers of a sovereign country for Quebec, but was careful to arrange for the sovereign country not to be independent. Indeed, his referendum question postulated that a sovereign Quebec would be associated with the other provinces and would continue to use the Canadian dollar as legal tender. Money, money, money!

So for 22 years the Quebec electorate has suffered the ignominy of having to choose between two provincial parties for whom the pride of being a Quebecer is negotiable for cash. And if by some stroke of ill fortune the rest of Canada seems disinclined to go along with the blackmail, as happened over the Meech Lake accord, it is accused of humiliating Quebec. In Quebec, humiliation is decidedly selective.

Except for a small handful of dyed-in-the-wool separatists, together with the sprinkling of Montrealers who exercised their vote in favor of the Equality party, just about all the cream of Quebec society approves of this shameful horse trading, and so without batting an eye has backed one or the other of the above-mentioned premiers for 22 years.

Artists in general parade as *indépendantistes*, but want the Canadian government to keep giving them money. Big business people and professionals endorsed the independence blackmail over the Meech affair, but with the economic crisis worsening are rediscovering advantages to "profitable federalism." The francophone media line up in great numbers on the side of sovereignty, but remain faithful to their hero and soft-pedal real independence because of the costs it would entail. Political scientists (and their students, of course), instead of analysing this spineless behavior with scientific detachment, subscribe to it almost unanimously; some openly advocate knife-to-the-throat negotiations with English Canada, maintaining that with a certain kind of independence, Quebecers could continue to elect federal members of Parliament (whence come equalization payments).

Curiouser and curiouser, as Alice said. Want more examples of this ludicrous political thinking?

• In 1964 and 1971, Quebec premiers scuttled two constitutional agreements that they had signed (Fulton–Favreau) or drafted and promised to sign (Victoria). In Quebec they were cheered. But when the premiers of two other provinces refused to back the 1987 Meech Lake accord, which they had neither negotiated nor signed, it was claimed that Quebec had been hurt and humiliated by the rest of the country.

• A Canadian prime minister is accused of having broken a promise made to Quebecers during the referendum of 1980, whereas the words interpreted as a promise were in fact addressed to the other provinces to urge them to resume constitutional negotiations after the referendum.

• Seven provinces that approved the repatriation of the Constitution in November, 1981, are accused of betrayal (on the night of Nov. 4, the so-called night of the long knives), after forming a common front with Quebec in April, 1981, to block the repatriation project. The truth is that during the negotiations on the morning of Nov. 4, it was the premier of Quebec who broke ranks with the other provinces of the Group of Eight and left them out in the cold.

• In 1992, the premier of Quebec considers a constitutional veto for Quebec a matter of life and death; yet in 1971 he himself rejected this veto when the federal government and the nine other provinces offered it on a silver tray. And his successor, who also considered Quebec's veto sacred, turned it down several times between 1978 and 1981; he even went to the Supreme Court to prevent the federal government, which had the support of Ontario and New Brunswick, from putting a veto for Quebec in the Constitution.

• Once the Supreme Court had defined the rules of the game, the repatriation of the Constitution was carried out in strict accordance with the rule of law and respect for convention; furthermore, it was backed by a weighted 65 percent of the combined totals of Quebec's members of Parliament in Ottawa and the Quebec National Assembly. Yet official Quebec history denounces the operation as "strong-arm tactics," and a number of worthy individuals (including a former federal cabinet minister who had supported the operation) have discovered retroactively that it had humiliated them.

In short, Quebec governments had blocked all Canadian attempts at repatriation since 1927, and here was a separatist Quebec government trying to do it again in 1980. The premier of Quebec, they say, loved to play the game. Well, he played at referendum and lost. He played at alliances and lost. He played at negotiation and lost. He played the Supreme Court game and lost. Finally, he played at getting votes from elected representatives and lost. How have Quebec's nationalist thinkers explained this succession of failures? Since it is out of the question for them to consider that a Quebec government might have played its cards atrociously, they have had to distort history once again in order to blame it all on some imaginary betrayal.

So it goes that, with myths and delusions, the Quebec nationalist elites falsify history to prove that all Quebec's political failures are someone else's fault: the Conquest, the obscurantism of Duplessis's time, slowness to enter the modern age, illiteracy, and all the rest. It is never our leaders' fault; it has to be blamed on some ominous plot against us.

II. The Distinct Society

The same glaring lack of professionalism is in evidence when nationalist thinkers in Quebec have used terms like "distinct society," which succeeded "sovereignty-association," which followed "equality or independence," which was preceded by "special status." None of these terms stands up to serious scrutiny.

The latest variation, the distinct society, turned up in post-referendum negotiations in 1980, when the premier of Quebec had to invent something to replace sovereignty-association, which had gone down with the referendum. The frivolity of the notion becomes apparent if we recall that its author considered his province so indistinct that he allied it with the other provinces of the Group of Eight in April, 1981, when all eight of them formally declared themselves equal to all the others, and approved an amending formula by which Quebec gave up its right of veto. Nevertheless, the phrase "distinct society" continues to be a hit.

That Quebec is a distinct society is totally obvious. The inhabitants of the province live in a territory defined by its borders. The majority speak French. They are governed under a particular system of laws. And these realities have been pivotal in the development of a culture which is uniquely theirs.

These are inarguable facts, arising from two centuries of history marked by intense struggles and juridico-political stubbornness. This produced the Canadian Constitution of 1867, whose federative rather than unitary form was imposed by French Canadians, led by Sir George-Etienne Cartier, on other Canadians. It was precisely this federalism which enabled and encouraged the development in Quebec of a province that is a distinct society.

This Constitution also gave birth to nine other provinces, all of them distinct from the others by reason of their territorial borders, their ethnic composition, their laws, and hence their cultures. (A society cannot be distinct in relation to another, in fact, without that other being distinct in relation to the first.)

Nonetheless, all these distinct societies share a considerable heritage, despite misconceptions to the contrary. Much is made of the fact, for example, that the civil law is the law in Quebec, whereas common law applies in the other provinces. Yet, however important the Civil Code may be, in reality it occupies a very small place in the total picture of provincial laws by which we in Quebec are governed. Just like the other provinces, Quebec has enacted a vast number of statutory laws; they apply to all aspects of our collective lives and are the product of a juridical culture far more closely related to that of the other provinces than to the laws of New France or the Napoleonic Code.

At any rate, it is a truism if not a platitude to assert that Quebec is a distinct society, since the Constitution we adopted in 1867 has permitted it to be a distinct society. Since this is constitutionally recognized already, why are so many Quebec politicians, public law experts and business people clamoring to have it inserted in the Constitution all over again? And why do they say they are humiliated when people wonder why this is so necessary?

Because, they say, the Constitution of 1982 recognizes the collective rights of other communities; ancestral rights of the native peoples, the multicultural heritage of many newer Canadians, even women's rights. So why such niggardliness when it comes to writing into the same Constitution "the promotion of Quebec as a distinct society"?

This is gross sophistry. Unlike Quebecers, neither the native peoples nor the "multiculturals" nor women are collectivities defined by a specific territory and enjoying executive, legislative and judicial powers. Consequently, the Constitution does not give them, as collectivities, any specific jurisdictional power to "promote" their distinct societies. The only effect of these charter provisions is to give individuals belonging to these collectivities an additional guarantee of protection against any interpretation of the charter whereby their rights could be overlooked. Somewhat in the same fashion, the charter has given to members of the French-Canadian collectivity scattered throughout Canada not the power to make laws to promote the French language, but the power to have the courts insist on the equality of French with English, to the extent guaranteed by the charter.

On the other hand, when the words "promotion of Quebec as a distinct society" are proposed for insertion either in the body of the

Constitution or in the charter, they would apply to a province – that is, a constitutional entity with power to make laws, give effect to them and have the courts impose respect for them. The courts will be called upon to define these words. First, they will need to determine what new powers the Constitution intends to give to Quebec in order to better enable it to "promote its distinct society." They will also need to consider how the province of Quebec is different from the other provinces, all of which are distinct societies, and all of which are empowered by the Canadian Constitution to promote the interests of their respective populations. Then they will ponder the wording of the proposed insertion whose purpose is to guide their interpretation of the charter; " 'distinct society' . . . *includes* a French-speaking majority, a unique culture, and a civil law tradition."

Now the consequences become clear. The charter, whose essential purpose was to recognize the fundamental and inalienable rights of all Canadians equally, would recognize thenceforth that in the province of Quebec these rights could be overridden or modified by provincial laws whose purpose is to promote a distinct society and more specifically to favor "the French-speaking majority" that has "a unique culture" and "a civil law tradition." There is a very good chance, then, that Quebecers of Irish, Jewish, or Vietnamese origin – even if they speak perfect French – would have trouble claiming to belong to this "distinct society" in any attempt to protect their fundamental rights as individuals against discriminatory laws enacted in a jurisdiction where they are in a minority. And even an "old stock" Quebecer would risk losing his fundamental rights if he were rash enough to pit them against Quebec laws passed for the promotion of "collective rights."

This most recent ideological fad in Quebec, collective rights, has an enthusiastic following. Journalists, academics, students, business people and politicians are all ready to man the barricades to protect the "collective rights" of Quebecers against any interference from the Canadian Constitution or the Charter of Rights and Freedoms. In this they are following the lead of their premier, who at the proclamation of Bill 178 banning signs in languages other than French, bragged that in the name of collective rights his government had trampled individual rights guaranteed by the charter.

III. Collective Rights

The poverty of nationalistic thinking in Quebec is abundantly clear from the dispatch with which so many of our Québécois thinkers have embraced the concept of "collective rights."

Under the charter, all Canadians stand as equals before the state. But Quebec's nationalist elites, who are fearless in the face of competition from the United States and even the whole world, are scared stiff of English Canada. Only in the St-Jean Baptiste parade are we a race of giants; when the next day dawns and we come to measure ourselves against other Canadians as individuals, we are afraid we are not equal but inferior to them, and we run and hide behind our "collective" rights, which, if need be, we invoke to override the fundamental rights of "others." But what politician or academic or business person will tell us which collectivity is supposed to have those rights?

Is it the French-Canadian collectivity living here and there across Canada? Of course not, since the preponderant ideology in Quebec doesn't give a fig about bilingualism in Canada, and Quebec has gone to bat in court for Alberta and Saskatchewan when they have denied French rights acquired even before these provinces joined Confederation in 1905.

Is it the collectivity of all Quebecers, then? No, because that collectivity is called a province, and the powers of the province as a collectivity were explicitly recognized long ago by the Constitution Act of 1867.

So it can only be some distinct collectivity within Quebec – but which? Certainly not the members of the anglophone collectivity, since Quebec law denies them any collective rights in relation to signs and certain aspects of education. We can rule out the native peoples, too, since they have been clearly given to understand that they cannot be a distinct society with the right to self-determination because the term has been reserved by Quebecers of another race.

When the nationalists talk about protecting collective rights, then, they are thinking only of French-speaking Quebecers. But are we sure we know what that means? There are plenty of anglophones who speak very good French and plenty of francophones of various cultural backgrounds who speak languages other than French. Will they all get protection of their collective rights at least for the French-speaking part of their being? If so, what will these rights consist of?

Can Haitian Quebecers, for instance, protect certain aspects of their own culture by claiming protection as part of the French-speaking collectivity? Or are they excluded from the "unique culture" which Quebec will have the power to promote through derogations from the charter? Can neo-Canadian Quebecers of whatever origin choose to renounce their heritage and origins so as to share with "old stock" Quebecers the protection sought for the French-speaking collectivity? Or are we dealing with a frankly racist notion that makes second- or third-class citizens of everyone but "old stock" Quebecers?

There are no certainties here, but what does seem clear is that it will not be for the individual to decide whether or not he or she belongs to the collectivity of "old stock" Quebecers. This will be decided by a Quebec government through laws adopted by majority vote in the National Assembly. And so from collective rights on down to the distinct society, thirst for power in some, together with apathy and sometimes stupidity in others, will have established that, as a basic element of Quebec society, a legislative majority will have justification for arbitrarily overriding the fundamental rights of any citizen who has the privilege of living in Quebec.

IV. Quebec's "Traditional" Demands

Max Nemni, professor of political science at Laval University, has shown in a book published last year[*] that between 1980 and 1992, Quebec's "traditional" and "minimum" demands have been anything but traditional or minimum.

---

[*] *Le Québec et la restructuration du Canada, 1980–1992*, Enjeux et Perspectives Septentrion (Québec: 1991).

Looking back further still, it can be seen that there has never been a definitive answer to the question "What does Quebec want?", which is still being asked by the few English-speaking Canadians who are not sick and tired of the evasiveness of Quebec nationalist thinking.

As far back as memory serves, French Canadians were essentially asking for one thing: respect for the French fact in Canada and incorporation of this fact into Canadian civil society, principally in the areas of language and education, and particularly in the federal government and provinces with French-speaking minorities. After two centuries of struggle and a few symbolic victories (bilingual money and stamps, for example), the Official Languages Act was passed in 1969 and minority-language education rights were entrenched in the Charter of 1982. The gates had suddenly opened and institutional bilingualism was recognized in Canada.

Then, equally suddenly, the Quebec nationalists no longer wanted the French language to be made equal with English throughout Canada. They denounced bilingualism as utopic at the very moment it was becoming a reality. With Bills 22 and 101, Quebec declared itself *unilingually* French and abandoned the cause of French-speaking minorities in other provinces, the better to marginalize the English-speaking minority in Quebec; the Quiet Revolution had suddenly empowered us to become indifferent to the first minority and intolerant of the second. It is as if we had practised virtue only out of weakness or hypocrisy.

Yet Premier Jean Lesage, the father of the Quiet Revolution, had spelled out Quebec's traditional demands at the federal–provincial conference held in July, 1960, a few weeks after the election that had brought him to power. In substance, they were as follows:

- Immediate resumption of talks on the repatriation of the Constitution and the constitutional amending formula;

- Insertion in the Constitution of a charter of rights, to include both language rights and education rights for French-speaking minorities outside Quebec;

• Creation of a constitutional court;

• Creation of a permanent federal–provincial affairs
secretariat;

• Annual meetings of provincial premiers;

• An end to conditional grants and shared-cost programs.

But whenever these objectives were about to be reached, Quebec's
"traditional" demands would begin to evolve. Then, in 1964, Premier
Lesage gave in to the nationalists and repudiated the Fulton–Favreau
agreement on repatriation, which his government had negotiated and
signed, and came up with an entirely new "traditional" demand, which
came to be known as "special status." The content of this notion
remained deliberately vague, for it was to become essentially an in
strument of blackmail: Quebec would never allow the Canadian Constitution to be brought home unless the country paid a ransom to
Quebec.

That ransom would vary from year to year, the only constant being
that, as soon as the ransom was paid, the Quebec government would
come up with a new one. Thus, under Lesage, there was a lot of "opting
out," by which various federal programs that were applicable throughout the country would be administered in Quebec by the Quebec government, but at the Canadian government's expense. There was also
much hoopla over the new *politique de grandeur*, through which it was
hoped that Quebec would gain recognition as an international power.

In 1966, Daniel Johnson's government took power, and Quebec's
new demand became "equality or independence."

In 1971, the profitable federalism premier scuttled his own agreement on repatriation and, as ransom, demanded the right to opt out of
family allowances. This had barely been paid when he demanded
another: cultural sovereignty.

In 1976, the sovereignty-association premier demanded sovereignty-association as ransom, failing which Quebec would become

totally independent. After the defeat in the referendum, this premier demanded merely a massive transfer of federal powers to the provinces (the Château Consensus of September, 1980) and refused to discuss even the possibility of repatriation until the transfer was assured. Then, in April, 1981, this premier allied himself with seven English-speaking provinces to demand an amending formula that provided for opting out with compensation.

On Nov. 5, 1981, the same premier spelled out his three conditions for agreeing to the constitutional deal that had just been made: an amending formula with a guarantee of full compensation to a province opting out of a transfer of powers; restrictions on the right to work anywhere in the country; and restrictions on minority-language education rights.

The federal government indicated that it was ready to talk, but less than two weeks later, on Nov. 13, 1981, these three conditions had disappeared and been replaced by three others: recognition of Quebec's distinct society, a constitutional veto and limitations to the charter.

After the federal election of 1984, the self-same premier recommended that Quebec give "the fine risk of federalism" a try.

The profitable federalism premier, when he had returned to power in 1985, demanded that Quebec's "distinct society" be mentioned in a preamble to the Constitution, failing which he would break off negotiations. A year or two later the "distinct society" was to be incorporated in the body of the Constitution as an interpretive clause (the Meech Lake accord), failing which Quebec would "resort to self-determination."

In February, 1990, while the Meech Lake accord was still being negotiated, this premier created the Allaire committee, whose mandate was to define the "traditional demands" to be made *after* the conclusion of the Meech Lake accord. The Allaire report, published less than a year later, demanded a massive transfer of federal powers just to Quebec. If this ransom were not paid, there would be a referendum on Quebec independence. As we know, this report was set aside by the premier at the policy convention of the Liberal Party of Quebec on Aug. 29, 1992.

Many in Quebec have the cheek to call this incredible grab bag "traditional demands"! And every time a new demand is announced, the self-appointed elites snap to attention, ready to feel humiliated if the ransom is not paid at once. Most incredible of all, there are still good souls in English Canada who are ready to take these temper tantrums seriously and urge their compatriots to pay each new ransom for fear of losing each "last chance" to save Canada. Poor things, they have not yet realized that the nationalists' thirst will never be satisfied, and that each new ransom paid to stave off the threat of schism will simply encourage the master blackmailers to renew the threat and double the ransom.

It has become clear that all the demands made of Canada by the Quebec nationalists can be summed up in just one: keep giving us new powers and the money to exercise them, or we'll leave. If Quebecers are offered the chance to have their cake and eat it, too, naturally they will accept. But as Canadians they also know that a country must choose to be or not to be; that dismantling Canada will not save it and the nationalists cannot be allowed to play the game of heads-I-win-tails-you-lose, or to hold referendums on independence every 10 years. And anyway, you cannot *really* believe in Canada and at the same time claim the right of self-determination for Canadian provinces.

"French Canadians have no opinions, they only have feelings," Sir Wilfrid Laurier said. For unscrupulous politicians, there is no surer way of rousing feelings than to trumpet a call to pride of race. French Canadians will be rid of this kind of politician if the blackmail ceases, and the blackmail will cease only if Canada refuses to dance to that tune. Impartial history has shown that it was exactly this attitude that pushed separatism to the brink of the grave between 1980 and 1984.

Separatism has regained a lot of ground since 1984, of course, but as the Portuguese proverb goes, "The worst is not always certain." However, to ward it off, our leaders will need a bit of courage.

Maclean's (September 28, 1992)

Lucien Bouchard, Illusionist

>‹

I accuse Lucien Bouchard of having misled the population of Quebec during last October's referendum campaign. By distorting the political history of his province and of his country, by spreading discord among its citizens with his demagogic rhetoric and by preaching contempt for those Canadians who did not share his views, Lucien Bouchard went beyond the limits of honest and democratic debate.

Truth must be restored in order to rehabilitate democracy in Quebec – this, I shall do by examining some of Mr. Bouchard's assertions between Oct. 14 and 27, 1995.

I – Failures and Their Causes

Mr. Bouchard's assertion:

"Countless negotiations have been held between Quebec and the rest of Canada over the past 30 years. All have failed. . . . Others have profited from our political weakness . . ." (Oct. 14, 1995 – Centre Communautaire de St. Justin, Rosemount).

The facts:

In 1964, in 1971 and 1981, it was the government of Quebec that sabotaged the negotiations by going back on its word. The Meech Lake Accord, in 1990, is a different matter, and I shall address it later.

1. In 1962, Premier Jean Lesage, with the strong support of his minister René Lévesque, had negotiated and signed the Fulton–Favreau accord to patriate the Canadian constitution. In 1964, Mr. Lesage changed his mind and repudiated the accord.

2. In 1971, Premier Robert Bourassa negotiated a constitutional agreement giving Quebec a veto as well as several other linguistic and legal benefits. The Canadian government convinced the premiers of the other provinces to accept this agreement. When the time came to sign the "Victoria Charter," Mr. Bourassa announced to his colleagues that he had new requests to present and that he needed a brief delay for tactical purposes. A few days later, he announced that he no longer wished to sign the agreement that he, himself, had negotiated and proposed.

3. On April 16, 1981, Premier René Lévesque signed, with seven other provinces, a constitutional agreement recognizing that Quebec was a province like all others, and did not have a constitutional veto ("This amending formula . . . recognizes the constitutional equality of each of Canada's provinces"). The objective of this agreement was to force the Canadian government to resume negotiating with a solid bloc of eight provinces. This tactic would eventually constitute an almost insurmountable obstacle to the patriation of the constitution once the Supreme Court of Canada, in September 1981, declared that, as conventions dictated, the Canadian government could not patriate without a "substantial level of provincial consent."

The Gang of Eight's solidarity was broken on Nov. 4, 1981, when, during a negotiation meeting and without warning his colleagues, René Lévesque accepted a proposal from Canada's prime minister to resolve the constitutional stumbling block through a referendum. By going back on his word to his seven allies, Mr. Lévesque forced them to regroup in a common front without him.

II – Demands and Their Consequences

Mr. Bouchard's assertion:

"For 30 years, the fundamental reason why . . . we were never able to convince English Canada [to concede] even Quebec's smallest historical demands is not that we sent people who were not good negotiators. We had the best ones. We had René Lévesque" (Oct. 18, 1995 – St. Léonard).

The facts:

Let us first examine the question of demands and then, that of the negotiators.

1. The true "historical" demands of French Canadians consisted essentially of one thing: respect for the French fact in Canada, mainly in the areas of language at the federal level and of education in the provinces where francophones were a minority. Thus the first two demands of Premier Lesage, presented in July 1960 at the start of the Quiet Revolution, were: first, to reopen negotiations for patriating the constitution and its amending formula, and second, to adopt, within the constitution, a charter of fundamental rights, including the linguistic and educational rights of French-speaking minorities outside Quebec.

Despite Mr. Bouchard's assertion, the Fulton–Favreau formula satisfied the first requirement; the Victoria Charter satisfied the first one fully and the second one partially; and the Constitution Act of 1982 entirely satisfied both requirements. In the three cases, these traditional demands were abandoned by successive Quebec governments when they went back on their word.

2. Let us examine the question of negotiators where, as Mr. Bouchard said, "we had the best ones." More particularly, how

can one explain that Mr. Lévesque, the master negotiator – who only had to hold his own for a few more hours to turn to his advantage the enormous enterprise of constitutional revision which had started in 1967 and was to end on Nov. 4, 1981 – could suddenly betray the Gang of Eight's accord to accept my offer of a public consultation via a referendum? Though this question will doubtless never be answered, I offer the following hypothesis. Did he fear that I would capitulate to the Eight and that, in order to accomplish patriation, I would accept their proposal? Mr. Lévesque would then have been caught at his own game since, by signing this accord, he had supported a patriation formula which included neither a distinct-society clause, nor a veto for his province.

But then, how can we explain that he then reneged on my referendum proposal which he had accepted a few hours before? Was he negotiating in good faith, or rather, was he trying to sabotage any federal–provincial co-operation designed to solve the constitutional problem?

III – The Night of the Long Knives: Sheer Fabrication

Mr. Bouchard's assertion:

"Although there was an alliance with René Lévesque to reach a reasonable agreement, these seven English-speaking provinces . . . abandoned him in the course of one night" (Oct. 23, 1995 – CEGEP de Limoilou).

It should first be noted that when Mr. Bouchard speaks of a "reasonable agreement" he does not know what he is talking about. This agreement explicitly rejected both the notion of distinct society and that of a veto, two items which Mr. Bouchard is constantly seeking for Quebec.

The facts:

The "night" in question is, of course, that of the so-called long knives, a label shamelessly borrowed from Nazi history by separatists suffering from acute paranoia. What really happened?

When René Lévesque betrayed his allies of the Gang of Eight by accepting my referendum proposal, he lost his credibility with them. The seven English-speaking premiers were in disarray and the session was adjourned to the following day, Nov. 5.

But it should be underlined that the seven English provinces did not, as Mr. Bouchard says, abandon Mr. Lévesque. Rather, it is Mr. Lévesque who abandoned them. He plunged the knife into the heart of the very accord he had signed less than seven months earlier.

And when Mr. Bouchard, in his Oct. 25 speech to the nation, says that Mr. Lévesque's "so-called allies . . . went to meet Jean Chrétien in an Ottawa hotel room in the middle of the night," this is historical falsehood.

Here is how the newspapers reported these events at that time:

As soon as the meeting was adjourned, around noon on Nov. 4, Mr. Lévesque is quoted as saying: "For us, it [the Trudeau proposal] seems to be a respectable and extraordinarily interesting way of extricating ourselves from this imbroglio." To which Claude Charron, one of his ministers, added: "For us, it is the ideal solution." *Le Devoir* reported that "at that point, the Quebec delegation was jubilant and, at the risk of offending its partners of the Common Front, did not hesitate to climb on board with Ottawa" (*Le Devoir*, Nov. 5, 1981).

The "risk of offending its partners" was not an imaginary one, the Quebec delegation finally realized in the afternoon of Nov. 4. This led René Lévesque to repudiate my referendum proposal without any explanation other than saying, "It is all Greek to me." Michel Vastel, a journalist then with *Le Devoir*, wrote: "By the end of the day, the bridges were burning between Lévesque and his former allies." He added that later, while everyone thought agreements were under discussion, "a senior Quebec official, who had been asked why he did not make a last-ditch effort to keep the provinces together, glumly answered: 'After what has happened this morning, we have lost all credibility'" (*Le Devoir*, Nov. 6, 1981).

For more details on the press commentaries, see "Le Désaccord du Lac Meech" in Max Nemni's book *Le Québec et la Restructuration du Canada* (pp. 177–79), and William Johnson's *A Canadian Myth* (pp. 180–83).

IV – Language, Education and the Veto

Mr. Bouchard's assertion:

The Constitution Act of 1982 "reduced Quebec's powers in the fields of language and education. . . . René Lévesque refused it. Claude Ryan refused it. The National Assembly of Quebec refused it" (Oct. 25, 1995, 7 p.m., Radio-Canada television).

The facts:

1. In the areas of language and education, the Constitution Act of 1982 enshrined precisely the "traditional requests from Quebec." Here is what Claude Ryan had to say about it the day after Lucien Bouchard made the above comment: "The Constitution Act of 1982 that Mr. Trudeau passed is not as dreadful as some like to pretend. It is a very reasonable law: it gave a Charter of Rights to all Canadians, Quebecers and others alike, and it reinforced the protection of linguistic rights for francophones throughout Canada." And elsewhere: "I heard Mr. Bouchard last night saying that [the Constitution of 1982] had stripped Quebec of important rights in language and education. In my humble opinion, it's not true. It's just not true."

While he disapproved of the "fact that the act had been enacted without Quebec's signature," Claude Ryan recognized that "objectively, the changes brought about by the act of 1982 were very good changes, except where the amending formula is concerned" (Oct. 26, 1995, Interview with Bernard Derome, Radio-Canada television and Château Frontenac, RDI).

2. I, myself, shared Mr. Ryan's reservations with regard to the amending formula. But it should be remembered that the formula used in the constitution of 1982 was based on the one

proposed by Mr. Lévesque and the seven other provinces that formed the Gang of Eight. This formula gave no veto to Quebec, while the one proposed by my government included a veto.

Thus, on Dec. 2, 1981, *Le Devoir* published my reply to a letter from Premier Lévesque dated Nov. 25, 1981, requesting a veto for Quebec. I said, in part: "Between 1971 and Nov. 5, 1981, every government I headed put forth an amending formula which would have given Quebec a veto. We only abandoned the principle after you had done so yourself" by signing the accord of the Eight and after "you had once again proposed [this accord] during our sessions of Nov. 2, 3, 4 and 5."

3. Furthermore, failing that veto, the accord of the Eight gave the provinces a right to opt out which was enshrined in section 38 (3) of the Constitution Act of 1982. This right allows each province to refuse any constitutional change that would diminish its "legislative jurisdiction" or its "rights and privileges."

Consequently, Mr. Bouchard is showing that he knows nothing about the 1982 constitution when he alleges that the Chrétien governments – after a No vote – will want "to perpetuate the current situation which gives the federal apparatus and the English-speaking provinces . . . the power to impose anything they want on Quebec" (Oct. 17, 1995, 7:25 p.m., Westin Hotel, Montreal).

Such stupid allegations – and they were legion – flow more from hallucination than from the science of politics.

V – The 1982 Patriation
Mr. Bouchard's assertion:

"In 1982, the constitution was patriated against our will . . . because the interests of English Canada impelled them to act in this fashion" (Oct. 27, 1995, Radio-Canada TV).

The facts:

Mr. Bouchard certainly has a strange way of interpreting our constitutional history! Wasn't it rather the French Canadians who had traditionally striven to free themselves from colonial ties with Great Britain by patriating the Canadian constitution from London? As for "interests," those of the predominantly English provinces were generally the same as Quebec's: to exchange their consent to patriation for increased provincial powers.

Since 1927, every Canadian government, from that of Mackenzie King to that of Bennett, St. Laurent, Diefenbaker and Pearson, had tried in vain to persuade the provinces to end this vestige of colonialism. All had failed and Canada was the only country in the world to have as its constitution a law located in another country which could be amended, for the most part, only by that other country. In 1982, we were emerging from an extensive constitutional debate begun in 1967 by the provinces. Canadian citizens had had enough of it and the matter needed to be laid to rest – 115 years after becoming a country, Canada still depended upon London's consent to amend its constitution. Could Canada face yet another defeat when the only opposition to patriation came from a provincial government set upon destroying the country? Would the project have to grind to a halt because of an adversary who wanted sovereignty for his province, but who refused it for our country?

Three provinces, including Quebec, had asked the Supreme Court of Canada to define the rules of the constitutional game. The ruling was that patriation could happen only in the presence of a "substantial level of provincial consent." This requirement was amply satisfied with nine provinces out of 10 giving their consent.

Quebec's premier was opposed to patriation but, as the rules of the above-mentioned game stated, he had no veto. In any case, he had explicitly waived this veto upon signing the accord of the Eight. It was clear that his government wanted nothing to do with a project that could be advantageous to the Canadian federation.

Moreover, 70 of the 75 members elected to the federal Parliament by Quebec had voted for patriating the constitution while, in Quebec's National Assembly, 38 members – led by Mr. Ryan – out of 108 had voted on Dec. 1, 1981, against a resolution which, for all practical purposes, slammed the door on the current efforts to seek compromises. Thus, less than 40 per cent of all elected representatives of Quebec were adamantly opposed to the constitutional agreement. One may dispute this arithmetic analysis by arguing that Quebec's government is the only body allowed to speak for Quebecers, but this claim is the very essence of separatism. If one believes in Canada, one must equally believe that, in matters constitutional, Quebec members elected to the Canadian Parliament represented Quebec's electorate just as much as the members of the Quebec National Assembly did.

Furthermore, polls have shown that patriation of the constitution was not being rejected by the people. In March 1982, a CROP poll indicated that 48 per cent of Quebecers blamed Mr. Lévesque's government for refusing to sign the accord, while only 32 per cent agreed with it. In June of the same year, a Gallup poll found that 49 per cent of Quebecers approved of the Constitution Act and only 16 per cent disapproved.

VI – Who Said No to Meech?
Mr. Bouchard's assertion:

"They [English Canada] rejected the hand offered by Quebec in 1990. . . . No one came to Montreal to demonstrate and claim 'We love you.' They simply said No to Meech" (Oct. 27, 1995, 7:30 p.m., Radio-Canada TV).

The facts:

Two days before the referendum, separatists would, of course, have preferred that a few English extremists trample the Quebec flag. But to mock the tens of thousands Canadians who came to Quebec from other provinces on Oct. 27, 1995, to express their support and their hope to the people of Quebec is, at the very least, inelegant. And, in fact, who had said No to Meech?

1. On June 3, 1987, the Canadian government and the nine English-speaking provinces said Yes to Meech and signed the Meech Lake Accord. Throughout Canada, the English press was generally in favor of it. In Quebec, the English press and

Alliance Quebec, standard-bearer of anglo-Quebecers, had said Yes to it from the outset.

2. In Quebec, French opinion-leaders generally said No to Meech. Only 18 per cent of the experts who spoke to the parliamentary commission set up by the Bourassa government in April 1987 said Yes to Meech – 70 per cent were against it. As for groups and associations, 19 per cent were in favor of Meech and 81 per cent were against it. And all these groups saying No to Meech were essentially French-speaking organizations such as the three largest labor federations (CSN, FTQ, CEQ) a teachers' group (l'Alliance des Professeurs de Montréal), an artists' group (l'Union des Artistes), a writers' group (l'Union des Ecrivains), a farmers' union (l'Union des Producteurs Agricoles) (see Nemni, op. cit.).

3. As for Quebec's political groups, the Parti Québécois and the NDP were firmly *against* the Meech Lake Accord. Then, surprisingly, Premier Bourassa, while saying he had to sign the accord, went on the record to say he had reservations. In fact, as early as May 12, 1987, even *before* the accord was adopted, he had declared to the National Assembly that his government had taken "another step toward a *temporary* solution to the constitutional problem. . . . There would be other requests and other discussions later, or a second series, or *other series* of constitutional reform." On June 18, 1987, Mr. Bourassa felt impelled to speak to the National Assembly about Quebec's "right of self-determination" and to recall that it was included "in the constitutional program of the Liberal Party." Finally, on June 23, 1987, he concluded the debate in the National Assembly with the following words: "The leader of the opposition [Mr. Pierre-Marc Johnson] constantly refers to constitutional matters which have yet to be settled. Does he forget that there will be a *second* round of discussions?"

4. But Mr. Bourassa himself did not forget: in February 1990, more than four months before the deadline for the final ratification of the Meech Lake Accord, his party adopted a resolution to "set up a constitutional committee (the Allaire committee) which would prepare the political content of the *second round* of negotiations which would start *after* the accord was ratified." It also contained a veiled threat: the committee would also examine scenarios "to prepare for a possible failure of the Meech Lake Accord."

Mr. Bourassa had dusted off his Victoria tactic from 1971: to negotiate an agreement but, even before its signature, announce that it does not satisfy Quebec and that other requests will follow. (He would again do the same with the Charlottetown Accord in 1992 when he compared the referendum to a lottery.)

5. One might assume that such actions would disillusion the good people of Canada who thought that acceptance of Meech would satisfy Quebec and bring constitutional peace to the country. But no! Astonishingly, on Jan. 23, 1990, after such inflammatory remarks and equivocal posturing coming from Quebec, including the use of the notwithstanding clause to ban English signs, seven English-speaking provinces and the Canadian government still supported Meech. Two provinces had yet to take a definitive stand, because of the hesitancy of *one* premier and the opposition of *one* native member of the Manitoba legislature.

How can one seriously conclude, as Lucien Bouchard does, that it is "English Canada" who "rejected the hand offered by Quebec in 1990" and who "simply said No to Meech"?

VII – I Accuse Lucien Bouchard

By calling upon fallacies and untruths to advance the cause of hateful demagoguery, Lucien Bouchard misled the electors during last

October's referendum. By his actions, he tarnished Quebec's good reputation as a democratic society and he does not deserve the trust of the people of this province.

The Montreal *Gazette*
(February 3, 1996)
(Published simultaneously in
French in *La Presse*)

A Reply to Lucien Bouchard

><

So I have written a whole page in *The Gazette* accusing Lucien Bouchard of having, on many occasions, "betrayed the population of Quebec during last October's referendum campaign." And the current premier of Quebec has filled a whole page in the same newspaper without refuting even one of my accusations.

True, Mr. Bouchard dug up a few of my old pearls of wisdom. True also, he vilified Jean Chrétien and praised Brian Mulroney. He certainly wrote at length on Quebec's indivisibility and neglected to mention Canada's divisibility. And he placed the responsibility for invoking the War Measures Act squarely on my shoulders without recalling that this was done at the express and written request of both the premier of Quebec and the mayor of Montreal.

In short, he has hidden behind historical relativism to avoid having to reply to my accusations. He wrote: "There will never be a single, definitive reading of the history of relations between Quebec and Canada over the past 30 years." It doubtless follows that he does not have to correct the historical falsehoods of which he has been guilty.

This relativism sometimes leads to strange conclusions. In one instance he describes as "Quebec's historical claims" the three contradictory programs of the three political parties existing in Quebec in

1969: "equality or independence," the "distinct status" and "sover-eignty-association." It is not surprising that the refrain "What does Quebec want?" was uttered so frequently in those days.

Elsewhere, to avoid having to reply to a precise accusation, Mr. Bouchard distorts it. About the events of Nov. 4, 1981, I wrote that "René Lévesque had betrayed his allies of the Gang of Eight by accepting my proposal for a referendum," a fact which was confirmed by the newspapers of the day. Mr. Bouchard turns this into "Here is what René Lévesque is being accused of: wanting for Canadians and Quebecers to express themselves through a referendum."

Toward the end, Mr. Bouchard waxes lyrical: "In Quebec, leaders such as Jean Lesage and René Lévesque, Daniel Johnson senior and junior, Jacques Parizeau, Claude Ryan and Brian Mulroney . . . all of them, at one time or another, have been repudiated, scorned, accused by Pierre Elliott Trudeau. . . . I have been admitted into that club of democrats. With them, and with all Quebecers, I plead guilty."

Mr. Bouchard, you misread me – I never accused you of being a democrat. What you must understand, however, is that all those people you named, and with whom you identify, were political adversaries in one way or another, and that words can sometimes be harsh between political adversaries.

I say "adversaries in one way or another," but I should explain: I have the nerve to possess a deeper confidence than these adversaries in the strength and the abilities of French Canadians from Quebec and elsewhere.

That is why I have always opposed the notions of special status and distinct society. With the Quiet Revolution, Quebec became an adult and its inhabitants have no need of favors or privileges to face life's challenges and to take their rightful place within Canada and in the world at large.

They should not look for their "identity" and their "distinctness" in the constitution but rather in their confidence in themselves and in the full exercise of their rights as citizens equal to all other citizens of Canada.

I do not doubt for one instant that they would be capable of making Quebec an independent country. But I have always believed that they have the stature to face a more difficult and nobler challenge – that of participating in the construction of a Canadian nation founded on democratic pluralism, institutional bilingualism and the sense of sharing.

In the era of the global village, the very notion of sovereignty is becoming obsolete, and it is to protect what is left of it that large-scale amalgamations are being formed.

But Canada already occupies half a continent. To weaken it by dividing it would be a historic blunder of infinite proportion. We must not rend the fabric of this still-young country, we must give it the chance to grow and to prosper.

This, premier, is what I had to tell you. I still have sufficient respect for political involvement to recognize that, in your own way, you believe that you are working for the good of Quebec. Because I do not believe your way to be the right one, I do not wish you success. But I say to you, all the same, "God bless."

The Montreal *Gazette* (February 17, 1996). (Published simultaneously in French in *La Presse*.)

From 1968 to 1984

"I was not in politics to acquire material to write a book. I was too busy doing my job and living my life to spend time keeping notes." Consequently, Pierre Elliott Trudeau neither wrote nor published anything during these sixteen years. But like all heads of government, he made many speeches and replied, on the most diverse subjects, to the countless questions put to him by journalists following in his train, abroad as much as in Canada. Here is a sampling of statements he made in public debates of the time.

Selling the Prairie Farmers' Wheat

>‹

Q: Mr. Prime Minister, I would like to know how and when you are going to sell the Canadian farmers' wheat?

A: Well, why should I sell the Canadian farmers' wheat? You know, the way I understand the system, the Canadian farmer has been very productive, very progressive, and very aggressive. He has increased his productivity enormously. He has founded co-operatives, he has organized the Wheat Board – which is not a political instrument once again, it is something which I think belongs as much to the farmers as to the Canadian government – and he has chosen to operate in a free-market economy. He is entitled, I think, the wheat farmer, to as much protection from the Canadian government as other producers get in other countries with whom he has to be in competition. And there are various forms of assistance. I shouldn't be telling this out in the West – I am only beginning to learn these things.

But there are crop insurances, and there are advance payments, and there is PFRA to help land assembly and irrigation and so on. There are various ways in which the State does intervene to help the farmer in distress. But every time there is a drought in another country and we sell more, or every time the other countries produce more and they don't have to buy as much from Canada, or every time our produce is not competitive with produce of other countries, which perhaps sell different kinds of wheat that are cheaper and of which you can produce more per acre, it's all of Canada's problem, because the wheat is so important to the Canadian economy. But it is, first and foremost, the farmer's problem. He makes his representations known, believe me, through his members of Parliament. We hear them every day and that is right. But I think we all realize that, as in the case of other sectors of the economy, the alternative is for the State to be the producer, to own the land, to own the wheat, to hire the farmers and to pay them a wage, and then it will be our problem to sell it and to market it. But if we want to have something of a free economy, we can assist – as we do politically – the farmer in various ways. We can also perhaps encourage and hope-fully prod sometimes the Wheat Board. But the Wheat Board, I think, on balance – and you would say this perhaps more than I – has done a very good job selling our wheat. In cases where we cannot sell it, we make it part of our external aid program.

Winnipeg, Address to Liberal
party, 13 December 1968

The United States

><

I have a very great respect for the United States and its institutions. I think it is an extraordinarily powerful society. It's vital. It's a tough society in the good sense of the word. It has lived through difficult problems and I'm sure that it has the wherewithal to answer difficult questions. As a student of the law, I would say that I have in particular a very great respect for the legal thought that you have developed there – I'm not talking of public lawmaking, but of the institutions which grew up around your political institutions, the Supreme Court, the federal system of government, and so on.

So, I think we are very fortunate to have as a neighbour this very great country. It has obvious economic benefits, it has obvious technological benefits, it has obvious cultural benefits; we are in a sense sheltered by the U.S. umbrella. But all these assets obviously are counterbalanced by the fact that it is such a large and strong power that, in the kind of good-neighbour relationship that has existed for a long while, the little guy always feels the rough edges more sensitively than the big guy does, and we have to be careful lest the economic benefits we draw from our relations with the United States lead to a form of economic domination which would then lead to atrophy of our political independence. We have to make the same assessment in the area of international relations, that what we gain by having such a strong big brother – I say that in a non-Orwellian sense – we lose by the fact that we cannot be a hundred per cent independent. Of course, no country can, not even the United States, but perhaps the measure of our independence is considerably reduced.

In the cultural field it is obvious too. I believe that the benefit that I have underlined, underscored, in the legal field can be extended to many other fields; the intellectual presence of the great universities, the cultural dynamism of a city like New York.

Interview with Jay Walz,
The New York Times,
November 22, 1968

Democracy and Minorities

＞＜

A democratic society and system of government, while among the grandest of human concepts, are among the most difficult to implement. In a democracy, it is all too easy for the majority to forget the rights of the minority, and for a remote and powerful government to ignore its protests. It is all too easy, should disturbances erupt, to crush them in the name of law and order. We must never forget that, in the long run, a democracy is judged by the way the majority treats the minority. Louis Riel's battle is not yet won.

That is why I suggest that we should never respond to demands for just treatment by pointing to other examples of injustice. If a certain right is attacked or denied in one province, it is not a valid reason for refusing similar rights in another. Yet such excuses are offered; and this leads to a vicious circle in which no improvement in human liberties is possible. The rights of individual Canadians are too important to be used as bargaining chips. Every government must accept responsibility for the rights of the citizens within its own jurisdiction. Canada as a whole suffers when any of her citizens is denied his rights; for that injustice places the rights of all of us in jeopardy.

Unveiling of Louis Riel Monument,
Regina, October 2, 1968

Parliament, the Opposition

><

The role of the Opposition is an important one and I do not wish here to embark on a judgement of their performance; I'd rather leave that to the Canadian electorate. I do think, however, that it is now more important than ever for the Opposition to present realistic alternatives, especially on fundamental questions. I don't think that at this sophisticated stage of our democracy people conceive of the Opposition as merely a tool with which to find scandals in the ranks of the government or to level criticism or jibes at specific actions. I think the Opposition will more and more be called upon to suggest alternatives, which means spelling out their own policy rather than merely attacking ours.

The Canadian public is participating in the discussion of many of the major issues. Academics are participating; editorial writers, newspapers, and the magazines are arguing for certain courses of action, and, I think, more and more the Opposition will also have to state its priorities and its solutions to specific problems.

A kind of game has been going on for a long while in the democracies where Opposition parties criticize the government for raising taxes and at the same time call for vastly increasing expenditures in various fields. I think this kind of game is gone and done with, and it's a good thing.

Answers to questions by
Charles Templeton, *Maclean's*,
April 3, 1969

Opposition to Separatism

><

Now, why am I such an opponent of separatism? I guess I just feel that the challenge of the age is to live together with people who don't have all the same values as yourself. I believe in pluralistic societies. I believe that the way of progress is through the free exchange of ideas and confrontation of values. Separatism is really an ethnocentric-based society which says all the French must live together, and all the Scottish, and all the Welsh, and all the Irish, and there should be no intercommunication between them except at the official level of the State. I think the wealth of a society and the wealth of a country like Canada, and no doubt New Zealand, is that we have immigrants who come from all parts of the world, and we have people who were there before we arrived, like the Indians and the Eskimos. And the challenge is to have all these values challenge each other in terms of excellence, and it is the challenge which permits a society to develop on the basis of excellence.

TV program *Gallery*, New Zealand Broadcasting Commission, Wellington, NZ, May 14, 1970

The Environment

⤞⤝

If part of our heritage is our wilderness, and if the measure of Canada is the quality of the life available to Canadians, then we must act should there be any threat to either. We must act to protect the freshness of our air and the purity of our water, we must act to conserve our living resources. If necessary, we must offer leadership to the world in these respects and withstand the cries of complaining vested interests.

. . .

Perhaps the responsibility for acting decisively in this area should fall with greatest force upon countries such as ours, which are gifted with almost limitless space. We have, after all, the most to gain. As we come to appreciate the great value of our wilderness, so should we take whatever step is necessary to preserve it. If we do not tackle systematically and effectively this simple problem – one which requires little more than determination and discipline – how can we suggest to some of our neighbours in this global village that they attack with more fortitude another of the great problems which threaten to stifle us, that of overpopulation? No complicated factors of religion, or culture, or lack of understanding compound our problem. Only greed and indifference stand in the way of a solution.

National Press Club, Canberra,
Australia, May 18, 1970

I Am a Believer

><

Ed: Now, I'm going to get personal. I have been told you are a devout Catholic. I know that you don't let photographers take pictures of you going to church and apparently you don't even want it mentioned that you go to church. I don't know whether you are a devout Catholic or not, I don't know whether the people know.

PM: I honestly don't know what they mean by a devout Catholic.

Ed: Well, you are a believer and you go to church?

PM: Yes. Does that make you a devout man?

Ed: No.

PM: I believe in life after death, I believe in God, and I'm a Christian.

Ed: Did you ever in your youth for a time leave your faith or find yourself severely shaken in it?

PM: I was shaken to the extent that people who criticized me used to say that I was Protestant more than a Catholic because I like to impose constraints on myself, but I don't like them to be imposed from the outside. You will remember that in Shaw's preface to *Saint Joan* he describes her as perhaps the first Protestant: sometimes I felt sympathy with that. I believe that the Catholic Church now would find much more accommodation for this type of person than did the particular

302

milieu I was brought up in school. But as to whether I had any philosophical doubts, about life and the hereafter and so on, I don't think I would like to answer that because I'm not sure how significant such doubts are. I mean, as does every young man studying philosophy, I naturally asked myself questions about the truth of all this, and about the meaning of freedom, predestination, and liberty of choice and so on. But to have asked questions of yourself about it, I think is not too important. Let's say that I remained – I remain – a believer.

United Church Observer,
September 1971

The Commonwealth

><

This is perhaps the greatest strength of the Commonwealth, this opportunity on a regular basis for men of goodwill to sit down together and discuss one with another the problems which affect them and the 850 million people whom they represent. All the other advantages of the Commonwealth relationship – the exchanges of people, the trading patterns, the economic assistance and cooperation schemes, the informality of diplomatic representation – these all assume their tone from the free and frank dialogue which takes place at the prime-ministerial meetings.

...

There is little headline material in that kind of decision; neither is there much domestic political advantage for individual leaders. But to a world burdened almost beyond endurance by incredibly complex problems of immense moment, an agreement to disagree and to search patiently for solutions and areas of agreement is of immeasurable value. Delegates can walk out of meetings in anger. But they cannot remove with them the underlying cause of their annoyance. Organizations can be broken apart by impatient members, but the act of disintegration contributes nothing to the easing of the original tensions.

As the Commonwealth grows in number of members it increases in diversity. The common ingredients, which were once the adhesive of membership, are now outnumbered by the unique institutions and practices of so many of the members. Nor, wisely in my view, have any steps been taken to create some artificial adhesive or binder. There is no charter, no constitution, no headquarters building, no flag, no continuing executive framework. Apart from the secretariat, which is a fraction of the size one might expect for an organization which encompasses a quarter of the people on this earth, there is nothing about the Commonwealth that one can grasp or point to as evidence of a structure. Even the use of the word "organization" creates an impression of a framework, which is misleading. The Commonwealth is an organism, not an institution – and this fact gives promise not only of continued growth and vitality, but of flexibility as well.

Commonwealth Conference,
Singapore, 1971

La Francophonie

><

It is a great honour today for Canada to welcome the representatives of so many countries, coming from almost every continent. This vast assembly is a sort of microcosm of the world; the fact that it should decide to hold its meeting in a country of the New World, a country still fulfilling itself, is for us a source of comfort, of profound joy, and of particular pride.

Over four centuries ago, the French fact laid down roots in our midst. In spite of many difficulties, in spite of the towering presence of the English language in North America, the French fact has held fast among us for over four centuries, the French language has been spoken and jealously guarded for four centuries. Not only is French being preserved, but as you will see during your visits, particularly in Quebec, French is celebrated and sung here.

We all know that La Francophonie has now become a reality. But you will appreciate how moved we are to see it brought together and given shape here. It's a little as if the permanence of French Canada were being confirmed.

This General Meeting of the Agence de coopération culturelle et technique has special meaning for Canada. And it marks a turning-point in the life of the agency.

In less than two years, the agency has moved so fast that we are already seeing the international dimensions of its character reach around the world. A generous idea has taken shape, and from now on that idea will make a difference to the human community. Because the agency is one of those all too rare structures which enable continents, races, and cultures to work towards a common cause. Indeed, the agency stands out in the world because it acts in the name of cooperation, exchanges, and development.

...

La Francophonie Is a Destiny

We now have an instrument derived from modernity. A welcoming presence in the world now emerging around us, the social and cultural integration of the boldest creations in science and technology – these are some of the important things our governments expect of the agency. La Francophonie is not a memory: it is a destiny.

Opening remarks, General
Meeting of the Agence de
coopération culturelle et
technique, 1971
Translation by George Tombs

The Future of Canada

><

Canadians by and large tend to think of Canada as a land of immense potential. Not just as a big land, which it unquestionably is. Or a privileged land, as many others enviously regard us. But as a land of limitless promise. A land, perhaps, on the threshold of greatness.

Toronto and District Liberal
Association, March 3, 1971

The Referendum

><

Mr. Lévesque has said himself that if he loses one referendum, he will not be bound by that loss; he will hold another. So, I do not think I will be bound by a win, particularly a win showing that 51 per cent were in favour of Quebec separating.

I do not think that the referendum itself will prove anything except the finding of an opinion poll at a particular time, and that opinion poll will be judged by the timing, by the wording of the question, and so forth.

. . .

Sure, Mr. Lévesque said there would be another referendum. I doubt whether he would be there to lead it. If he lost a referendum very badly, he obviously would have failed in his *raison d'être* for being a politician and I would suggest he would go away. And at the converse of that, I say it before you say it, is that if Québec were to vote very massively for a separation in an election or in any other forum, I would have failed and I would silently go away, perhaps to fight another day in another field.

Interview on the CTV Network
Broadcast, December 28, 1976

Capital Punishment

✦

I do not deny that society has the right to punish a criminal, and the right to make the punishment fit the crime, but to kill a man for punishment alone is an act of vengeance. Nothing else. Some would prefer to call it retribution, because that word has a nicer sound. But the meaning is the same.

My primary concern here is not compassion for the murderer. My concern is for the society which adopts vengeance as an acceptable motive for its collective behaviour. Vengeance and violence damage and destroy those who adopt them, and lessen respect for the dignity and rights of others among those who condone them.

Respect for human life is absolutely vital for the rights and freedom we all enjoy. Even the life of the most hardened criminal must be accorded some degree of respect in a free society. If we take that life without proven purpose, without proven necessity, then we weaken dangerously one of the fundamental principles which allow us to live together in peace, harmony, and mutual respect.

. . .

It is because I have an enduring confidence in mankind, and confidence in society's ability to protect itself without taking human life, that I am eager to support this bill and vote for the abolition of capital punishment.

House of Commons, Debate of
the Bill to Abolish Capital
Punishment, June 15, 1976

PART VI

Einstein and Ralston Prize Lectures

*After leaving active politics, Pierre Elliott Trudeau received
many accolades, including two prestigious awards: the Albert Einstein
Peace Prize (in Washington, D.C., on November 13, 1984) and
the Jackson H. Ralston Prize "for distinguished contributions
to the development of the role of law in international relations"
(at Stanford University, on January 30, 1990). Here are the
two acceptance speeches he made.*

The Nuclear Peril

><

I should state at the outset that I do not believe nuclear war to be either imminent or inevitable. If I thought otherwise, I would not be talking to you now; rather, I would be stocking up with canned goods in some remote hideaway, preferably in the Southern Hemisphere.

But I do believe total nuclear war to be *possible* . . .

[However,] I believe Einstein gave us justifiable cause for hope and involvement when he stated, albeit in another context: "Der herr gott ist raffiniert, aber boshast ist er nicht" – ("God may be subtle, but he is not plain mean"). In other words, the problem of making peace more likely than war in a nuclear age may be extraordinarily complex, and the solution may be agonizingly elusive. Indeed, it may be at once the most important and the most difficult intellectual question of all time; but there is no conspiracy of nature, no diabolical force making the problem insoluble.

As a matter of fact, in reviewing the literature on the subject over the past several years, I am very impressed by the massive intellectual effort which is being directed – particularly in the United States – toward reducing the likelihood of nuclear war. . . . Let me just mention the Harvard group's *Living with Nuclear War*, and subsequent studies.

Scholars, in and out of universities, institutes and think-tanks; moralists, both clerical and lay; military strategists, active or retired; members of the liberal professions, particularly doctors: all are contributing to a body of thought, which continues to grow in breadth and in depth, on the subject of avoidance of nuclear war. That in itself should be cause for great optimism if it were not for the following fact.

On the whole, government leaders seem unwilling or unable to contribute much to the solution of the problem. I do not suggest that they are not concerned. I bear evidence to the contrary in that some two dozen heads of state or of government, over a period of three months, adjusted their agendas, sometimes at great inconvenience to themselves, to discuss with me Canada's peace initiative of a year ago.

Equally, 42 Commonwealth leaders at their meeting in India, with the late, lamented Mrs. Gandhi in the chair, devoted some two days to discussing the nuclear peril. And the initiatives of the Parliamentarians for World Order led to a most welcome statement by a distinguished group of six officeholders. . . .

But this show of concern is generally sporadic, and can only occasionally be characterized as seminal. More important, it is not being translated into political action by the political community as a whole.

Compare the past ten years to the previous ten. From 1963 to 1974, multilateral and bilateral (U.S.–U.S.S.R.) arms control agreements or treaties included: the Limited Test Ban Treaty, the Hot-Line Agreement, the Outer-Space Treaty, the Non-Proliferation Treaty [NPT], the Seabed Arms Control Treaty, the Accidents Measures Agreement, the Anti-Ballistic Missile Agreement, the SALT I Agreement, the Biological Weapons Convention, the Prevention of Nuclear War Agreement, the Threshold Test-Ban Treaty.

Since 1974, there has been only one multilateral treaty, the Environmental Modification Agreement, and two U.S.–U.S.S.R. agreements, SALT II and the Peaceful Nuclear Explosions Treaty, and both have remained unratified. But no progress on the START, no agreement on the INF* Talks, no results on MBFR† in Vienna, no advance in Stockholm, no movement yet on the NPT, even though the treaty is up for review in 1985.

One might surmise that such a dismal record would spur heads of government, both East and West, into action. But consider the following: for the first time since the Harmel Report of 1967, NATO attempted a comprehensive analysis of East–West relations in May 1984. And though one must welcome the desire for dialogue and the call for increased levels of security at lower levels of armaments, as set out in the report, one must sadly recognize that the report fails to deal with the Alliance's most important hard issue: military strategy. Efforts to open up that can of worms have been rejected as premature and divisive.

Alas! Having attended four out of the six Summits held since NATO's inception in 1949, I bear solemn witness to the fact that NATO heads of State and of government meet only to go through the tedious motions of reading speeches, drafted by others, with the principal objective of not rocking the boat. Indeed, any attempt to start a discussion, or to question the meaning of the communiqué – also drafted by others long before the meetings began – was met with stony embarrassment, or strong objection. Is it any wonder that the value of NATO as a political alliance is increasingly being questioned?

Discussions of the nuclear threat among leaders at the Economic Summits are somewhat more tolerated. But the pressure to conform is every bit as strong as at NATO Summits. Efforts at Williamsburg to send out a message of peace as well as one of military preparedness, and attempts in London to include on the agenda a discussion of areas of common ground between East and West, were characterized as "giving comfort to the Russians"!

I cannot, of course, vouch for what happens at Warsaw Pact

---

* Intermediate Nuclear Force.
† Mutual and Balanced Force Reduction.

Summits, but having had discussions with several of the participants, I can fairly guess that the party line is adhered to every bit as much on their side as it is on ours. And I do know for a fact that a Ceausescu's initiatives are no more eagerly welcomed over there than a Papandreou's over here.[*]

Meanwhile, a handful of scientists and technocrats, in their genius and devotion to what governments believe to be right, have brought the human race to the brink of extinction. In ten years, their shortsighted dedication has moved us back from the fearsome but stable balance of terror which we called nuclear deterrence, and taken us into an era of highly destabilizing weapons systems.

I relate these facts, not in a spirit of grievance, but in order to provoke reflection on a most astonishing reality: it is the political leaders in office who will decide whether the possibility of nuclear war will be transformed into a likelihood, and from a likelihood into a reality; it is they who will be held accountable for the success or failure of efforts to turn back Armageddon. Not the scientists, not the military commanders, not the arms merchants, not the negotiators; but the politicians. And yet, they are the ones who are mostly absent from the discussion and attempted resolution of the nuclear impasse. Why?

I had long sought the answer in terms of the personalities of leaders and the mood of nations, as influenced by their political misfortunes: Watergate, Vietnam, Teheran, in the case of the United States; the lost showdown over the Cuban missiles, the Polish upheaval, and the continuing leadership crises, in the case of the U.S.S.R.

I was wrong. The explanation lies in a much more simple paradox: the politicians who once stated that war was too important to be left to the generals now act as though peace were too complex to be left to themselves.

In saying so, I intend no offence to the political leaders. The subject-matter is esoteric, the literature is voluminous, replete with

---

[*] A reference to the unease caused by Greek premier Andreas Papandreou's questioning of NATO Alliance policies and the proposed nuclear-freeze initiative with non-aligned nations – Ed.

jargon and laced with contradictions. Any government leader who
wanted to master the topic completely would have difficulty in dis-
charging all his other duties, particularly when the difficult economic
situation calls for so much attention. Hence the temptation to rely on
others, be they ministers, ambassadors, chiefs of staff, technocrats, or
negotiators. In the last analysis, this means that the nuclear accountants (as Carrington called them) on both sides hold the world to
ransom. And judging by their performance these past years, the world
is entitled to ask questions.

Who, for instance, aborted the "Walk-in-the-Woods" Formula –
which might have brought the INF negotiations to a successful conclusion a couple of years ago? And why? I tried to find out, both in the
White House and in the Kremlin, and it is a fair guess that neither
leader knew the answers. The closest I came to knowing why was that
the Pentagon did not want to give up the Pershing IIs. A remarkable
position, since Helmut Schmidt, who, as Chancellor of the Federal
Republic of Germany, had asked for the Pershing IIs in the first place,
has stated that *he* would have *welcomed* the Walk-in-the-Woods
Formula! As for the Soviets, it would appear that their generals saw no
necessity of reducing the number of *their* Euro-Missiles, if they could
rely on the peace movements in the West to prevent deployment of
ours. Thus, we are left with the bizarre result that, in matters pertaining
to peace, even when the decisions are *political*, they are enveloped in
such technical complexity that they cannot be taken by the politicians!

An interesting corollary of the foregoing is that – since only the
superpowers are present in the [strategic and intermediate nuclear
arms] negotiating chambers – the rest of us, in the East and in the West
– will never know for sure how intelligently or effectively each side
played its cards.

I am not implying that the various leaders on both sides play *no role
at all* in their respective alliances. On the contrary, where armaments
and military budgets are concerned, political will is generally quite
apparent. On our side, the U.S. are developing the MX and ASATs;
Britain and France are busily modernizing and increasing their nuclear
arsenals; West Germany insists on forward deployment of NATO

forces, thus making a policy of *no early* first use difficult to conceive. The rest of us, realizing that we are the beneficiaries of the American nuclear umbrella, do what we can to be good members of the club: some accept deployment of Euro-Missiles on their soil, some beef up their defence expenditures, Canada tests the Cruise. One way or another, we all make our little effort to strengthen the Alliance; that is to say, we all dutifully contribute to the arms race.

On the other side, as beneficiaries of the Soviet nuclear umbrella, the behaviour of the Warsaw Pact countries seems to follow much the same pattern.

All of which is to say that government leaders everywhere are very much involved in the politics of war. They are not much involved in the politics of peace, except insofar as the adage goes: *si vis pacem, para bellum* [If you want peace, prepare for war].

This is not the place to review and assess the various aspects of my proposals and peregrinations. Suffice it to say that between East and West the shouting has subsided, the insults are less pointed, and the meetings have become more frequent and less frowned upon. Time is right for the involvement of government leaders in the politics of peace. President Reagan has been re-elected; NATO has demonstrated stead-fastness by showing that it could, without splitting the Alliance, carry through with its two-track decision. The Soviets realize that they cannot modernize their SS4s and 5s into SS20s without provoking a parallel response on our side.

Having proved that it could follow through on the second track of its 1979 decision (modernization, i.e., deployment), NATO is now well placed to give the first track (negotiation) another try.

Surely in such circumstances, one ought no longer to be suspected of disloyalty to NATO for saying: *si vis pacem, para pacem*. [If you want peace, prepare for peace]. Indeed, it is official NATO policy to seek parity with, rather than superiority over, Warsaw Pact forces, and to recognize the legitimate security interests of the Soviet Union. President Reagan has stated that a nuclear war could not be won and should not be fought. President Chernenko's recent interview with the *Washington Post* also provided a positive message.

Of course, everything remains to be done! A climate of trust will not replace suspicion without a vast reassessment of the principles guiding East–West relations. In that regard, the Aspen Institute's *Project on East–West Relations*, soon to be released, deserves enormous respect and influence.

Economic insecurity and political instability in the Third World will also have to be recognized as one of the main causes of war. Since 1945, the world has witnessed 130 conflicts which killed some 35 million people, all of them located in the Third World. Aside from the so-far successfully managed NATO–Warsaw Pact [relationship, the politics of] East and West concentrates on developing-country geopolitics: Western Asia, Southeast Asia, Arabian Gulf, Middle East, Horn of Africa, Maghreb, Southern Africa, Caribbean, Central America. Vast energies will have to be expended by the North in the South if the conditions for peace are to be created there.

I refer here to much more than economic aid. The fact of regional conflict and the danger of such conflict leading to confrontation between the U.S.A. and the U.S.S.R. stand in stark contrast to the inertia shown in recent years by the Security Council in acting to keep the peace. Restraint in the use of the veto is most urgent, in order that the carefully constructed conflict-resolution machinery of the U.N. may be brought to bear in some of the flash points I just mentioned.

Another grave obligation rests on the five permanent members of the Security Council, since they also happen to be the five nuclear powers. In their never-ending quest for security, they are actively in breach of solemn international obligations such as the Non-Proliferation Treaty. By failing to observe article six of the NPT, they are directly encouraging the wider spread of nuclear arms, and that in turn increases the likelihood of a total nuclear war caused by the cataclysmic use of such arms by others than the big five. I renew my call for a Summit of the five nuclear powers which they viewed so cautiously when I appealed to each in turn last year. But I will return to this point in a minute.

Most important of all, NATO must be transformed into a vital political alliance, as had been intended in the beginning, and the new

Secretary General of NATO, Lord Carrington, has both the intellect and the nerve to oversee such a transformation. NATO Summits must be frequently held, and sufficient time must be allowed for fruitful and creative exchanges. If heads of government allow themselves to behave like the democratic leaders that they are, their thoughts and actions will soon gravitate to peace. And this is not wishful thinking. A vibrant democratic alliance will have no need for bombast or pusillanimity. Once macho posturing is replaced by self-confidence, everything becomes possible.

NATO should respond constructively to the several positive proposals made by the Warsaw Pact countries . . . rather than react only to the shrill propaganda in which they were couched.* In turn, the Warsaw Pact could be invited to look constructively at the Brussels declaration of . . . December [1983]. Carrington could put out feelers for exchange visits between the political and military leaders of the two Alliances. . . . NATO should do the following:

1. Declare that upon the achievement of the reduction of forces to the MBFR goals (900,000 total on each side), and given adequate verification provisions, it . . . will adopt a *no first use* of nuclear weapons policy;

2. Enjoin those of its members participating in the MBFR talks in Vienna to respond more constructively to the Soviet proposal of mid-1983;

3. Request of its members who are nuclear powers that they take part in exploratory five-power talks under the aegis of the Secretary General of the U.N.;

---

* The Prague Declaration, January 1983.

4. Support the French proposal or the one I made a year ago, for banning the testing and deployment of those anti-satellite systems designed to operate at high altitude;

5. Announce a temporary moratorium on the deployment of INF weapons in Europe, making it clear that it expects a reduction of equivalent Soviet weaponry, as well as a Soviet undertaking to resume negotiations immediately.

Envisaging any one of those five steps is likely to cause a flap among those bureaucrats of NATO who still believe that peace is too important to be left to the politicians. But I am convinced that many others will heave a sigh of relief that common sense is finally taking charge, and that the downward spiral of paranoia and distrust is finally being broken.

Of course, this can happen only if such gestures are matched by equivalent signals from the Warsaw Pact. *Both* sides must do their part. And so I call upon the Soviet Union and its Allies to show by similar concrete actions that they too have sufficient self-confidence to make a gesture, to take some small risk in the interest of reducing the threat of war.

[M]ankind now possesses the power to prevent . . . all opportunity, all life: the power to create a permanent winter, in Carl Sagan's words "a Nuclear Winter." In a world with untold riches yet to be discovered, with countless symphonies and novels yet to be written, with massive human wants yet to be alleviated, in this world a handful of men and women have dedicated their energies to the design of explosive power so overwhelming that the use of only a small portion of it endangers the continued existence of life on this planet. The decision to destroy the brilliant accomplishments of seven millennia of poets and architects, musicians and scholars, theologians and artists, to destroy all of God's handiwork, to place in jeopardy the lives of almost five billion people – that decision lies essentially in the hands of two men, one in Washington, the other in Moscow.

I know them both. Neither, in my judgement, is evil. Each, in my judgement, profoundly hopes that the vicious genie contained in each of their bottles will never be released.

C. David Crenna, Ed.,
Lifting the Shadow of War
(Edmonton: Hurtig, 1987)

On the Eve of the Third Millennium

><

It's an honour to be associated with a man (Jackson H. Ralston) who, if I judge from his autobiographical notes, had a tendency to stick up for unpopular causes, to defend the weak against the strong, and who had the opportunity to be asked to leave Stanford University around 1932 as a teacher because he was probably a Rooseveltian Democrat. In that I share the experience with him, having been refused admittance to teach at the University of Montreal in my own province because I was too much of a liberal. I read a phrase in Mr. Ralston's notes which endeared him to me, and I'm sure it will endear him to many of you: "My course in life was not such as to commend me to the good graces of those who had large favors to give." So I'm very happy to be here, to be associated with his name and with the name of the four gentlemen who received the prize before me – all of whom I knew, and with two of whom, President Carter and Prime Minister Palme, I was closely associated in my work, and also as a friend. The dean and I thought that maybe if I didn't speak too long we could have a period of questions and answers later, so I'll try to shorten some of my remarks in the hope that you might have some questions to throw at me.

Therefore I won't spend too much time on the first few pages of my notes, where I say that since January 1, 1900, the world has changed enormously in every area, and that during this coming decade, as we approach the third millennium, we'll have the occasion to be entertained, perhaps educated, at great length on the subject of change. I then quote Schlesinger, who, in his *Cycles of American History*, calculated that the last 2 lifetimes have seen more change than the planet's first 798 put together. Or as Ehrlich and Ornstein of this university put in *New World, New Mind*, if all of "Earth's history were charted on a single year's calendar . . . all that has happened in recorded history would occur in the final minute of the year." Consequently, they add, "the world that made us is now gone, and the world we made is a new world, one that we have developed little capacity to comprehend."

All of which may assist us in fathoming the nature and cause of the apocalyptic times we seem to have entered, as we cross the threshold into this last decade of the second millennium. Even though millenarians have not yet emerged in great numbers, we would be wise not to discount the possibility that they are already among us, spreading their gospel of irrationality and proclaiming that "the end is near."

Early in the first millennium, fathers of the Church had read the Book of Revelation, Chapter XX, to prophesize that the end of the world would come after the saints "had lived and reigned with Christ a thousand years. And when the thousand years are expired, Satan shall be loosed out of his prison, and shall go out to deceive the nations which are in the four quarters of the earth." And Matthew, Chapter XXIV, tells us of Jesus' answer when asked by his disciples on the Mount of Olives about the second coming and the end of the world: "Ye shall hear of wars and rumours of wars. For nation shall rise against nation . . . and there shall be famines, and pestilences, and earthquakes in diverse places. . . . Ye therefore shall see the abomination of desolation" and so on.

But, of course, the year 1000 came and went, and the world soldiered on. Though much sorcery, hysteria, and unreason had held sway, historians assure us that the period was not one of universal terror, nor of unmitigated fear.

Nevertheless, by the sixteenth century, millenarianism had again reappeared, with the Anabaptist sect, to be followed by various religious leaders, mainly in France and England of the seventeenth and eighteenth centuries. The end of the world was then predicted – now hear this – for some time in the 1900s, during the closing years of the second millennium. So perhaps it's not too soon for us to start itemizing the signs of madness and to look for the signals of a coming apocalypse. I leave to astronomers and seismologists the task of deciphering the messages sent to us by heavens and earthquakes. But perhaps some prodromes can be found in the temper of the times, well expressed by William Butler Yeats in his poem "The Second Coming." I shall refer to it a few times, so let me read the first ten lines:

> Turning and turning in the widening gyre
> The falcon cannot hear the falconer;
> Things fall apart; the centre cannot hold;
> Mere anarchy is loosed upon the world,
> The blood-dimmed tide is loosed, and everywhere
> The ceremony of innocence is drowned;
> The best lack all conviction, while the worst
> Are full of passionate intensity.
>
> Surely some revelation is at hand;
> Surely the Second Coming is at hand.

Item: The richest country in all of history went in eight short years, during the presidency of the man elected and re-elected to balance the budget, from being the world's greatest creditor to being the largest international debtor (just under half a trillion dollars in 1988, and still growing). It is kept out of insolvency by repeated borrowings from the two countries it had defeated in the Second World War, whose economies it had destroyed, and for whose defences it has been paying these past forty years. In fact, the sum it was spending to defend Europe in 1987 alone, some $150 billion, was roughly equal to its current-account deficit in that year. And, of course, it continues to pay for the defence of Japan, though that country can now boast of having the world's third-largest military budget. In order to finance its repeated external deficits, the world's largest economy is siphoning out most of the current-account surpluses of its aforesaid enemies, thus preventing sufficient capital from flowing to the developing nations, where investment is desperately needed to break out of the cycle of poverty.

Meanwhile, we incongruously enjoin these Third World nations to do what we cannot do – "live within our means" – and we force them to compress their already meagre standards of living in order to transfer, in 1988 for example, some $43 billion of their earnings from trade surpluses to the rich industrialized countries in a futile attempt to repay earlier borrowings. Since those savings are no longer available to them to build infrastructures and modernize production facilities, the debtor nations cannot possibly generate the quantity and quality of exports which alone would permit them to satisfy their creditors. As a consequence, from 1984 to 1988, the net transfer of funds to the developing world has been negative. Those countries, in fact, transferred some $140 billion to the wealthy North in a Sisyphean effort to pay their debts, while at the same time their indebtedness – a large part of it in the form of compound interest – grew from $950 billion to $1.24 trillion!

Adding insult to injury, those very institutions set up at Bretton Woods to help reconstruction and development were net recipients, in 1987 for example, of transfers to them from Third World countries. In the case of the International Monetary Fund, the net flow from the developing countries, the poor countries, to the IMF was $8.6 billion; net transfers to the World Bank were more modest, a mere $350 million.

Things fall apart; the centre cannot hold;
Mere anarchy is loosed upon the world . . .

Item: In the world's greatest democracy, the lack of vitality of the political process could be measured by the fact that its president was elected in 1988 with roughly 50 per cent of the electors not bothering to vote; that, in the House of Representatives, 20 per cent of the members won their seats unopposed, and 98 per cent of those who sought re-election were victorious. Meanwhile, in Eastern Europe, in Latin America, in South Africa, citizens had risked persecution, imprisonment, and even death in order to win the right to vote. And in Tiananmen Square, students were raising a statue to the goddess of democracy as the tanks rolled in.

> The best lack all conviction, while the worst
> Are full of passionate intensity.

Item: Soviet troops marching across the border of Afghanistan commit a crime against humanity, but U.S. troops landing in Vietnam, in Grenada, and in Panama are deemed legitimate interventions in one's sphere of strategic interest.

One superpower is condemned for waging wars by proxy in Angola and Ethiopia, while the other is absolved for doing the same in Cuba and Nicaragua. It was all right for our side to base nuclear missiles near the Soviet border in Turkey, but not all right for the other side to base nuclear missiles in our vicinity in Cuba.

If General Jaruzelski seizes power to prevent the entry of Soviet troops into his country, we light candles and impose sanctions in order to "let Poland be Poland." But if General Pinochet takes power in a coup d'état involving the assassination of democratically elected President Allende, he is acclaimed for restoring law and order, and he gets our support.

Bombing of Libya is justified as a retaliation against a government that supported terrorism, but dealing with Iran, which also supported terrorism, is okay if the money that's raised thereby is used to flout Congress by arming the Contras.

When the Soviet air force shoots down a Korean passenger plane, which in the dark of night strayed a great length into Soviet air space, we call them murderers and impose worldwide sanctions. But when the U.S. Navy in broad daylight shoots down an Iranian passenger plane on a scheduled flight over international waters, we commend the ship's captain for doing his duty.

General de Gaulle, in a visit to Canada as head of State, issues a call for independence to one of its provinces, which already exercises the largest measure of sovereignty to be found in any federal constitution anywhere. But when the Corsicans or Basques or Bretons agitate for a small measure of devolution within unitary France, the French government arrests them as traitors and throws them in jail.

> The blood-dimmed tide is loosed, and everywhere
> The ceremony of innocence is drowned . . .

Or, as Blaise Pascal put it three centuries earlier: "Vérité en deçà des Pyrénées, erreur au delà." [Truth this side of the Pyrenees; error on the other.]

Item: Global warming is with us. If current trends continue unchecked, rapid and continuous shifts in climate, including possible droughts in mid-continents and increases in frequency and intensity of tropical hurricanes, accompanied by increases in sea level, will occur over the next decade. These changes are bound to endanger the well-being, perhaps the survival, of humanity, as well as the security and physical integrity of entire countries. The principal cause of global warming is the greenhouse effect: the increasing accumulation of a variety of gases in the atmosphere which trap heat and reflect it back to the earth's surface. And carbon dioxide alone accounts for more than half of that gas build-up, largely caused by energy-consumption patterns and by deforestation. Yet all scenarios about energy requirements until well into the next century agree that considerable increases in fossil-fuel use causing carbon dioxide will happen unless corrective action is taken.

Notwithstanding various undertakings at international conferences for carbon-dioxide reductions, most experts consider proposed corrections as grossly insufficient, and furthermore the undertakings have not been followed by the needed legislative action. In addition, there are threats to the ecology and human survival from many other sources, such as nuclear testing, radioactive substances, ozone depletion, acid rain, pesticides, and other chemical pollutants.

Thus, an entire generation has barely escaped from the fear of nuclear annihilation when it is asked to come to grips with the threat to human survival coming from ecological destruction. The managers of public affairs in the superpowers had been so intent on an arms build-up, ensuring to each of them the capacity to destroy the other many times over, that they failed to heed the Club of Rome's early warnings of destruction coming from the misuse of the earth's resources.

"Mere anarchy is loosed upon the world," wrote Yeats. But perhaps T.S. Eliot said it even better. I'm sure you remember the lines: "This is the way the world ends / Not with a bang but a whimper."

Have the benefits of freedom and democracy given our side an advantage in averting either apocalypse – that of the bang or that of the whimper? Hardly! From the onset of the cold war until deep into the Gorbachev era, the NATO powers generally remained so obsessed by the fear of communism that, even in the coming and going of Khrushchev, they perceived no clue that the rival system was crumbling from within and ceased to be a threat to Western-type societies, politically, economically, or ideologically. The only potential threat posed by the Soviet Union remained the military one. Yet instead of concentrating all our diplomacy and statecraft to the end of reducing *that* threat, we used every stratagem to cause its build-up, from the early use of nuclear blackmail, to the MIRVing of warheads, to the madness of "Star Wars."

On that score, the first glimpse of sanity came from the so-called evil empire, with its unilateral suspension of nuclear testing in 1985 and proposals for force reduction in all of Europe, from the Atlantic to the Urals. Here are the words of General Secretary Gorbachev, as he then was, barely in office for some months, at the November 27, 1985, session of the USSR Supreme Soviet:

> The people of the whole world are today facing a host of ques-
> tions which can only be resolved jointly and only under condi-
> tions of peace. . . . [O]ur generation is already witnessing the
> mass extermination of forests, the extinction of animals, the
> contamination of rivers and other bodies of water, and growing
> "desertification." What will the world be like that future gen-
> erations will see? Will they be able to live in it if the rapacious

destruction of nature is not stopped and if the economic, technical and scientific achievements of our time are directed at perfecting weapons of destruction rather than ensuring conditions for the existence and progress of humankind and the natural environment?

Gorbachev then addresses the problem of "the growing gap between a handful of highly industrialized capitalist nations and those developing countries . . . whose lot is poverty, hunger and lack of hope." And he continues: "Humankind is capable of resolving all these problems today if it pools its forces and intellect. . . . [L]ife itself calls not for competition in armaments, but for joint action in the name of peace." Then he goes on to discuss some of these joint actions: "a program of peaceful cooperation in space . . . fundamental research projects and the application of their findings in geology, medicine, material studies and studies of the climate . . . global satellite-aided communications systems and remote probing of the Earth," and so on.

Not since the death of my friend and distinguished predecessor Olaf Palme have we heard the leader of a Western state speak so convincingly of the importance of using the "economic, technical and scientific achievements of our time" for "the existence and progress of humankind and the environment" rather than for "perfecting weapons of destruction."

Thus, on the one hand, the leader of the Eastern bloc that we had declared to be intellectually and morally bankrupt was subordinating class interests to human interests, and setting the agenda for the next century, proposing the vision of an interdependent world wherein nations would cooperate for the benefit of all humankind. On the other hand, the leaders of the free world remained hidebound by strategies of containment developed for yesterday's cold war, and seemed totally incapable of participating creatively in a dialogue about tomorrow.

NATO, though conceived as a political as well as a military alliance, had found it unnecessary to hold more than half a dozen meetings of its heads of governments during the first forty years of its existence. And the record would show that such Summits rarely lasted more than one day, the waking hours of which were devoted to food, music, and the endorsement of a communiqué prepared in advance by the minions of the United States. The last time NATO had considered the problems of East–West relations for the purpose of formulating a military strategy somewhat appropriate to the times went back to the Harmel Report in 1967.

As for the annual Summits of the Economic Seven, an examination of their communiqués from 1975 onwards would reveal that their sights were firmly set on the past and the present, never the future. They seldom strayed far from the economic or political crisis immediately at hand, that is to say, the ones that had recently caught the fancy of their experts or the attention of their electorates: monetary policy, unemployment, OPEC, Afghanistan, the Falklands, terrorism, or acid rain.

Indeed, the most recent Summit occurred just six months ago, when the magnificent seven forgathered in Paris on July 14 to commemorate the storming of the Bastille in the name of *Liberté, Egalité, Fraternité*. It will remain one of history's great ironies, perhaps worthy of pre-apocalyptic times, that most of the seven presidents and prime ministers assembled there would be leaders of extremely conservative regimes, as far to the right as democracies can produce, and that if they were thinking anything at all, they could only be giving thanks that the Revolution was two centuries dead, and that the *sans-culottes* could now only be imagined in some distant Third World country. Indeed a case of history happening the first time as a tragedy and the second time as a comedy!

Liberté perhaps they could be celebrating, if they had in mind the political processes whereby inherited privilege as a source of civil authority had gradually been replaced by electoral systems in which the dominant role was increasingly played by a media controlled by the power of money. And economic liberty they could also acclaim, since the economies of the world were either turning to or were currently being governed by principles which Adam Smith had formulated some fifteen years before the French Revolution. These principles of *laissez faire* were undoubtedly instrumental in bringing about the extraordinary growth in wealth which accompanied the industrial revolution. But the industrial revolution, it will be recalled, was hardly a tale of equality and fraternity. In terms of misery, disease, injustice, wanton indignity, and sheer wastage of human lives, it easily surpassed the years of the Terror. Indeed, if a tally could be made in the four quarters of the globe, one wonders if it would not be a match for the tens of millions sacrificed by Stalin in the name of the dictatorship of the proletariat, when he attempted to force the backward Soviet society through its own industrial revolution.

In any event, the excesses wrought in Western societies by economic Darwinism and the indiscriminate reliance on "the invisible hand" eventually led to T.H. Green's liberalism, to Fabianism, and to social democracy, just as some hundred years later the excesses of totalitarian central planning would lead to Deng Xiaoping's economic reforms and to Gorbachev's *perestroika*. But of course, the two cycles were out of sync. In the 1980s, the so-called socialist countries were rising against totalitarianism and centrally planned economies, whereas by that time the capitalist countries were reacting against welfare-statism's attempt to ensure a fairer distribution of the fruits of progress, and its inability to continue doing so when economic growth had faltered. Consequently, in both East and West, the accent was more on liberty, and less on equality and fraternity. In reality, the world of 1989 appeared to be celebrating 1794, the Thermidorian triumph of the Bourgeoisie over the people. It was trying to bury not only the French Revolution of 1789, but also the Russian and Chinese revolutions of 1917 and 1949.

In America, we saw the Democratic candidate for the presidency cringing when he was accused of being a liberal. In Western-type economies, many social democrats were supporting the trends towards deregulation and privatization and putting all their faith in the market. In Eastern Europe, Soviet ideology chief Vadim Medvedev was advocating market exchange as "an indispensable means of gearing production to fast-changing demand." In Hungary, Politburo member in charge of ideology, Janos Berecz, was stating: "the production of goods and services should be driven by the market. If the market gets into conflict with the plan, the plan will have to be modified." And he reported that entrepreneurs were complaining about a new income tax as "something that blocks the entrepreneurial spirit." In Poland, the new prime minister, Tadeusz Mazowiecki, was stating in his investiture speech that the strategic aim of his government would be a return to the market economy and to a role for the state approaching the one prevailing in the economically developed countries. In China, Hu Qili, member of the Politburo, stated: "Our final objective is to expose all enterprises – individual, state, private and collective – to market competition." Then he went on to explain the advantages of competition between firms. The manager, he said,

> will have to put his bank account and his family property as a deposit on the property of the factory. . . .
>
> A director selected through such a system will inevitably be very strict with the production and highly responsible. . . .
>
> The workers will duly understand why the particular director is so strict. . . .
>
> Now, the director can say to the workers, "You must work very hard because you put me at risk of bankruptcy. . . . So if you don't work hard, I'll sack you."

I feel there is something quite touching about the abiding faith in the market system shown by all those reformers who are trying to free themselves from the dead hand of central planning. Yet I cannot help but wonder how many of them realize that, even in the best of circumstances, our so-called free markets are not always free, and that even though the market has proved to be the main condition for the efficient production and accumulation of the wealth of nations, it can hardly be claimed that its purpose and effect are to ensure that the distribution of that wealth is either fair or just. Nor can it be held that in our market societies the efficient production of goods and services will guarantee

the people's health or the preservation of their environment, or that
the slogan "let the consumer decide" produces beneficial choices in
those who are manipulated by advertising and conditioned by a
society dedicated to acquisitiveness. For example, a few decades ago,
the dream of America was that of a reduced work week and increased
leisure, but in spite of computers and robots, it is estimated that over
the past fifteen years leisure time for the average American family has
fallen by 30 per cent.

It should be obvious to us by now that, if the centrally planned
economies have failed for having made too little use of the market, our
Western capitalist societies are failing because of their too great reliance
on the market. The law of supply and demand is not an objective law
found in Nature, like the law of gravity. It's a law whose operation is
based on subjective variables such as human decisions and feelings.
Absent a social contract whereby people direct their governments to
define the conditions and limits of production, distribution, and consumption, the market will simply turn out more of everything desired
by those wielding some form of power: more arms for the military,
more profits for business, more goods and services for the consumer, to
each according to his rank. The market is not equipped to consider and
report that, as by-products, it is also producing more misery for the
underclasses, more health hazards for the community, more drugs and
crime for the cities, more carbon dioxide for the greenhouse effect,
more depletion of the ozone layer, more destruction of rain forests and
of genetic varieties.

In some cases costs can be internalized and be reflected in market
decisions, but competition will prevent this from happening unless
there is regulation by public authorities. The competition of the mar-
ketplace will also prevent newly empowered business élites from producing a fairer set of rules. For instance, entrepreneurship in the hands
of women or of new minority groups seems incapable of moving to
other values than the sacrosanct bottom line. As Thomas More had
predicted four centuries ago in a book that we well know, "When I
consider . . . all these commen wealthes . . . I can perceave nothing but

a certein conspiracy of riche men procuringe their owne commodities under the name and title of the commen wealth."

What is to be done? We're living in an age where the only constant factor is rapid change. The question is: Can we harness change in order that our human societies now and in the future be equitably governed, that is to say, so that every human being be enabled to fulfil himself or herself to the utmost? In other words, can mankind develop the self-control and sense of fairness that would permit reason and justice to govern the earth? Or must we forever lament with Emerson that "things are in the saddle and ride mankind"? To answer such questions, one would have to examine the role of ideologies in the governance of civil societies, and that cannot be my purpose here and now. Suffice it to say that I have yet to be convinced by those who claim that the world is moving towards a convergence between socialism and capitalism, and I strongly disagree that we are witnessing the end of history in the form of the universalization of Western liberal democracy as the final form of human government. Even though I claim to be a liberal in the twentieth-century meaning of the word, it will be obvious from my earlier remarks that I believe that liberal democracies have a long way to go before they can claim to be victorious in many crucial areas, from arms control to controlling carbon-dioxide emissions.

Indeed, if ideas are the stuff of which history is made, governments in the Western world seem singularly unprepared to shape their own destinies. In the field of disarmament, Gorbachev has dominated the negotiations by basing defence on the concept of sufficiency, an idea which had been around a long time in the West but which had been rejected by NATO, with its mind set on flexible response and possible first use of nuclear weapons. In terms of East–West relations, the Soviets have set their former satellites free, whereas the United States – in utter contempt for the international law of nations – continues to determine what governments have its leave to stay in office in the Western Hemisphere and elsewhere in the world. Events in Central America seem to demonstrate fairly clearly that "containment of communism" was only a gambit in the policy of empire. In the absence of the rationale for containment, the State Department has now returned to the justification it had been using in Latin America since the turn of the century: the punishment of bad guys, in this case the drug barons. In terms of diplomacy, the Soviet group of countries is busily establishing commercial and diplomatic relations with Asian countries, while North America looks helplessly at events in Eastern Europe, and while the governments of the European Community debate whether upheavals in the East should cause the speeding up or the slowing down of European integration.

On the economic front in the West, the private sector rather than the government continues to determine the pace and direction of change. In the European Community, big business has taken the lead in the march towards integration by 1992, just as in the Canada–U.S. trade accord it was big business that decided what was good for the people of Canada. As things now stand, it is also big business that will decide whether competitive forces will oblige the Canadian government to trim down its social legislation. On that score, I must say that the European countries have at least envisaged some structures to protect their people and their social-welfare legislation. (I am thinking of Jacques Delors's social charter.)

More important still, market economies have yet to make a choice between: (a) untrammelled economic growth of the kind that has prevailed until now; (b) sustainable growth, as advocated by the Brundtland Commission; or (c) rejection of the entire growth mystique, as advocated by Ivan Illich and Wolfgang Sachs. If our democracies are enlightened enough to go for choice B or C, the art of government will entail a different kind of planning than that currently practised on the people's behalf by the international corporations. And it will certainly necessitate a return to a more regulated economy, where the public interest would have priority over private profits. Thus, true equality of opportunity for all, regardless of the condition of their birth or the size of their bank account, may some day become the goal of life in civilized societies.

So the contest between political systems, if not ideologies, is bound to continue. On the one hand, the capitalist countries are still far from having resolved their internal contradictions; and, if this be true in the United States of America, it is even more so in the Koreas, the Brazils, the Chiles, and the South Africas of this world. On the other hand, the centrally planned economies, having at last discovered that progress is no longer possible under totalitarian state planning, must ponder their choices. No doubt some of them will opt for Western-type democracies with free markets, but others will certainly strive to preserve the egalitarian aspirations of collectivism, reconciling the virtues of a free market with the form of democratic planning.

So there is hope that we will continue to live in a pluralistic world for a while yet. And we will continue to struggle with problems raised by Plato and Aristotle, by Rousseau and Locke. How can individuals remain free, yet be restrained by the State? How can the exercise of liberty lead to a society of equals?

Yet many dangers will continue to lurk. Horizontal and vertical nuclear proliferation, though currently subdued, has not ceased. Ecological threats continue to grow relentlessly. The Third World is a cauldron, more ready than ever to boil over now that official development assistance is being redirected from there to Eastern Europe. And no exorcist has yet appeared to protect political stability, East and West, North and South, from the demons of tribalism forever in search of an ideological or spiritual void.

Only if statecraft and public law are diligent in the constant reshaping of social contracts appropriate to the rapidly changing times will our crowded world feel secure from the terrible vision of Yeats.

The Second Coming! Hardly are those words out
When a vast image out of *Spiritus Mundi*
Troubles my sight: somewhere in sands of the desert
A shape with lion body and the head of a man
A gaze blank and pitiless as the sun,
Is moving its slow thighs, while all about it
Reel shadows of the indignant desert birds.

The darkness drops again; but now I know
That twenty centuries of stony sleep
Were vexed to nightmare by a rocking cradle,
And what rough beast, its hour come round at last,
Slouches towards Bethlehem to be born?